A Crisis of Leadership and the Role of Citizens in Black America

A Crisis of Leadership and the Role of Citizens in Black America

Leaders of the New School

Stephen C. W. Graves

LEXINGTON BOOKS
Lanham • Boulder • New York • London

PublishedbyLexingtonBooks
AnimprintofTheRowman&LittlefieldPublishingGroup,Inc.
4501ForbesBoulevard,Suite200,Lanham,Maryland20706
www.rowman.com

UnitA,WhitacreMews,26-34StannaryStreet,LondonSE114AB

BritishLibraryCataloguinginPublicationInformationAvailable

ThehardbackeditionofthisbookwaspreviouslycataloguedbytheLibraryofCongress
asfollows:

LibraryofCongressCataloging-in-PublicationData

Names:Graves,StephenC.W.,author.
Title:AcrisisofleadershipandtheroleofcitizensinBlackAmerica:leadersofthenewschool/
    StephenC.W.Graves.
Description:Lanham:LexingtonBooks,2016.|Includesbibliographicalreferencesandindex.
Identifiers:LCCN2016009552(print)|LCCN2016013473(ebook)
Subjects:LCSH:AfricanAmericanleadership.|AfricanAmericans--Politicsandgovernment--21st
    century.|AfricanAmericans--Socialconditions--21stcentury.
Classification:LCCE185.615.G67182016(print)|LCCE185.615(ebook)|DDC305.896/073--
    dc23
LCrecordavailableathttp://lccn.loc.gov/2016009552

ISBN:978-0-7391-9790-5(cloth:alk.paper)
ISBN:978-0-7391-9792-9(pbk.:alk.paper)
ISBN:978-0-7391-9791-2(electronic)

♾TM ThepaperusedinthispublicationmeetstheminimumrequirementsofAmerican
NationalStandardforInformationSciencesPermanenceofPaperforPrintedLibrary
Materials,ANSI/NISOZ39.48-1992.

PrintedintheUnitedStatesofAmerica

Contents

Introduction

What does it take to be an effective Black leader in America today? Who are the Black leaders in America today? My purpose in writing this book is to assess the effectiveness of current and past Black leadership figures. What major role have they played? What major contributions and significant gains in the Black community have they played a role in? There are two main topics explored in this proposal: leadership and citizenship. In particular, the elements of effective leadership and the habits of citizenship needed to make the "good citizen" are questioned. Perceptions of African Americans and historical depictions of the Negro as a "second class" citizen permit African Americans to devalue their American identity and reinforce the idea that provisions in the U.S. Constitution do not apply to them. Through the historical injustices forced upon Blacks, many have the impression that American institutions cannot help them, perceive themselves as enemies of the state, or believe that the rights and privileges awarded to citizens of the U.S. have not been afforded to them. Subsequently, many African Americans suffer from detachment and disassociation from American identity, and consequently, abandonment of a part of themselves. Whether African Americans are able to find identifiable and effective leadership is imperative to the solutions that African Americans face. It is the duty of its leadership to lead the development of new citizenship habits that will ensure the sustainability and viability of a successful African American community in the future so they will not be confronted with the same, or similar, problems and conditions in the future. The sustainability of a viable and effective African American community in the U.S. is important to the racial dialogue and the overall protection of U.S. values in a changing racial dynamic.

Contemporary African Americans have a corrupted conception of citizenship, or bad citizenship "habits." It is my argument that leaders of the Black community have failed to develop innovative and creative institutions to stimulate good citizenship habits among African Americans. An effective Black leader is one who will influence the change of patterns of behavior of African Americans to make positive changes in key areas that demonstrate "bad habits" of citizenship. The corruption of Black citizens and the community is also manifested by Black leaders' inability and unwillingness to put the good of the community over self-interest and self-aggrandizement. Additionally, a devotion to self-help, community-building on a national as well as local level, and a commitment to improving the impoverished Black community, are key elements missing among the majority of Black leadership.

Today's Black leaders are not willing to sacrifice their individual "self" to accomplish the goals of the community at-large. Such sacrifices include devoting themselves to creating previously unexplored opportunities for African Americans and representing the previously scapegoated members of society and the most suffering populations. The standard for Black leadership that I will apply is described as such: the ability of an individual to arouse new attitudes and a new creative type of follower and stimulate untapped possibilities and originalities in other people. These attributes make for the greatest type of leadership. The ideal type of leader must have the following attributes: (1) virtue (moral and political); political in the Machiavellian sense, meaning, whatever works or enables the leader to accomplish their vision for the people; (2) flexibility; (3) sacrifice; (4) humility; (5) responsibility; (6) courage and determination; and (7) innovation and creativity.

The role of the leader is to shake the bad habits from the community before they become engrained behaviors in perpetuity, by any means necessary, regardless if they are agreeable or not. This will require the use of a variety of political tools. A leader of the Black community must address the habits of negative interaction and resentment that Blacks feel about one another. African Americans commit crimes against other Blacks because value in being a member of the Black community is that low. Such negative interactions amongst each other are based on feelings of resentment, disdain, and mistrust. Consequently, citizenship, or the membership into a national community, must be earned or gained through a process in which individuals demonstrate the capacity to willingly participate actively in order to attain national interests and the betterment of their community. Short periods of limited or premature exclusion may be a necessary component of developing good citizen habits, and may be a tool used by an effective leader in shaking the people out of their corrupt and innate state. In particular to Black leaders, this may include the creation of institutions that build trust and allegiance to the community, but require a membership based on obligation and commitment to sustaining the community and work to its best interest.

The theoretical framework for this research takes place within three phases of political thought. First, Aristotle's definitions of citizenship and the citizen, plus the emphasis on the "common good" and the attributes of citizenship related to the "good life," provides the basis for how citizenship will be conceptualized. Aristotle identifies citizenship with the holding of public office and administration of justice. Only some in his view are by nature fit to exercise the virtues of citizenship. Slaves, women and non-Greeks were not only excluded from the statutory privileges of citizenship, but their exclusion was viewed as rational, in that, these individuals were deemed not to possess the virtues of mind, body, and character that were essential to the practice of citizenship. Thus, citizens are distinguished from other inhabitants within the territory.

A citizen is defined by Aristotle as a person who has the right to participate in deliberative and judicial office; subsequently, there is more to citizenship than living in a particular place, sharing in economic activity, or being ruled under the same laws. Citizens must actively participate in politics if they are to be happy and virtuous. Participating in deliberation and decision-making means that the citizen is part of a group that discusses the good and bad, and the just and unjust, and then passes laws and reaches judicial decisions based on this deliberative process. This process requires that each citizen consider the various possible courses of action on their merits and discuss these options with other citizens. By doing so the citizen is engaging in reason and speech and is therefore fulfilling his *telos*; engaged in the process that enables him to achieve the virtuous and happy life. Citizenship in this manner is not just a set of privileges; it is also a set of duties. The citizen has certain freedoms that non-citizens do not possess, but also has obligations that they do not have. The citizens of a political community are partners, and as with any other partnership, they pursue a common goal good citizens must have the type of virtue that preserves the partnership and the regime.

Danielle Allen's conception of the "habits" of citizenship espoused in *Talking with Strangers* will be used as the basis for conceptualizing "bad habits" associated with my conception of citizenship and the interaction among members of the Black community. Allen argues that democracy can survive only when the people adopt the habits of political friendship that allow us to communicate meaningfully through our differences, most importantly the differences supplied by race. Such "habits" of citizens are defined as *those habits that guide citizens in how to interact with each other*. The habits of citizens determine the shape of the public sphere and the quality of political life for the people in that community.

The habits of everyday interaction comprise the substance of democratic citizenship. These customary habits are more significant than institutional practices such as voting, to the practice of citizenship. Developing "good habits" is a fundamental part of achieving maturity as individuals and as members of a community. Allen proposes that current habits limit our ability to cultivate the kind of trust amongst Blacks and Whites in this country to live together in a democratic (rather than autocratic) community. This entails learning and being educated on the practices and obligations of citizenship. Our "bad habits" have often hardened into "congealed distrust" and even "settled patterns of mutual disdain," to the point where Allen suggests that our current lives as citizens are ones of suspicion, alienation, anger, and resentment. Consequently, Allen implores us to cultivate "good habits" to establish the desirable relationship between citizens. My primary focus is the interaction and "membership" within the African American community and as members of the American community, including, the necessary habits to establish desirable relationships among African Americans and their relationship among other citizens of the U.S.

Citizenship and leadership are related based on Machiavelli's standard of leadership and his depiction of the citizen. He declares that the role of citizens is to practice civic virtue by essentially putting the needs of the community over their needs as private individuals. In Machiavelli's *Discourses* he urges citizens to practice civic virtue to prevent the decline of the city. Civic virtue meant the patriotic love of the republic that led citizens to place the welfare of the political community above individual interests. To foster the type of civic virtue needed to sustain the practices of the state, Machiavelli suggests that good laws and institutions are necessary.

According to Machiavelli, due to corruption, citizens lose their freedom by putting their own self-interest over the needs of the city. During these times, cities need leaders to come forth and shake the people out of their corrupt state. To accomplish this, leaders have to develop new political systems or institutions to reinvigorate good laws and habits amongst the people. There are three essential elements of excellent leadership according to Machiavelli: innovation, *virtù*, and responsibility. Excellent leadership requires the ability to bring something new to the political world using the resources provided in the current political climate. Leaders have to do something new for the people that is worthy of public honor and glory.

If the goal of a leader is to be remembered forever as someone who did great deeds, the first thing he or she must do is create an innovative vision that enables one to put their own stamp on the world. Machiavelli states that "nothing makes a prince so much esteemed as great enterprises and setting a fine example."[1] He regards greatness and excellence in terms of the accomplishments that an individual achieves. Great leaders display their excellence by bringing something new to the political system or institutions, exercising political skills that enable one to attain their innovative vision, and finally, by taking responsibility for the outcome of the administration and the stability of the city. To conclude, Machiavelli's framework lays the foundation for my theory of leadership. Today's Black leadership does not emulate Machiavelli's "great leaders." Those claiming the throne of Black leader do not have the characteristics provided by his ideal type. Today we have a selfish, uncreative leadership that is incapable of leading Black Americans to healthy habits and conversely, into good citizens.

These theoretical models provide the foundation for my conception of citizenship and leadership. Accurately conceptualizing citizenship and leadership is imperative to promote and advance those necessary attributes that will generate the desired results within the Black community.

Thus, I will explore how the habits of trust, sacrifice, and allegiance to the national community enable people, in particular African Americans, to be good citizens. These habits are what need to be cultivated by the Black community, and these are the habits that the effective Black leader must instill in the people to shake them out of their complacent state and turn them into contributing citizens.

The central problems that I seek to address are: (1) the erosion of "good" citizenship habits within the African American community, and (2) Black leadership's inability to develop initiatives at the national level to improve the socioeconomic conditions of the African American community. Thus the research is centrally focused on a model of Black leadership that will lead to the development of new practices of citizenship and the training of citizens that will result in constructive behavior that will facilitate improvement in the lives of African Americans. In order to adequately explore Black leaders' role in improving the lives of African Americans, a number of additional questions must also be investigated, including:

1. Why is the concept of citizenship tied to the concept of the national community and the common good?
2. What are the new and essential citizenship habits that need to be developed?
3. What are the key issues facing contemporary Black leaders pertaining to the common good of the Black community?
4. What political strategies and tactics have been unsuccessful in (1) instilling good citizenship habits, and (2) improving the trust and well-being of the Black community?
5. What new model of leadership can achieve points (1) and (2) in point #4?
6. What characteristics must a Black leader possess to achieve points (1) and (2) in point #4?
7. How do these ideal traits lead to good habits?
8. Do bad habits cause negative socioeconomic conditions and standing in society or is it the other way around?

Particular leadership qualities of Malcolm X closely resemble the attributes found in my alternative theory of leadership. There are essentially two different versions of thought attributed to Malcolm X. First there is Malcolm as the leader of the Nation of Islam (NOI) beginning from his parole in 1952 to 1964, who expressed criticisms against the civil rights movement and White America for crimes committed against Black Americans. Originally, as a member and leading advocate of NOI, Malcolm taught Black supremacy and the separation of Blacks and Whites. Messages of Blacks' willingness to bear arms and protect themselves by any means necessary were consistent images within Malcolm's early Black Nationalism.

One aspect that demonstrates Malcolm's effective leadership is his flexibility and willingness to change with the times. After Malcolm's departure from the NOI, his trip to Mecca, and witnessing anticolonial revolutions in Africa, there was a shift in Malcolm's teaching into a human rights approach that looked to combat racism in a more Pan African approach. Upon his return from visiting Northern Africans in Morocco and Algeria who were by all measures of appearance, White, Malcolm reconsidered his Black Nationalist approach and emphasized the impact of racism as not just a Black and White issue in America, and expanded the problem of African Americans as a human rights issue. This transformed the condition of African Americans into an international issue by concentrating on the "direct connection" between the domestic struggles of African Americans for equal rights with the liberation struggles of Third World nations. In his case, the message of international human rights, the willingness to work with civil rights groups, and a reassessment of the impact of racism that affected all disenfranchised people. In the end, an essential part of the greatness of Malcolm's leadership is that he was literally willing to use any and all means to advance the cause of African Americans, whether that included Black separatism and self-determination, or if the times changed, willing to employ another message. Not only did he apply lessons learned from post-World War II anticolonial revolutions and social movements to the liberation of Blacks in the U.S., but his break from NOI symbolized a willingness to change tactics, admit any flaws in a previous strategy, and try another way. Flexibility and the ability to change strategy and tactic is an exercise in political virtue, according to Machiavelli, which demonstrates an essential element of effective leadership.

Malcolm X's impact on changing the attitudes, behaviors, and patterns of interaction among African Americans is extensive. First, he is credited as being largely responsible for the spread of Islam in the Black community throughout the U.S. and with raising the overall self-esteem of African Americans. In 1953 he established Boston's Temple Number 11 and would later expand the membership of Temple Number 12 in Philadelphia and lead Temple Number 7 in Harlem.[2] These are associated with good habits of citizenship in that he articulated African Americans taking pride in their community and being Black, protecting themselves, educating themselves, and doing whatever it takes to ensure their safety and sustainability. These are important attributes that must be reintroduced and promoted within the Black community today in that they may play a significant role in producing the good habits needed to make productive citizens by reinforcing the people's commitment to the group.

The quality of effectiveness of today's Black leaders will be measured by their ability to turn bad habits of citizenship into good ones. More specifically, how one turns African Americans from people of resentment, mistrust, and anger, into a people with trust, honor, and allegiance to their community and its best interest. Four specific areas will be used to measure the effectiveness of Black leadership based on the improvement of the Black community: (1) crime, (2) education, (3) health, and (4) economic status and behavior. My analysis of the statistics in these areas will demonstrate how bad habits of citizenship are played out and ultimately lead to the unproductive and unworthy citizen or member of the national community. Economically, Blacks earn 65 cents to every dollar of their White counterparts and spend 90 cents of every dollar earned outside of their own community. Educationally, Blacks attend college at half the rates of Whites, are more likely to drop out of high school, and less likely to graduate from college. In regards to the general health of the Black community, Blacks have a lower life expectancy on average than Whites and are more likely than Whites to not have a source of health care. Lastly, 90 percent of Blacks are murdered by other Blacks, and continue to be incarcerated at twice the rate and are more likely to be victims of homicide than their White counterparts. Combined, all of these elements demonstrate the bad habits associated with our membership in the Black community and our standing as U.S. citizens due to the laceration of self-inflicted wounds, such as committing violent acts against one another, and at the same time refusing to spend our capital in predominantly African American neighborhoods.

Although the concept of citizenship is one that can be applicable to many different populations, for the purposes of the argument to be made, I will concentrate on the aspects of American citizenship and how African Americans perceive their membership in national communities, specifically, as members of the Black community and their standing as U.S. citizens. The particular negative socioeconomic conditions and standing of African Americans selected resemble the "bad" habits of resentment, disdain, mistrust and contempt among them. The socioeconomic realities facing African Americans are related to "bad habits of citizenship" because they are the manifestation of their distrust, alienation, and resentment as a community; destructive habits that must be turned around to create the bonds of trust and good habits to be good citizens.

The objective is to apply my theory of citizenship and leadership to the contemporary condition of African Americans and offer an interpretation of how African Americans should evaluate their membership in the Black community, their role as U.S. citizens, and evaluate our leaders for the purpose of accomplishing the "good" society. My theory of leadership implies that effective leadership will turn these bad habits of mistrust and resentment into institutions that create bonds of trust. Economically, the effective leader will lead the Black community into habits that will enable them to earn a wage and income more comparable to their White counterparts and have faith in buying products within predominantly African American neighborhoods; educationally, will instill the attitude of the importance of education and restore graduation rates and access to higher education to competitive rates; criminally, lead the Black community to a trust and respect for one another that decreases the number of incarcerated Black males, who suffer disproportionately and more severely than their White counterparts and women, and reduce Black on Black crime. In regards to health, create institutions that may provide greater access to health care, develop habits to increase life expectancy and decrease disease within the Black community. I propose to provide the Black community and any potential Black leader with a philosophical foundation with which the needs of African Americans can be met. This will be done by interpreting key texts to develop my own argument into the ways in which Black leaders can cultivate the proper habits of citizenship among African Americans in order to lead them into the good life, and by measuring their effectiveness (measured by their success in improving the socioeconomic condition in the four variables) in changing the proscribed bad habits.

I will measure the effectiveness and quality of Black leaders by their ability to address the negative habits and make improvements in the aforementioned key socioeconomic areas. Again, using Allen's framework, the good habits are trust, sacrifice, respect, and allegiance to the interests of the community, in contrast to resentment, anger, and disdain, which I suggest play a significant role in the outcome of the socioeconomic variables. My analysis of the statistics regarding crime, education, health, and economics lead me to propose that African Americans have little faith in one another, and despise and resent one another to the point that their membership and value in the Black community diminishes. My theory of leadership and citizenship will provide the best opportunity for the Black community to develop the necessary habits and patterns of behavior to be "good" citizens. Thus, effective leaders will be the ones who are most efficient in changing the attitudes, behaviors, aspirations, and opportunities of African Americans.

The weakness in my approach to studying the habits and meaning of citizenship and Black leadership in this way are two-fold. First, African American interests are varied and the level of intensity, meaning how strongly or weakly an individual feels about a particular issue, fluctuates by education level, sex, religion, and economic status. These factors make it difficult for any one leader or possible group of individuals to represent all of the varied interests of the group. However, there is more in common among African Americans than acknowledged; for example, the impact and effects of slavery and segregation, economic depravity due to result of being withheld from the opportunity to earn a living, and the impact of racism. Whatever differences there are in age, sex, class, and religion, the footprint of these experiences remains present for African Americans.

Secondly, my theory of leadership cannot explain the cause or origin of the "bad" habits; whether "bad" habits are the cause of negative socioeconomic status and standing in society, or if the socioeconomic condition of African Americans causes "bad" habits. It is possible that the research may point in each direction as to the origins of mistrust and resentment among African Americans. My approach to measuring the effectiveness of leadership and the practices of proper citizenship habits by the individuals' willingness to put the good of the community over their own self-interest, measured by the improvement in status and standing of the Black majority in key socioeconomic areas, is softened by the assumption that any potential leader can reasonably be expected to tear down the perceived barriers of class, education, and religion, and reinforce the shared elements of the African American experience. This predicament between reinforcing the shared experiences that can mobilize and unite African Americans, and recognizing the interests among multiple demographics are difficult to be achieved by one individual.

Additionally, the dilemma between the interests of affluent Blacks and their willingness to cultivate many forms of change in order to be perceived as different and separate from their uneducated, poverty-stricken brethren, presents an example of the lack of value, resentment, and disdain that Blacks have for their community and their membership in it. African Americans should find gratitude in the success of other African Americans, but what I question is whether it comes at the cost of erasing the memories of struggle that less educated and poor African Americans still experience.

The African American experiences and perceptions of American citizenship play an integral part in their history and the role that politics plays in the development of the expression of their rights and access to the privileges of citizenship. Carter G. Woodson's *Fifty Years of Negro Citizenship* (1921) argues that the citizenship of the Negro in the United States is a fiction. According to Woodson, the U.S. Constitution guarantees him every right vouchsafed to any individual by the most liberal democracy on the face of the earth, but despite the powers of the federal government, it has studiously evaded the duty of safeguarding the rights of the Negro. Immediately following the Civil War, the undoing of the Negro as a citizen was easily affected throughout the American South by general intimidation and organized mobs. Belz (1977) agrees that Reconstruction legislation, lacking any commitment to social, economic, or even full political equality for Blacks, made little headway at the time in overcoming centuries of racial discrimination, but the wartime definition of the freedmen's rights served as the basis for the 1866 Civil Rights Act and the Fourteenth Amendment.

W. E. B. Du Bois (1935) suggests that three common theses resulting from the Fourteenth Amendment during the Reconstruction era were: all Negroes were ignorant; all Negroes were lazy, dishonest, and extravagant; and Negroes were responsible for bad government. For Du Bois, a problem concerning the implementation of Black citizenship is that the White majority "cannot conceive Negroes as men."[3] Derrick Bell (2001) suggests that support for the Fourteenth Amendment reflected Republicans' concern after the Civil War that the Southern Democrats, having lost the war, might win peace. When it served White interests, the Supreme Court, along with the rest of the nation, ignored the original stated purpose of the Fourteenth Amendments equal protection guarantee.[4]

Regardless of which model or particular bundle of rights you apply to the American conception of citizenship, the experience of African Americans in the United States as they vowed to express their citizenship rights has played an integral part in their history. Since the days prior to the Civil War, African Americans have fought an uphill battle to achieve the status and standing generally associated with the citizenship experiences of the White majority. This includes the ability to vote, earn a decent living, and be protected by the laws and privileges outlined in the Constitution. Today, this battle rages on as African Americans still find themselves unable to acquire, successfully, meaningful equality under the law, and a practical conception of citizenship that will enable them to flourish in the U.S. and achieve group-centered goals. Black leadership is central to the mechanisms by which African Americans can achieve and meet the expectations of citizenship. Who is the identifiable leadership; those at the forefront of expressing and communicating the people's need and interests? What does it mean to be an effective leader? These are recurring themes in the dialogue of African American history and fight for equality.

Leadership is the special influence that an individual exercises over others by arousing their dominant behaviors and beliefs, changing their attitudes, or arouses new attitudes. In each of these ideal type-situations, the "other persons" are as important a factor as the leader, and the process by which one person succeeds in affecting the attitudes of others is most important of all. To arouse the dormant attitudes of one's fellows and become a leader is relatively easy. By being enthusiastic along traditional lines of activity, by "ballyhooing," by raising the cry of "danger," and by the use of other cheap devices, a member of a group may shoot up into the rank of leader without much difficulty.[5] But to change human attitudes and political behavior requires greater skill by the individual.

BLACK LEADERSHIP: MODELS AND PATTERNS

Hugh H. Smythe's "Changing Patterns in Negro Leadership" (1950) argues that leadership involves a group of individuals in which one assumes dominance over the other; the attitudes and values of the group being changed by the dominant person.[6] A Negro leader is subsequently defined as a person who exerts special influence over a number of people for a period of a decade or more and who has helped to change significantly the position of the Negro in American society.[7] A leader stands as a distinctive symbol in the struggle, growth, and development of the Negro. Ralph Bunche's models of Black leadership were influential in what would later become Gunnar Myrdal's analysis in *American Dilemma*. *A Brief and Tentative Analysis of Negro Leadership* (1940) saw Black leadership as motivated primarily by notions of escape—either from racism and oppression or from the deprivations suffered by Blacks as a whole. For Bunche, being a leader suggests transcendence over a community of peers, and thus, transcendence to a place of enhanced material prosperity.

Black leaders might be divided into three broad categories: (1) those who openly and deliberately seek a fundamental change in the political, economic, and social order, (2) those who believe in struggling entirely within the existing framework of the society, and (3) those that are quite willing to accept things as they are.[8] Within these three categories, Bunche identifies six leadership styles: (1) the dynamic and aggressive, (2) the cautious or timid, (3) the "undercover" agent, (4) the "symbolic leader" (5) the "prestige personality," and (6) those appointed by Whites. The dynamic and aggressive type of leadership bases its appeal on the fighting attitude, on boldness, or on the uncompromising stand. This is often merely "bombast" and rabble-rousing, but in many communities, it provides a sure basis for followers. The cautious and timid type of leader is often "pussy-footing" and frequently exerts its influence because of the favor which it wins with influential Whites. Blacks in governmental positions of responsibility, both local and national, sometimes fall into this category. The "undercover" agent performs the role of stooge for responsible Whites and who, because of the favors he is permitted to distribute among Blacks, assumes a position of considerable, but substandard influence in the community. White professional politicians often employ Black intermediaries as public-relations or goodwill ambassadors to their Black constituents; Black bankers and other "big shot" Black racketeers would be included in this group.

The "symbolic leadership" type exerts its influence because of the position it holds. In many Southern communities, Bunche observed that the head of Black schools, irrespective of their merits, and even though they may not be respected by the Blacks in the community, are accepted as the Black leader or spokesperson for their people. The "prestige personality" attains leadership because of the eminence connected with their name. Artists, athletes, and other individuals in this group possess influence because of the reputation of their name, team, or organization. Lastly, there are those Black leaders who are appointed by Whites, which is similar to the characteristics of the "Uncle Tom." Individuals within this leadership type appear more than willing to accept the conditions of

Blacks within the status quo due to the benefits they receive as an intermediary or representative of the race among Whites, in addition to the benefits he or she may receive socially, such as higher education, better living conditions, and access to certain circles.[9]

ACCOMMODATION VS. PROTEST AND
THE BLACK ELECTED OFFICIAL

It is important to note consistencies that have been established in the literature concerning Black leadership. Much of the consensus relates to the new form of "accommodationist" style leadership and the influx of elected officials and Black politicians. Additionally, business managers and leaders of large corporations have entered into the sphere of influence and demonstrated a willingness to work within the system in order for African Americans to advance. Ronald Walters and Robert C. Smith (1999) found that from 1970–1972 a major shift coinciding with the impact of the Voting Rights Act of 1965 occurred in Black politics. The transition from protest to electoral politics elevated Black elected officials to the forefront of Black leaders, signaling a preference for institutional rather than non-institutional strategies. Eventually, disruptive protest demonstrations gave way to conventional methods for pursuing public policy.[10]

The accommodation paradigm accurately defines the incorporation of moderate, middle-class Blacks into mainstream institutions and civic organizations, culminating in moderate Black leadership styles and strategies. Tilman C. Cothran and William Phillips, Jr. (1961) argue that the changing character of Black leadership has become one of the significant forces initiating change in the area of race relations. Prior to May 17, 1954, Black leaders were predominately of the "accommodating" rather than the "protesting" type. Situations of racial harmony are conducive to the accommodating type of leadership. In contrast, in situations of racial crisis, protest leadership seems to become dominant. The emergence of protest leadership indicated diminishing influence of the White community in determination of Black leaders. Protest leadership gains widespread vicarious, if not always active, support from Blacks because it is an effective expression of latent hopes and aspirations of the "inarticulate" Black masses. In the Black community, leadership dynamics are inextricably interwoven with the total complex of forces operative in the relationship between Whites and Blacks.

Robert Smith (1996) argues that in the post-civil rights era, Black leaders have become incorporated into the electoral system, which rendered them largely ineffective in addressing the problems of urban decay and entrenched poverty. Lastly, he maintains that Black leaders have spent too much time pursuing racial and political integration, which may have benefitted middle-class Blacks but left poorer African Americans marginalized. Among Black politicians, the fight against oppression is frustrated by co-optation into the very political positions that marginalize the masses.[11] The "waning" of Black leadership is correlated with the rise of Black conservatives, anti-government rhetoric, and Black elected officials. Nelson (2003) concludes that "unlike Black leaders of the previous century who devoted themselves to ending racial discrimination and creating opportunity for African Americans, high-profile Blacks on the eve of the twenty-first century acted to help the White establishment maintain hegemony in the judicial, executive, and legislative affairs of the nation."[12] The fact that some of these so-called leaders are interested in self-aggrandizement rather than the best interests of their constituents has not been a deterrent to their election and re-election.[13] As a result, a new group of White "anointed" Black leadership defined by its ability to "carry the White folks' water," in government and political and cultural debates has resurfaced. This new group has only an ephemeral connection to the Black masses.

Middle-class, and church-centered leadership have been the primary examples of Black leaders. Mabee (1964) agrees with Gunnar Myrdal's (1944) suggestion that middle-class Blacks, the natural leaders of the Black community, often do not fight hard against segregation because they are ambivalent toward it. On the one hand they feel segregation blocks their opportunities, and therefore they have reason to oppose it; on the other hand, they see that segregation provides them with much of the opportunity they have, and therefore they have reason to favor it. For example, Black ministers, politicians, and doctors, while they publicly deplore segregation, often depend on segregation for their patronage and so do little to destroy it. The rising Black middle-class, accepting as it does the values of the White middle-class, often craves White approval.[14]

THE MULTIPLICITY OF BLACK LEADERSHIP

The areas of contention within the literature of Black leadership are vast and represent a pressing dilemma in the development of identifiable Black leadership. There is debate on whether African Americans rely too heavily on the notion of "one" or "a" Black leader, or rather the idea of many spheres of Black leadership are more conducive to progress. The acceleration in the changing social status of Blacks created a different framework in which Black leadership had to operate. The results were a shift from a pattern favoring an all-dominant, single individual, to one calling for several leaders. As Blacks strove for assimilation and developed a new conception of themselves, the appeals of the early leaders had to give way to current trends, resulting in multiple patterns of leadership.

Hugh Smythe (1950) argues that the multiplicity of leadership has brought a consciousness of group disunity on the part of many Blacks. This new pattern created a dilemma; Blacks complained of the need for a great leader, yet it became questionable whether they wanted or really needed one. A single recognized leader makes for speed and efficient progress, where the "masses are ignorant" and leaders are "wise and honest." Blacks have progressed to the point where their activity has penetrated into almost every aspect of the general society; their interests span more situations than any one person can handle. Contrasting techniques may result in greater speed toward the attainment of ends than a single consistent approach, which may be suited to handle some, but not all, problems or people. Donald Cunnigen (2006) argues that Black leadership has never flowed from a few individuals but has always been amorphous with a wide range of views, and this very nature makes it a dynamic force that has the potential for introducing and sustaining positive structural changes within society.

Another aspect of the scholarly debates on Black leadership is the variety of attitudes and ideas on procedures. Questions of what techniques to employ on given issues, the problem of pace and timing in pushing for civil rights and social integration, and where to attack first face each leader and are met with different reactions. The pattern of Black leadership is the result of the development and maturing of Blacks as a people. Marable (1999) argues that African Americans now require the same varieties of spokesperson as do their White companions, mainly, those capable of developing new techniques to meet current problems and anticipate future ones. There are questions within Black leadership about the speed of success. Optimistic proponents of working within the current political system and institutions see the expansion of Civil Rights to Blacks as symbols of progress and future hope.

On the other hand, proponents of Black Nationalism see less significance in the symbolic gestures and privileges generally associated with citizenship. The ability to vote and attend White schools are hardly symbols of progress and success. Black Nationalists perceive African Americans' ability to advance in the current state of things less optimistically. Optimists argue Blacks have made splendid progress in the over one hundred years since they were slaves. In the pessimistic view, despite considerable success in improving upper class Blacks' job opportunities, jobs for the semi-skilled and skilled Black worker are being wiped out. Both the optimistic and pessimistic schools have their validity, but it was the pessimistic view that was more characteristic of the growing impatient leadership of the 1960s.[15] As unemployment continues to rise disproportionately in the Black community it will be intriguing to see how optimistic African Americans continue to be despite having an African American President, or potentially a return to Republic presidential leadership after the 2016 election.

RACE, CLASS, AND SEXISM

Issues of growing class divisions and the emphasis on male-dominated, charismatic leadership are areas of contention within the literature focusing on Black leadership. Bell hooks (1981) argues that Black men never viewed themselves as protectors and providers of Black women and have always been primarily interested in self. Hooks considers Black Nationalism as a patriarchal and misogynist movement, one that sought to overcome racial divisions by strengthening sexist ones and readily latched onto the idea of the emasculating Black matriarch. Similar to hooks, Michelle Wallace (1999) argues that the aim of the Black political movement became the "pursuit of manhood" and the open denigration of Black women was its consequence. Black men argued that they had been emasculated by Black women and the time had come for Black women to be silent and assume their proper place behind or under the Black man.[16] Black liberation, therefore, was aimed at liberating Black men, not Black women. Unfortunately, "[t]he movement had ended and the system had not changed: it was no less racist or sexist."[17] Where Black men had the opportunity to completely overhaul the system by making the women partners in the fight for liberation of the Black community as a whole, they reverted back to traditional American patriarchal stereotypes, which in the end hurt their cause more than it helped.

Marable (1999) argues that Black liberation has been inhibited by the community's reliance upon charismatic, authoritarian leaders and by a limited theoretical vision that has failed to recognize that Black progress is contingent on addressing class, as well as race, issues. The current Black leadership's ineptitude and impotence emanates not only from the widening of the White-Black divide, but also because of the increased differentiation between the treatment meted out to different sections of the Black population.[18] Although a lucky few in the middle class are offered visible and lucrative positions in Washington and elsewhere, the vast majority of their people are being pushed further and further into poverty and marginalization.

The over-arching problem which plagues Black leadership, political or otherwise, is that many are, or aspire to be, members of the capitalist bourgeois elite themselves.[19] Consequently, they balk when faced with the reality that the only course of action that may alleviate Black suffering is the dismantling of hegemonic capitalist structures. One clear reason why Black elites, inside and out of politics, resist serious challenges to capitalism is because they have positioned themselves to be the members of the Black community who are most likely to enjoy its fruits. Black capitalists conveniently suffer from selective amnesia when loyalty to the struggle of the masses does not benefit them economically. After economic benefits are garnered at the expenses of the Black masses, Black capitalists desert the people as well as the projects that may benefit the Black community, but are not sufficiently profitable. In the midst of this fray of greed, Black leadership often engages in political and economic competition to determine who has the "right" to become "sub-oppressors." This seems to only further commodify and exploit the masses. For Jones (2001), the great issue with Black leadership is that it has reached a historic moment in which it no longer seeks to liberate the people or transform the world, but often languishes in vulgar careerism and selfishness that reinforce, rather than oppose, African American peripheralization. Such peripheralization only bolsters the division in factions within the Black community, further dividing the rich and successful from those most in need.[20]

Black leadership has been an essential and integral part of African American culture, history, and their relationship with the White majority. Effective and excellent Black leadership is essential to the advancement and improvement of the socioeconomic conditions of the African American community in the United States. Additionally, President Obama's presidency reveals a new era and symbol of Black leadership; expectations are high in the African American community for the first African American president, and thus a new element to the effectiveness of Black leadership surfaces. If President Obama fails to meet expectations and the Black community emerges from his presidency degraded, devalued, and discouraged about their potential to achieve justice and equality in the U.S., they will be left looking for leadership in a more difficult and worst-off condition than where they began. Where, then, will the Black community look for leadership? Where should they look? And, what exactly should they be looking for?

It is important to realize the necessity and value of serving and uplifting Black communities based on their own perception of their culture, values, and needs, and thus without necessarily having access to White dominated institutions, and without their approval or recognition. The battles taking place within African American communities must ultimately be won by African Americans themselves, and only a commitment to this method, once revealed nationally, will enable them to attain their goals and objectives, and consequently preserve the legacy and stability of their communities for the future.

NOTES

1. Niccolo Machiavelli, *The Prince* (New York: Random House, 1992), 102.
2. Bruce Perry, *Malcolm X: The Life of the Man Who Changed Black America* (Station Hill Press, 1992).
3. W. E. B. Du Bois, *The Souls of Black Folk* (New York: W. W. Norton, 1999).
4. Derrick Bell, *Faces at the Bottom of the Well: The Permanence of Racism* (New York: Basic Books, 1993).
5. Emory S. Bogardus, "Leadership and Attitudes," *Sociology and Social Research* 13 no. 4 (1929): 377–81.

6. Hugh H. Smythe, "Changing Patterns in Negro Leadership," *Social Forces* 29 no. 2 (1950): 191.

7. Ibid.

8. Ralph Bunche, *A Brief and Tentative Analysis of Negro Leadership* (New York: New York University Press, 2005), 47.

9. Ibid.

10. Ibid., 257–58.

11. Ricky L. Jones, "Permanent American Hegemony: Liberalism, Domination, and the Continuing Crisis of Black Leadership," *Black Scholar* 31 no.2 (2001): 38–48.

12. H. Vincent Nelson, *The Rise and Fall of Modern Black Leadership* (Lanham, MD: University Press of America, 2003), 311.

13. Ibid., 27.

14. Gunnar Myrdal, *The American Dilemma: The Negro Problem and Modern Democracy* (New Jersey: Transaction Publishers, 1999).

15. Carlton Mabee, "The Crisis in Negro Leadership," *The Antioch Review* 24 no.3 (1964): 365–78.

16. Michelle Wallace, *Black Macho and the Myth of the Superwoman* (Verso: Verso Classics Edition, 1999).

17. bell hooks, *Ain't I A Woman* (Boston: South End Press, 1981), 181.

18. Kofi Buenor Hadjor, *Another America: The Politics of Race and Blame* (Boston: South End Press, 1995).

19. Jones, "Permanent American Hegemony," 44.

20. Ibid.

ONE

Constructing Black Citizenship and the Second-Class Citizen

The concept of citizenship is composed of three elements. First is the idea of citizenship as a legal status, defined by civil, political, and social rights. Citizens in this instance are legal persons free to act according to the law and having the right to claim the law's protection. This does not, however, mean that the citizen takes part in formulating the law, nor does it require that the rights of citizenship be uniform between citizens. The second dimension of citizenship considers citizens specifically as political agents, actively participating in society's political institutions. Within this element the ability of citizens to participate in political parties and eligibility to run for political office are significant. The third dimension refers to citizenship as pertaining to membership in a political community that furnishes a distinct source of identity. In this instance, the sharing of specific cultural, historical, or religious practices are essential elements that relate the people of a particular region or territory into the sharing of particular values that unite the individuals.[1]

The theme of citizenship pertaining to social rights and benefits derives from T. H. Marshall's (1950) analysis that citizenship can be understood as a status that entitles individuals to the possession of a certain bundle of entitlements and benefits as well as obligations. Marshall's log of civil, political, and social rights is based upon the cumulative logic of struggles for the expansion of democracy in the nineteenth and early part of the twentieth century. Civil rights, in their most basic sense, entail the rights to protection of life, liberty, and property, the right to freedom of conscience, and certain associational rights like contract and marriage. Political rights, in their narrow sense, refers to the rights of self-determination, to hold and run for office, to enjoy freedom of speech and opinion, and to establish political and nonpolitical associations, including free

1

press and free institutions of science and culture. Social rights involve the right to form trade unions as well as other professional and trade associations, health care rights, unemployment compensation, old-age pensions, child care, and housing and educational subsidies.

In regards to collective identity, citizenship implies membership in a political entity that has been formed historically; that has certain linguistic, cultural, ethnic, and religious commonalities, and that can be distinguished from similar political entities.[2] In this instance, the concepts of citizenship and national identity are to be distinguished from each other since political communities are generally not composed of nationally and ethnically homogenous groups. The privilege of citizenship confers upon its holders the right of political participation, the right to hold certain offices and perform certain tasks, and the right to deliberate and decide upon certain questions. Struggles over whether women should vote, whether non-White and formerly colonized peoples are capable of self-rule, or whether a gay person can hold certain kinds of public office are illustrations of the tension between the social and naturalistic dimension of citizenship.[3] The naturalistic dimension of citizenship is represented by the notion that birth in a certain territory confers citizenship, while the social dimension is characterized by the impacts of culture and religion that unite individuals into a national community.

TWO MODELS OF CITIZENSHIP:
REPUBLICANISM VS. LIBERALISM

The liberal and republican models of citizenship present different depictions of the role of citizenship. The key principle of the republican model is the notion of civic self-rule, which is embodied in the traditions of classical institutions and practices like military service and rotation of offices. Under this model, citizens are first and foremost those who share in office-holding; it is their co-authoring of the laws via the general will that makes citizens free and the laws legitimate, as in the case of Rousseau. Thus, active participation in processes of deliberation and decision-making ensures that individuals are citizens and not subjects.

The civic-republican position articulates a "thick" conception of citizenship, community, and belonging. It expresses stricter criteria of incorporation and citizenship of foreigners and immigrants than liberal or Universalist theories. In the modern world this has meant membership in a bounded political community that was either a nation-state, multinational state, or a federation of states. The political regime of territorially bounded sovereignty, exercised through formal-rational administrative procedures and dependent upon the democratic will-formation of a more or less culturally homogenous group, can function only by defining, circumscribing, and controlling citizenship.[4] Max Weber (1968) argued

Table 1.1.   The Liberal and Republican Perception of Citizenship

Liberalism	Republican
• A legal status; protection by the law • Entitlement to certain rights (right to vote, due process, etc.) • In return, legal responsibilities (taxes, jury duty if called, serve as witness if summoned, etc.) • Membership in common law community • Bundle of civil, political, and social rights	• Based on tradition and classical institutions • Emphasis on the duties of citizens; qualifications over citizenship • Strict criteria of incorporation and citizens of foreigners and immigrants • State defines, circumscribes, and controls citizenship • Membership rights to reside within a territory subject to the state's administrative jurisdiction

that this "unity of residency, administrative subjection, democratic participation, and cultural membership constituted the 'ideal typical' model of citizenship in the modern nation-state of the West."

Under the liberal tradition, which developed from the seventeeth century onwards, citizenship came to be represented primarily in the protection of a legal status; political liberty is thus important as a means to protect individual freedoms from interference by other individuals or the authorities themselves. Peter Reisenberg (1962) understands citizenship in the liberal tradition to mean the entitlement to certain rights, such as the right to vote or to be a federal government official. In return, all citizens have certain legal responsibilities, such as paying taxes, serving on a jury, serving in the nation's armed forces if called, serving as a witness in court if summoned, and obeying the nation's laws. Virginia Leary (1999, 2000) follows up Reisenberg's interpretation by conceiving citizenship as connoting a "bundle of rights"—primarily, political participation in the life of the community, the right to vote, and the right to receive certain protection from the community, as well as obligations. Walzer (1989) suggests that in the liberal model, citizenship became an "important but occasional identity; a legal status rather than a fact of everyday life."

To be a citizen conveys the willingness and ability of an individual to contribute to the good of the state or community to which he or she belongs. It is the joining into civil society in order to achieve a common objective or common good that designates one as a citizen and thus the individual citizen is recognized by the contribution he or she makes. Being a citizen and belonging to a national community requires individuals to put the needs of the community above their own self-interest. Through sustainment of the community and the persistent effort to attain the common good, the concept of citizenship is preserved, in that, the

Table 1.2. Gravy's Theory of Citizenship

Gravy's Theory of Citizenship

- Focus on the obligation the citizen has to the sustainment, protection, and improvement of the community.
- Restrictive membership necessary to ensure commitment of the individual to community goals.
- Citizenship has a value that increases or decreases depending on how members of the community perceive their role in the community.

values and attributes that make a national community to belong to in the first place are recognized and sustained.

For the values of the national community to be sustained by the efforts of its citizens, any privileges or rights of citizenship must be earned or gained through a process by which individuals demonstrate their capacity to willingly participate actively in the conquest of the objectives and the betterment of their community. Citizenship, in this way, represents a commodity or good that has value, and in such cases, must be nurtured and guarded against depreciation and erosion. Citizenship can go through a process of devaluation in which individuals are no longer attached to the objectives of their national community, subsequently putting in jeopardy its stability. Additionally, this erosion of the national community results in the continuing process of creating citizens who are not able to adequately perform the rights and duties that come with the obligations of citizenship.

Individuals must be trained to be citizens and fully accept the privileges, rights, and responsibilities associated with it because most will not naturally put the good of their community over their own self-interests, even though the two are essentially interconnected. Individuals need the national community to continually recognize their rights, privileges, and responsibilities, thus, it is in each individual's self-interest to work for the common good and the preservation of the national community. This ability requires each individual to understand their place or role within the national community to which he or she belongs. Within the national community each individual must apply whatever skills or talents they possess that are most useful to the common good, and not attempt to go beyond one's own limitations, which is an act of their own self-interest.

Each citizen identifying with his or her place in society is essential to this discussion because it expresses that leaders must be given the power and resources to lead, workers must be given ample resources to work, and defenders of the national community must be adequately supplied to defend; each person subsequently given the resources to do what they are best at in the use of attaining the goals and objectives of their community. This is essentially the role of leaders; putting individuals in the proper place to fulfill and achieve their objective within the national community, or putting the people in the best possible scenario for a common goal to be achieved. The leaders may then be those people of political knowledge, or knowledge of the rights, responsibilities, and privileges of citizenship, that would then train and prepare the masses and lead them into their new role within the national community. Leaders are those individuals that lead people to self-sufficient, fully active participation in the national community.

THE MEANING OF AMERICAN CITIZENSHIP
AND THE AFRICAN AMERICAN EXPERIENCE

Another area of contention is the perception and meaning of citizenship in the United States. The distinction worth noting is how American citizenship came to manifest itself for African Americans and how the Fourteenth Amendment, which clearly defined the citizen in the United States, was perceived differently by the White majority versus the Africa-American minority. This area of contention is pivotal in explaining the current state of race relations in America today. In the perception of the framers of the Constitution, citizens were autonomous beings whose individual needs had value, and governments that interfered with the fulfillment of these needs; specifically "life, liberty, and the pursuit of happiness" were tyrannical and unjust. But even this conception was not absent of exclusionary criteria. The framers' stipulation that the President of the United States be a "natural born citizen" represents an implicit rule making a distinction between different types of citizen. The President of the United States was required to fit into one of these models of the framers' interpretation of citizenship, either as naturally born on the territory of the new state, or born to parents who are naturalized citizens.

Edward J. Ennis (1943) argues in "The Meaning of American Citizenship" that U.S. citizenship means many things common to citizenship in other nations, but it also possesses unique and invaluable qualities to be found in no other model of citizenship, modern or ancient. Judith Shklar's *American Citizenship* (1995, 2001) declares that American citizenship provides citizens with status attainments which set them apart from others, who are not citizens. The entire history of the idea of status in this nation has based itself on differentiating the people who matter, from slaves who do not. Citizenship is how Americans become equals, and ballots and jobs are how equality expresses itself. For Shklar (2001), the point is to be able to vote, to be able to earn, not necessarily to go to the polls or hold a job at any one moment. In America, citizenship has been about standing; one's position in society relative to others.

Blacks are unable to express their full citizenship rights in America. The conception of slavery led them to question the value of the Black community, and the devaluing of labor and producing things with your hands. Meanwhile the fight for voting rights gave them the notion that all their problems could be solved through political institutions and electing Black candidates. Through the historical injustices forced upon them, many Blacks have the impression that American institutions cannot help them, perceive themselves as enemies of the state, or believe that the rights and privileges awarded to citizens of the U.S. do not apply to them. Attempts to dissociate from American identity and the misperception of their standing and contribution to the founding of America, is a problem facing Blacks. More importantly, a misperception of what it means to be a citizen has produced destructive patterns of behavior inconsistent with their need for unity and solidarity to adequately protect and serve the Black community.

ON SLAVERY, LABOR, AND THE ECONOMIC CONTRIBUTIONS OF EARLY BLACKS

The perception that Blacks have about the institution of slavery contributes to their negative conception of themselves as Americans. As cruel and reprehensible as the institution of slavery was, making it distinct from previous forms of slavery, the contribution from the labor and resources produced by Blacks permitted the existence of the great economic structure of contemporary America. Blacks' understanding of slavery must be reinterpreted to acknowledge the fact that without their contributions, America would not exist as it does today. The value and dignity associated with labor and the physical contributions to the community are being devalued as essential elements in one's active participation in the fate of the community. Blacks should have pride and be commended for the products of their labor and contributions that founded a nation.

Locke substantiates the traditional liberal value that honors labor as a commodity. According to Locke, an individual who develops and cultivates land as a result of labor advances the condition of humanity. It is labor that turns something ordinary into something that people value; "for it is labor indeed that puts the difference of value on everything."[5] In this respect, it is the physical contributions that improve the conditions of the community and establish the value of one's commitment and contribution to the community. It is this commitment to the community's improvement where the value of citizenship is found; through the value of labor individuals improve the conditions of their community.

Judith Shklar (2001) perceives labor and the ability to earn as an attribute of American citizenship. The dignity of work and personal achievement, and the contempt for aristocratic idleness, has been an important part of American civic self-identification since colonial times.[6] Martin Delany highlights the importance of Blacks in all aspects of American labor and the daily privileges and accommodations afforded to Whites as a result. Hemp, cotton, tobacco, corn, rice, sugar, and many other essential products contributing to the economic success of America were the by-product of the labor of Blacks. An ability to earn a wage is a materialistic expansion of labor and is outside of the boundaries proposed by Locke. It is derived first, from the prices individuals are willing to sell their labor for, and two, from the individual's excessive concerns for physical comfort through the acquisition of more money. Rather than labor sprouting from humanity's need to produce the things needed for survival, wages has transformed labor into the means in which individuals isolate themselves from the rest of the community. For Karl Marx, this separation of individuals from the products of labor causes alienation. The ability to earn does not remove the value of an individual's labor nor the value of one's contribution to the community. Whether or not an individual receives a wage does not lessen the importance or necessity of labor and contributing goods to the sustainment of the community. Nor does it diminish the individual values and lessons learned through labor and hard-work. If a person gets paid minimum wage or $150,000 annually, the merit and necessity to contribute one's labor to the community is just the same. The truth is, people should labor or work, and would need to, whether or not they receive a wage. Despite the significance placed on the ability to earn, admiration for labor and producing things with your hands were still understood as valuable assets and inherent elements of active participation in the community.

The mastery of agriculture and endurance through miserable conditions introduced another significant attribute to the value of labor. Although plantation owners technically owned the land on which the goods were produced, the majority had very little skill or aptitude for cultivating the land and sustaining efficient farming for economic growth on their own. While the institution of slavery reservedly put Blacks in a state of dependence on Whites for their right to life, Whites undoubtedly had come to rely on Blacks as a means to sustaining their way of life. Through the labor of their forefathers, Blacks became the backbone to America's economy and consequently its development as a world superpower. Blacks should admire the contribution of those who so largely supplied the labor for which the great things of this America have been accomplished.[7] They must, with the same spirit and resolve, contribute their labor to supply the Black community with resources and products to empower the future of Black America to accomplish great things and preserve the value of labor.

The demeaning and intolerable conditions of slavery set the foundation for Blacks to question their commitment to America, in addition to the overall value of the Black community in America. Nevertheless, the value and inseparable nature of labor to the individual creates the conditions where Blacks can cherish and recognize the U.S. as their own; a land in which their forebears not only fought for independence, but mixed with their labor, have acquired as property. The greatest riches in America have risen from the blood and tears of Blacks.[8] Delany offered a similar position based on the contributions made by Blacks to the economic success of America through the effects of their labor. For Delany, these contributions are sufficient to establish Blacks' claim to America as legitimate as those who fill the highest stations by the suffrage of the people.[9] It is such an understanding and interpretation of Black history that must be developed and nourished to establish a legitimate perception of their contributions as Americans, and thus, the value of their participation in their community as citizens.

ON VOTING: A SYMBOL OF CITIZENSHIP

There has been a false impression that the privilege of voting constitutes, or necessarily embodies, the rights of citizenship.[10] Voting represents more than merely a political act of participation. It requires a political voice; the opportunity to have one's interests represented and be an active participant in government as one of the governed. The Fifteenth Amendment states "the right of citizens of the United States to vote shall not be denied or abridged by the United States or by any state on account of race, color, or previous condition of servitude."[11] Yet, after the ratification of the Fifteenth Amendment in 1870 Blacks still faced institutional and systematic obstruction of exercising and practicing this newfound right. The vote could not protect Black southerners against grotesque registration requirements, literacy tests, poll taxes, grandfather clauses, White primaries, and more chicanery than they could possible defeat.[12]

Shklar suggests that voting is one of the main emblems of public standing in America and a main attribute of citizenship for people who have traditionally been excluded, such as Blacks. What ex-slaves wanted was to be citizens like everyone else, and for them that meant voting.[13] Frederick Douglass perceived the right to vote as a means of self-protection and a form of political agency, which would empower Blacks and allow them to promote their own interests.[14] Whether the right to vote would secure and promote the interests of Blacks, or merely subjugate them to the will of their oppressor, had yet to be determined. To demand the right to vote and participate in government as equal citizens conforms to traditional American principles. Blacks not only fought for the freedom of America in battle they struggled for the right to vote and have their interests represented and acknowledged by its government. Barring both of these elements, voting takes on a symbolic connotation instead of a tangible meaningful act of freedom. When this happens, the whole definition and interpretation of citizenship and the role of voting comes into question.

Without the individual's interests being represented and expressed within government, voting is essentially a meaningless act. Many prominent early Blacks have inquired about the value of voting despite the lack of representation of their political, social, and economic interests. Delany attempted to deconstruct the very definition of citizenship by questioning the perception of citizenship as defined by the right or privilege to vote. At the beginning of the period of Reconstruction (1863–1877), 1,500 Blacks held public office in the South.[15] With large Black minorities and even majorities in Mississippi and South Carolina, coalitions of Blacks and White Republicans elected governments that expanded civil rights for Blacks, culminating in the passage of the Fifteenth Amendment. More than a half-million Black men became voters in the South in the 1870s, mostly for the Republican Party. Du Bois (1917), writing about Reconstruction and its effects, highlighted the crucial role that Blacks played in government contributing to the first public school system in the south.[16] In addition, Blacks played leadership roles in encouraging industry expansion and limited redistribution of plantation property.[17]

Even though Black men voted freely and in large numbers, Whites were still elected to a large majority of state and local offices.[18] By the end of Reconstruction, White legislators passed laws and new constitutions that created barriers for Blacks. After the compromise of 1877, which saw the last of federal troops leave the south, Blacks were progressively stripped of political, social, and economic powers previously practiced. Blacks' voter rights provided power to coalition with Whites and lead opposition movements, but not enough power to eradicate the obstacles of violence and terror by the Ku Klux Klan (KKK), the institution of Black Codes and Jim Crow laws, and other social institutions built to obstruct progress in the Black community. For Delany, this is unacceptable and unworthy of being considered the equal political participation of citizenship. What Delany meant to convey is that voting is more than an act of political participation; it is for the people to have an active role in governing themselves. No people can be free who themselves do not constitute an essential part of the ruling element in the country in which they live.[19] Therefore to consider themselves citizens in America for Blacks means more than the act of voting, it requires an active role in determining the fate of their community.

As a result, Blacks need to adopt new systems and institutions to promote their group interests, while taking an active role in determining the fate of their communities, and thus, recapturing the essence of their rights as citizens. One example of this need for new political forms is the experience of the Mississippi Freedom Democratic Party (MFDP). The MFDP attempted to be recognized as the official Democratic Party in the state of Mississippi since the "regular" Democratic Party had continuously denied participation by Blacks. This would have broadened the base of political participation and given Blacks the opportunity to begin making decisions that affected their daily lives. The MFDP challenged the seating of "regular" Mississippi Democratic Party delegates due to a completely segregated process that violated federal law and both parties' regulations.[20] After some of the all-White southern delegates threatened to leave the convention and the party, Lyndon Johnson ordered a "compromise" that offered the MFDP two at-large seats that allowed them to watch floor proceedings but not participate.[21] Though ultimately the MFDP was unsuccessful, the major moral of the experience was that it was imperative for Black people to fight for an independent base of political power first, realizing that they would need to have new institutions outside the two dominant political parties to bring about social change.

The experiences of the Lowndes County Freedom Organization (LCFO) in Tuskegee, Alabama in 1966 resembles that of the MFDP and the need for the Blacks to develop new forms of political structure and systems within America to promote their collective interests. Blacks in Lowndes County set up a voter registration and participation program in which they educated and trained each other on the concept of voting and attempted to elect Black representatives. They established a system making sure that Blacks were able to locate polls and be able to vote safely without interference from Whites, working together to defeat such attempts to stifle and destroy their political voice like the voter "helper" program. Focusing on slow integration and assimilation into White culture and norms, Blacks in Tuskegee, Alabama, hoped to be gradually given the privilege of gaining political power in their community. Consisting of a significant middle class population who worked at the colleges and hospitals, the people simply wanted to work hard in hopes that Whites would "accept" them fully as citizens. This meant taking an active role in determining the future of Blacks in the community. When this meant electing Black officers and representatives, LCFO advocated electing only a few and not trying to "run the whole thing."[22] Ultimately, when Blacks had the ability to control the political arena in Lowndes and Macon County, they were met with strong, systematic resistance from the White power structure. This led to the defeat of the large goals and aspirations of the Black community in Lowndes and Macon County.

It has been a misrepresentation of the concept of citizenship and a mistake by the Black community to assume that voting exemplifies the rights of citizenship. The experiences of MFDP and LCFO illustrate Blacks' diligence in fighting to have a political voice, more than merely a token vote. A token right to vote is hardly considered a right or a privilege, and the willingness to fight for representation in the promotion of Black interests is admirable. Yet, there are other ways for Blacks to take an active role in determining the conditions of their daily lives. Voting is not the only way to promote Blacks' collective interests, and the experiences of MFDP and LCFO symbolize the need for Blacks to view their commitment as citizens beyond the notion of voting, and seek alternative methods to actively participate in the expression of the values and interests of the Black community. Access to the ballot is a useful tool when it directly influences or brings resources to the community. Blacks devaluing and feeling detached from their commitment and perception as citizens based on their inability to adequately exercise their right to vote means they must readdress the significance of voting and their interpretation of citizenship.

If Blacks aspire to fully exercise the rights and privileges of American citizenship, they must operate within a framework that restores commitment and obligation to protecting and promoting the collective interests of the Black community and encourages them to actively explore ways to determine the conditions of their daily lives. Such a commitment can be derived from an appreciation for the contributions made during the period of slavery and the value of labor, and the shared history and experiences of members in the Black community. Any attempt to achieve the social changes they desire resides in realizing the significance and necessity of embracing community values and a commitment to one another. Making this commitment is vital to the Black community and thus, it is important to investigate why this essential element to the improvement of the Black community is lacking.

ON THE CORRUPTION OF CITIZENS
AND THE BLACK INDIVIDUAL

Due to the perception of slavery, labor, and voting rights that helped conceive of Blacks as second class citizens, the habits of proper citizenship among Blacks have undergone corruption and erosion. Corruption *is the process in which peoples' original intent is changed to become or caused to become morally debased or disloyal*. Machiavelli introduces the concept of the corrupted spirit of citizens in his *Discourses*, where his main objective is to reinvigorate the citizens of Florence whom he feared would be incapable of defending themselves. For him, corruption is manifested in the inability of the community to maintain social cohesion. In such instances, a sect or group of people acts for the purpose of personal or sectional gain, or in a way that harms the maintenance and development of the people.[23] Corrupt men will eventually corrupt the rest of society. Thus the problem is that a corrupted people cannot defend itself, nor its members against a corrupted government.

The corruption of the Black citizen means *the inability and unwillingness to put the good of the community over the good of individual self-interest*. Such emphasis on personal advancement over group advancement leads to moral perversion and debased character. Individuals become so fixated on the "self," the ways and means to satisfy their own desires and tastes, that the aspirations of the community at-large are lost. This results in the individual asserting their individuality and exploiting their talent or skills as members of the community, but *despite* their community and with little or no participation in its improvement. Ultimately the individual comes to realize that the community at-large is an inhibitor to reaching one's goals, and the wisest thing to do under such circumstances is to separate one's self from the Black community as far as possible.

While narrowly focused on accomplishing one's individual goals, the aspirations and the interest of the Black community become an afterthought. The selfish struggle for personal aggrandizement blocks the social and economic progress of millions of innocent people.[24] In the end it is the poverty-stricken and uneducated Blacks who suffer the most. Those with the greatest potential to help and serve those with fewer opportunities have found economic success and multiple opportunities in a more diverse America. Yet the majority of Blacks suffering from economic disparity and social inequality have had their opportunities diminished. The ability to mobilize for group desired goals is the most efficient way that the rights and privileges of citizenship can be extended and assured to all.

Blacks' ability to unify and be mobilized is significantly associated with the level of intensity of one's racial identity. Sellers et al. (1997) defined racial identity profiles as the extent to which one's blackness or race is central to one's sense of self. One of the most popular and widely used theories of racial identity is Cross's (1971, 1991) Black Racial Identity Development model (BRID). The BRID focuses on the process of how an individual's racial identity is formed and changes over time. Change is conceptualized as moving from a negative, unhealthy view or attitude about Blacks to a more positive healthier one. Racial identity profiles labeled as either psychologically unhealthy or reflective of Black self-hatred are considered negative. Blacks who do not consider race as an important component of identity are identified as psychologically unhealthy.

Sellers et al. (1997) outline four dimensions to describe the significance and meaning of race in the self-concept of Blacks: (1) identity salience, (2) the centrality of identity, (3) the ideology associated with the identity, and (4) the regard in which the person holds Black people. Salience and centrality refer to the significance of race, whereas ideology and regard refer to the qualitative measuring that individuals ascribe to their membership in the Black community.[25] Salience identifies the prominence or importance of a person's race in the individual's self-concept at a particular point in time. It allows for the consideration that certain events will bring into consciousness a person's racial identity, regardless of that person's racial awareness or ideological views about Blacks. Centrality refers to the stability and dominance of a person's race in the individual's self-concept. It implies the existence of a hierarchical ranking of several different identities such as sexual orientation and gender, in terms of how close they are to the individual's core definition of self. For example, when one calls himself a "Black man" he is assuming the ranking that being Black is a priority of equal or greater value to being a man.

How intensely individual Blacks identify as members of the Black community will determine the probability of Blacks improving their socioeconomic status as a whole. If members do not feel like being Black or that their membership in the Black community is important or relevant to the individual's condition, it is less likely the individual will feel like contributing to the cause of the group, or that their contribution is relevant to the condition of the whole. To effectively unify and mobilize as a group, each member must feel like being Black is important to their identity and their contribution to the other members who identify as Black is reciprocated.

This inability to unite and mobilize for a central cause or group desired goals exposes the alienation Blacks suffer from as a result of corruption. Alienation *is the separation of things that naturally belong together or to put antagonism between things that are properly in harmony*. In a Marxian sense, alienation results in the inability of people to define their relationship with others. Rather than a social relationship between people involved in a common effort for survival or betterment, alienation affects a false consciousness where the mutual interests of the people is concealed. As a result, the progress of the community is impeded because the people are deficient of any communal action or satisfaction.[26] Blacks are alienated in that their political, economic, and cultural decision-making power is located outside the group.[27] Their relationship with each other and with other citizens in the U.S. is completely designated and determined by members outside of their community. One of the most important aspects of Blacks' inability to define and set the parameters around their own relationships has been the failure to commit to continued involvement for the common effort of Black survival and betterment in America. Rather than Blacks defining their relationships in a common effort to combat the consequences of slavery, segregation, and the effects of racism, they have continually sought success at the individual level, putting their commitment to the group on the back burner, particularly emphasizing that participation in a community effort diminishes the individual's ability to achieve success. There is no identification with selfhood; the individual's future cannot be separated from the future of one's community,[28] and yet everywhere Blacks trying desperately to rid themselves of the future of other Blacks.

EROSION IN THE BLACK COMMUNITY

Once the corruption of the Black individual has begun to set in, the erosion of good behavior and citizenship habits begin to impact the Black community. The erosion of citizenship means *to destroy the elements that unite a community that share a history and are involved in a common effort for survival or betterment by slow consumption or disintegration.* Erosion takes place when people devalue membership in their national communities. This occurs amongst Blacks within their own community and as citizens in the U.S. Thus, erosion is the wearing away of the individual's affinity for the community and the gradual wearing a way of community values. When erosion sets in, the values of the individual are no longer aligned, or there is a separation between their needs and the needs of the community.

Erosion further takes place when the individual believes that the rights and privileges of membership in the national community or as a citizen are given away too liberally. This happens when inclusion into the group comes without almost any obligation or stipulations that equal the contributions and sacrifices of original members. If it does not take much to gain the rights and privileges of membership, the people will value membership in that community less. When the rights and privileges of membership are highly valued, the process in which individuals become members is generally extensive. In regard to community membership, this means the ability to contribute to the sustainment and future of the community and its existence; the most important duties of citizenship. If individuals do not show the capacity to contribute to the existence and well-being of the community, what rights and privileges have they earned to be granted from the community in the first place? Without demonstrating the ability to contribute to the betterment of the community, there can be no rights and privileges extended to the individual. And when rights and privileges are granted to members who have not contributed to the protection of the values and interests of the community, value in belonging to the community is diminished.

The erosion of citizenship and value in the community also takes place when individuals no longer see their advancement through the attainment of group goals. Again, in the Black community you are more likely to see Blacks celebrating their success despite their involvement, however little there may actually be, in the Black community. Although they may see a successful Black individual win a court case or achieve success in a particular field, more than likely they see one less spot available within a limited amount of Black success stories available to them. Thus, the perception is that it is in the best interest of Blacks to do whatever they can to not only separate themselves from their own community, but tear the others down if for no other reason than to make themselves stand out and look better than the rest. They are glad to see Black group success, if for no other reason than they may find the ability to exploit their own individuality within the newfound freedoms of the group; any wiggle room for the individual to make more for themselves is gladly accepted.

THE PERPETUATION OF CORRUPTION AND
EROSION IN THE BLACK COMMUNITY

This perception of Blacks as second class citizens, their subsequent cor-ruption, and the erosion of value in the Black community continue for four reasons: (1) manipulation, (2) cultural invasion, (3) division (lack of trust), and (4) over-reliance on liberalism and the Democratic Party. Ma-nipulation *takes places when Whites falsify the existence, status, and conditions of Blacks to suit their own purpose and advantage.* This falsification takes places in the historical depictions of Blacks and the denial of contribu-tions made by African civilizations. Additionally, manipulation consists of making Blacks feel inferior and that the best way for them to achieve their group-desired goals is within a system to which they have very little access and influence. During slavery, Blacks knew what the odds were and what was needed to defeat the power exercised over them by Whites. But in a society which pronounces them free but makes them behave as a slave, all of the strength and will power to identify the enemy is under-mined; the structures of oppression are camouflaged and the enemy is elusive. Blacks have been told that their oppression is due to their ignor-ance and mental inferiority. They have been duped into believing that if only they were like Whites, they would no longer be ridiculed.[29] Thus, it is because Blacks have been told that they belong to an "inferior" race that they try to resemble the "superior" race.

As a result of manipulation, Blacks are anxious to have everything that White Americans have even if it's harmful and detrimental to their collective survival. This takes place through Whites deconstructing and manipulating the values and objectives of Blacks and incorporating the "approved" elements into mainstream, White American values. Whites have indoctrinated Blacks with the belief that the good life is one of individuality, and the devaluing of everything that is Black; that the Black individual cannot achieve full potential while clinging to the mem-bership of the Black community and representing its collective interests. Somehow the interests of the Black community have been demonized to represent everything that is un-American, against the freedom and liber-ty of the individual, and the ability to accumulate wealth and property. Thus, one of the methods of manipulation is to inoculate Blacks with the White upper-class appetite for personal success and achievement.[30]

Another method of manipulation is to give Blacks the impression that they are being helped.[31] This takes place in the form of social and assis-tance programs provided by the state to "serve" the poor and under-served members of society. This is not to argue that access to such pro-grams make Blacks dependent on the state, Whites, or any specific pro-gram. Merely that Blacks' disillusionment concerning the intentions of Whites and the government is magnified by having access to these pro-grams to the point they feel that Whites generally care about solving their problems by providing any programs at all. Blacks have false ideas about the intentions of Whites, the purpose and use of such programs, and whether or not the social programs aimed at the "poor and disadvantaged" are really meant to improve the daily lives of Blacks. Access to social programs aimed at the "poor and disadvantaged" give the false impression to Blacks that Whites are sincerely concerned about the conditions in the Black community and taking considerable steps to improve them. One could look at unemployment benefits, housing and rent subsidies, Medicare and Medicaid, and instances of affirmative action in hiring practices and college access, and have the impression that Whites and American institutions seek to rectify the problems in the Black community. Simply by providing social programs as a "safety net" for the poor, those responsible for the perpetuation of the plight in the Black communities are able to pass off as though they are actively trying to serve their interests. In particular, liberal Democrats love to mobilize the Black vote around such issues as social programs and minimum wage for lower class, working Americans, and that Blacks will be the beneficiaries.

The most significant ploy of manipulation experienced by Blacks is the concept of freedom, particularly what it means to be "free" in the U.S. Whites enforce individuality and the freedom from community involvement and obligation based on the conception of personal success as the chief expression of freedom and citizenship. Freire (1986) identifies this concept as the "fear of freedom," in which people confuse freedom with the maintenance of the status quo so that consciousness of their repression threatens to place that status quo in question thereby constituting a threat to freedom itself.[32] Blacks have been conditioned into believing that they are free because they have been allowed to participate in the exploitation and manipulation of other Blacks.

Blacks have come to believe that freedom is the practice of the strong and privileged to dominate and oppress others; they are only displeased currently because they are not in a position to exploit their White counterparts, or some equivalent. Wealthy and privileged Blacks already dominate and exploit their position in society, mainly over the Black poor, whom they formerly were, and are still not very far from returning to. This level of detachment and blindness to the injustices of the Black poor demonstrates an advanced level of adhesion in the Black community today. Adhesion *is the steady and devoted attachment and allegiance that Blacks have toward Whites that encourages them to follow and imitate them so exactly.* The majority of Blacks believe freedom is the maintenance of the status quo, but with the Black individual as the oppressor and not the oppressed. They do not care who does it as long as they can participate in some form of exploitation. The system itself is in no need of change, Blacks just wish to participate in the system and exploit others with the same freedom, success, and frequency as Whites. Ideally they would be in a position to reverse the circumstances and exploit Whites, but pragmatically, Blacks are content with exploiting the poor and uneducated members of society, a good proportion of which tend to be Black. Blacks simply want in the game, and under the current rules of the game, exploiting all groups including their own, is fair game. Freedom would require Blacks to reject the image of the oppressor and replace it with autonomy and responsibility.[33]

Blacks have become so assimilated into the value system of White America that they are no longer able to contemplate the injustice and oppression of their former selves; no longer are they able to understand the severity of their former conditions, how far they have come through the road of oppression, and how far they still have to go to achieve equality. How degrading was the attitudes towards Blacks and horrifying the treatment and conditions of their forefathers? Under the current state of assimilation into the cultural values of Whites, the acceptance and lack of knowledge of such practices and the diminishing anger and frustration over the historical treatment of Blacks results in a less than enthusiastic effort by members of the Black community to seek retribution for previous injustices for which they are still suffering from the effects. Blacks adopt an attitude of adhesion to Whites, thus their perception of themselves as oppressed is impaired.[34]

The second element that contributes to the corruption of citizens and the erosion of value in the Black community is cultural invasion. Culture represents the behaviors, beliefs, and inherited ideas and values that constitute the basis for social action which may signify the range of activities and ideas of a group of people with shared traditions. Freire emphasizes that cultural invasion is on the one hand an instrument of domination and on the other a result of domination because it implies the "superiority" of the oppressor and the inferiority of those who are oppressed.[35] Whites have penetrated the cultural context of Blacks by imposing their own view of the world upon them while inhibiting the self-expression and determination of the Black community.

At times cultural invasion is camouflaged with Whites assuming the role of a helping friend (remember the liberal Democratic Party and its emphasis on social programs to help the underprivileged). As a result, Blacks begin to respond to the values, standards, and goals of the White community, thus it is essential that Blacks come to see their reality with the outlook of Whites rather than their own. For cultural invasion to succeed, Blacks must become convinced of their intrinsic inferiority, until the values of Whites become the values of Blacks. The more cultural invasion is accentuated and Blacks are alienated from their own culture and themselves, the more they want to be like Whites: to walk like them, dress like them, and talk like them.[36] They feel an irresistible attraction towards Whites and their way of life. Sharing this way of life becomes an overpowering aspiration of Blacks. Fanon describes this dilemma as the "Black Subject."[37] In this instance, the "Black Subject" will try to appropriate and imitate the cultural code of the oppressor. The behavior, Fanon argues, is even more evident in upwardly mobile and educated Blacks who can afford to acquire the trappings of White culture.[38]

A third component to this perpetuation of the corruption of the Black individual and erosion of value in the Black community is division, or lack of trust. The more alienated Blacks are the easier it is to divide them and keep them divided.[39] Given the circumstances that have presented Blacks with such resentment and suspicion of their own community it is only natural that they distrust themselves. In order for the condition of the Black community to perpetuate itself and the system remain intact, Blacks must remain divided. Accordingly, Whites uphold a political and social system that halts any action which in even incipient fashion could awaken the Black oppressed to the need for unity. Thus to isolate them and create and deepen the rifts among them is of vital importance.[40]

The only harmony which is viable and demonstrable is that found among Whites. Although they may diverge and upon occasion even clash over group interests, they unite immediately at a threat to the racial and social order. Favoring certain "representatives" of the Black community, promotion of individuals who reveal leadership capacity and could signify a threat if they were not "softened up," and the distribution of benefits to some and penalties to others, are ways of dividing Blacks in order to preserve a system which favors Whites.[41] Whites want to save their riches, their power, and their way of life: the things that enable them to subjugate others. Their interests lie in merely "changing" the consciousness of Blacks, not the situation which oppresses them.[42]

Lastly, an over-reliance on liberalism and the Democratic Party produces the perpetuation of the corruption of Black citizens and the erosion of value in the Black community. Keeping Blacks passive is accomplished by Whites depositing indispensable myths about the political culture in America; for example, the myth that the current system and state of affairs is the manifestation of a "free" society and all persons are free to work where they wish; or the myth that the street vendor is as much an entrepreneur as the owner of a large factory, and private property as fundamental to personal human development; and finally, the myth of the industriousness of Whites, the laziness and dishonesty of Blacks, and the natural inferiority of Blacks and the superiority of Whites.[43] The fact that over 80 percent of the Black population consistently votes Democratic only reinforces their commitment to "tweaking" the status quo.

As a political ideology, Liberalism has continually bombarded Blacks with an emphasis on individual rights and freedoms, meanwhile entire groups of people are subject to discrimination. Thus what the Black community needs is a group effort instead of relying on the protection of individual rights and relying on the assumption of upward mobility based on private property. Additionally, voting and participating in the American system as a minority is being overemphasized as the main methodology of Black progressive action eventhough Blacks remain politically isolated in America's two-party system. The perpetuation of corruption and erosion within the Black community is based, partly, on Blacks' inability to explore ideas and opportunities outside of the liberalist model and pursue political accountability outside of the Democratic Party. To change the habits and behaviors of the Black community will require innovative ideas and methods beyond the scope of Liberalism and the Democratic Party.

Rescinding the perpetuation of corruption and erosion of value in the Black community begins through a reinterpretation of Black history, portrayed and confessed by Blacks. What others have written about Blacks during the last three-plus centuries has been mainly for the purpose of bringing them to where they are today and holding him there.[44] The whole conception of Black history as it has been continually played out by Whites and depicted in textbooks, on screen, and in our institutions, is to keep them in a place in society behind that of Whites. To deny Blacks a history, a heritage, and a culture of their own ultimately makes them dependent on the oppressive White culture, history, and heritage. Ultimately this makes it easier to manipulate Blacks and get them to conform to practices and behaviors outside of their will. This transition is aided by the destruction and annihilation of Blacks' previous culture and history, and replaced with a more repressive history and culture to program Blacks into a mental environment of dependency and inferiority.

Dependency on liberalism and the over-reliance on the Democratic Party can be opposed by Blacks being reintroduced to the "meaningful vote" and new methods of impacting the way decisions are made and resources are allocated in Black communities. This implies not just the right to vote as a means of electing White candidates who have no real interest in the betterment of the Black community, nor a vote for Black candidates who are in no better position than White candidates to deliver resources to the Black community and only plan on using their position of power as spokesman for the Black community to enhance their own political power, influence, and wealth. The Black vote should represent a way to hold elected officials accountable. Rather elected officials, Black or White, wish to be accountable to the Black community at all remains uncertain. The Democratic Party has "captured" the Black vote. Based on the perceived racist and discriminatory rhetoric from Republicans, Blacks overwhelmingly vote Democratic essentially resulting in a lack of accountability to Black interests from the Republican Party who has been successful in winning elections without any significant proportion of Black votes. Yet at any time the interests of the Black community can be abandoned and ignored by Democrats as well when Blacks are not a determining factor in an election cycle. More importantly, "Black issues" are considered divisive and most politicians are taught to stay away from issues pertinent to the Black community to keep from being seen as a

"Black candidate," as if such a title reinforces negative connotations and feelings towards Blacks. Yet, the Black vote is not the only way to hold elected officials accountable, and thus cannot be all the focus of Blacks' attention to emancipate themselves from their current status and inadequate living conditions. A new perception of the reality of Blacks' history, their conditions, and their contributions to America will propel Blacks to combat their manipulation, cultural invasion, division and their over-reliance on liberalism and the Democratic Party.

THE AFTERMATH OF CORRUPTION AND EROSION: WHAT'S LEFT?

The consequences of corruption and erosion in the Black community are self-depreciation and a lack of race consciousness within the Black community; characterized by a lack of self-worth, self-respect, and holding negative perceptions of the community. Self-depreciation in the Black community is derived from Blacks' internalization of the opinion Whites hold of them.[45] Ultimately, Blacks have become convinced of their own unfitness and the unfitness of their community. Such self-depreciation results in a "culture of silence" in which Blacks' ignorance and lethargy becomes the product of their economic, social, and political domination.[46] Lack of self-worth and self-depreciation amongst Blacks is also the result of a perception that the U.S. government cares less about the well-being of the Black community than it does its other, more privileged members. When Black people fail to see their interests and aspirations being paid adequate attention by elected officials they feel that such institutions see little value in the Black community. They also rarely see their needs being addressed by any one of significance, or anyone who can reasonably be expected to have the resources to do anything about it. This opens the door to a wide array of individuals who, although not elected officials and unable to enact policy, can contribute resources to improve the condition of Blacks. And yet, the majority of Blacks see their concerns for adequate health care, quality education, jobs, and housing, go largely ignored by wealthy elites, both White and Black.

To determine the value and commitment that individuals, organizations, and the government have toward the Black community one can look at the allocation of resources to predominantly Black areas, or allocated specifically to those who identify as Black. Organizations and people generally allocate their money and resources into things that are important to them. Thus, housing, food, and the necessary essentials for sustenance are typically given top priority. In regards to government, defense, education, and taking care of the elderly and handicapped are typical priorities, in addition to other social programs such as assistance to the unemployed. Thus, one way to measure how much value is placed in the Black community is by the allocation of resources sent to solve Blacks' most pressing issues, and how efficient those resources are at achieving their desired outcomes. The majority of Blacks rarely see resources allocated to Black communities with the purpose of solving their declining employment, quality of housing options, and their health care needs. While Blacks continually find themselves at the bottom of the socioeconomic ladder, and no foreseeable aid coming from anyone with the resources to help, the lack of value and self-worth perceived by the Black community by Whites and other elite Blacks is not surprising.

Correcting the perception of citizenship among Blacks, the corruption of the Black individual, and erosion of value in the Black community is of vital importance to the sustainment of the Black community. Accurately depicting the conditions and shortcomings of Blacks' participation in the current system and the historical contributions made by Blacks creates value, self-worth, and self-respect, which in turn combats and slows down corruption and the erosion process. This can be done by pointing out the "nuclei of contradictions" in the American system and the functioning of its institutions. Blacks must consistently and continually point out the inherent flaws and inequalities in American society, perceptions of history and ultimately, the negative and contradictory perceptions of Blacks and the Black community. Disadvantaged members of the community must point out all discrepancies in earning power and wealth by Blacks despite doing equal, and sometimes more work than their White counterparts. The contradictions of American history based on liberty and freedom while at the same time annihilating Native Americans, expanding into another nation's territory, while enslaving millions of others must never be overlooked and neglected. These realities demonstrate how justice benefits the wealthy and privileged classes, while average working class Americans seldom find justice in America's courtrooms where high price lawyers and legal teams appear to have advantages rarely given to the poor. For all of the rhetoric about freedom, justice, equality, and the pursuit of happiness in America, Blacks must play a significant role in making sure that the nation lives up to its obligations and never stops reaching to achieve its ideal.

Once Blacks come to perceive themselves as less than free despite their assimilation into White society, they will be eligible to accept a "new" reality. Freire calls this process "submersion," in which individuals analyzing their own reality become aware of their prior, distorted perceptions and thereby come to have a new perception of that reality.[47] Blacks' new reality must confront their perceived inferiority to Whites, the insincere support by liberals and a Democratic party that has captured the Black vote, and the realization of their own self-worth and value in the Black community. Blacks must become aware of not only their distorted perception of freedom, but also what it means to be a citizen, or member of a national community, both the Black community, and as citizens of the U.S.

Conquering erosion and corruption creates value amongst Blacks that makes them easier to mobilize, thus, easier to sustain and accomplish group-desired goals. Sooner or later Blacks will have to comprehend their corrupt state and determine that as long as they are divided they will always be easy prey for manipulation and domination. Unity and organization can enable them to change their weakness into a transforming force.[48] Blacks' ability to unite on key socioeconomic issues that affect them directly will make it more difficult for them to be divided and will promote and sharpen their quest for universal freedom. Mobilizing Blacks around issues essential to their freedom and quest for equality strengthens the will and the resolve of the collective by reinforcing their commitment to the group. This requires more than just mobilizing around the Black vote and attempting to use it to get an elected official to consider Black interests. *Blacks need to reinterpret their conception of citizenship and association with the national community to establish the unity and solidarity required to adequately confront the American system from a position of strength.*

Blacks must think of themselves as citizens and members of the Black community in such a way as to successfully transform their conditions and change their daily lives. To be a member of the national community and continually look after the stability, sustainment, and betterment of the community takes a conception of citizenship currently not realized by Blacks. It is time to explore citizenship and the citizen in a way that addresses the dilemmas surrounding the misperception and corruption of citizenship and erosion of value in the Black community.

A THEORY OF CITIZENSHIP

Proper citizenship is established by a healthy relationship between individuals and their commitment and obligation to the national community to which they belong. A healthy relationship is defined as one where each individual is committed to the stability, protection, and betterment of the national community. Such a commitment can only be realized in an uncorrupted state; one in which the individual puts the collective interests of the community over their own self-interest.

Citizenship is something that must be earned or gained through a process in which individuals demonstrate the capacity to participate willingly and actively in attaining national interests and the betterment of their community. As Shklar suggests, citizenship can go through a devaluing process if people feel they are not adequately able to perform the duties and responsibilities associated with being a citizen. Subsequently, citizenship is valued as a good or status that is sought after so that individuals aspire to attain its rights, privileges, and more importantly, the responsibilities. Citizenship is devalued when people feel it is too liberally granted, which causes it to lose its esteem; similar to belonging to an exclusive club that comes with certain amenities included with the dues of membership. The more exclusive and admired the rights and privileges of membership are, the more valuable and respected they become.

Who, then, is a citizen? Any member of a national community that actively participates and contributes to the sustainment, protection, and improvement of that community is a citizen. Citizens identify as members of their national community; a group sharing certain physical and biological traits, a particular culture, identity, and values within a specific area or territory. Thus, America is a national community, as well the Black community represents a national community; Blacks ultimately owe their allegiance to both as members of both communities.

To willingly be a member of any national community confers certain obligations and responsibilities that non-members do not receive. The benefits of and obligations in being a citizen of the U.S. includes legal protection and civil rights, such as due process, and voting rights in exchange for obeying the laws of the constitution and paying taxes. As a citizen or member of the Black community, one should expect to receive protection and asylum within the Black community from oppressive laws, racist Whites, or any other enemy to the interests and sustainment of the Black community as a whole. The Black community offers to its members a place of retreat and a people who understand and defend their interests. In return for protection from the community, members of the Black community are obligated to contribute to the sustainment and protection of the group. You do not pay taxes necessarily as one does as a citizen of the U.S., but individuals should contribute to the economic well-being of the whole and protect the interests of the members and the values of the group. Just as there are certain rights and privileges associated with being a member or citizen of the U.S., the same is true for being a member of citizen of the Black community; mainly, contribute to the groups' sustainability, betterment, and protect its interests.

Citizenship is essentially the conferring of rights, privileges, and obligations between members of a national community; what you can expect from the group in return for one's contribution to it. To get something out of the Black community, members of the community have to put something into it. Thus the problem with the Black community today is that the people have not deposited anything of significance into the Black community. As a result, there is nothing to benefit from or take away from the Black community that its members view as a privilege. Ultimately, the Black community does not get much in return from its members, mean much to its members, or *have* much to provide its members. Being a member of the Black community demands one's active participation in contributing to the sustainment, protection, and improvement of the Black community; those who do not contribute are unworthy of the rights and privileges (protection) from the Black community. Anyone, Black or White, who does not defend, but rather causes the value of the Black community to diminish, does not deserve protection from the group, or the rights and privileges it confers. Consequently, short periods of limited or premature exclusion may be a necessary component of developing good citizenship habits.

Why is exclusion a necessary component of developing good citizens? First, requiring individuals to earn the rights and privileges of citizenship develops value; assigns worth and importance to the rights and privileges that citizens possess with an equitable worth to what citizens surrendered to earn those rights and privileges in the first place. To gain the protection that only belonging to a community can provide means that the individual must relinquish something of equal value, in this case excessive self-interest. Individuals give up the ability to unrelentingly go after their own self-interest in order to have the opportunity to attain a much higher, more significant collective interest. The more the individual is required to expend to attain the rights of citizenship, the more value placed in citizenship and the more individuals will also revere citizenship for all the hard work and effort they had to go through to attain it. Conversely, if required to put in and contribute nothing to the community to earn the rights and privileges of citizenship, the amount of value that the community can expect members to hold in it will be naught.

Protecting the value of the community and ensuring that citizens have the right relationship to the community is achieved through the exclusion of certain individuals from the rights and privileges of the community. The proper relationship between the citizen and the national community is one where the interests of the community are top priority; mainly the sustainment, defense, and protection of the interests and way of life of the community come first. This relationship ensures that there is a community in existence for future generations to tell its history and maintain its culture and heritage. This also establishes the rights and privileges of the individual. Without the community to recognize these rights, the individual citizen does not exist. Thus the relationship between the citizen and the national community is one of interdependence. No one wants to be isolated and separated from their history, culture, and heritage; all the things that make a national community come into existence. On the other hand, a national community cannot maintain itself without citizens who will stick up for it, defend it, and keep the stories of their history and heritage alive.

Citizenship, or the transfer of rights and privileges from the community to the individual membership, must be earned or gained through a process in order to protect its value. The rights and privileges associated with belonging to a community is a commodity or good that has value; if it has value then it must be nurtured and hoarded, not just issued nonchalantly. The relationship that individuals have with a national community has to continually be defended and guarded from attack or loss by people outside of the community, whose character is more destructive than conducive to the healthy environment that the community needs. Membership in a national community and identifying with a larger collective of individuals who share a history, culture, and language, has merit and importance in terms of what individuals will be willing to go through in order to obtain it. It's worth is essentially the level of contribution one is willing to exchange for access to the rights and privileges of the group. Members have the ability to acquire certain rights and privileges that people outside of the community do not share in exchange for their commitment and responsibilities to the collective. Thus, one's membership in the national community is to be considered with respect, worth, and regarded with high esteem. The best and most efficient way to ensure such loyalty to the community is through a process in which citizenship and its rights and privileges are earned.

Secondly, citizenship must be earned because it enables the people to be trained and educated in the ways of productive membership. This means not just taking from the community, being a detractor or contributor to its decline, but rather learning the ways of yielding favorable or effective results for the community overall. Not every individual will readily or willingly be able to accomplish such feats, nor are they inherently capable of doing so without proper education or training. Being a productive member of the Black community means producing goods and services that have favorable results for the community and contribute to its value. Thus, any person worthy of calling themselves a citizen must adhere to certain principles of contribution and obligation to the national community to which he or she belongs.

THE CITIZEN AND THE COMMON GOOD

The stability and sustainment of the community is based on the role of the citizen. An individual becomes a citizen only through their participation and involvement in the national community. A citizen cannot be a citizen alone, he or she must be recognized by a state or community of others. Citizens must work for the good of the community, or the common good, for no other reason than self-preservation; preservation of the citizen through the expression of trying to attain the common good. The common good represents those resources that are good for the entire group as a whole, or what preserves what the people or inhabitants of the national community have in common. Thus the most important thing a citizen can do is contribute to the preservation of the community in which the person belongs; most importantly, defend the community against that which seeks to destroy it.[49] In working toward the common good, citizens are then able to preserve themselves, the state, or constitution that makes them a unit or recognizes their rights and privileges. Through the common good, a community and its people are able to preserve themselves. It is working toward the common good that the citizen preserves oneself and the institutions that ensures future citizenship. As a result, the concept of citizenship and the "good" citizen is tied to the national community and the common good.

The common good represents specific goals that are shared and beneficial for all or most members of the national community. This is broken down to individual persons in regards to the basic requirements for staying alive, such as food, water, or shelter that are always good for all people. Similarly, there are the basic requirements that all communities need to "stay alive:" self-preservation, stability and sustainment of the shared history, culture and heritage, and protection from members outside the community who do not have the community's best interests. John Rawls defined the common good as "certain general conditions that are equally to everyone's advantage."[50] The common good, then, consists primarily of having the social systems, institutions, and environments for which all members of the community depend on and work in a manner that benefits all people. In the Black community today the common good is generally associated with the liberal Democratic agenda: concerns for employment, quality education and health care, and fairness in the justice system and other institutions of authority.

The rights and privileges associated with being a member of the Black community are the same as being a citizen of the U.S. There are certain claims and benefits enjoyed as immunities or exemptions for special treatment under certain circumstances. Those circumstances are associated with the obligations or duties associated with membership. Meaning, there are certain expected or required actions to do by position, function, or status in the Black community to contribute to the common good; to protect, defend, and be a productive member of the national community and work towards its best interest. Protecting the Black community from harm, including further corruption and erosion, can only be achieved with other invested members of the Black community. Collectively the people have power to change their socioeconomic conditions and influence government, but no single person has any significant power that lasts.

As a citizen of the U.S., individuals expect to receive the rights and privileges of protection, loyalty, and access to resources and decision makers through institutions that represent the common good. Thus, the rights and privileges of membership in the Black community are protection of their history, culture, and shared experiences from attacks and invasion by Whites and other communities, and loyalty to protecting and sustaining institutions that ensure the rights and privileges of membership for future generations. For example, when individual Blacks receive unfair treatment, or feel like the system or institutions have done them a disservice or treated them unfairly, the Black community should be there to provide a sanctuary to which the individual can retreat and be given not only the benefit of the doubt, but be defended and protected by the collective of individuals who will hold whoever is responsible accountable. But to continually be able to get such rights and privileges from the Black community, individuals have to make contributions to the common good of that community; otherwise there will be no sanctuary of unified group that is capable of protecting the community and holding others accountable. Thus, to make withdrawals on the rights and privileges of membership, individuals have to pay dues of contribution to the community for its stability and health in the long run. Without individual contributions to the common good of the Black community, there will be no Black community to retreat to.

The concept of citizenship and membership in a national community is essentially tied to the concept of the common good. A citizen must work for the good of others, or the common good, if for no other reason than self-preservation; preservation of the citizen through the expression and realization of the common good. It is in the community that values are chosen, because the community provides the structure in which our being as persons is realized. It is not possible to transcend the community; it frames our being because being is always being in relation to others.[51] The common good represents the preservation of those characteristics that members of the national community have in common. In other words, in working for others, citizens are then able to preserve themselves, the state or national community to which they belong, and the history and culture that makes them a community in the first place. Such a community is then able to recognize the rights and privileges associated with membership, and ensure that people are fulfilling their obligations to the community. Working towards the common good empowers the citizen to preserve themselves, the institutions that ensure future citizenship, and the stability of the national community to which they hope to belong to in the future.

Citizens need the national community to continually recognize their rights, status, responsibilities, and obligations of belonging to the community; otherwise they would not exist as a national community in the first place. Knowledge of the common good is stored in the community. The further one departs from their community, the less comprehension they will have of the common good. As a result, Blacks must reassess how we value membership in our communities: both as citizens of the U.S. and as members of the Black community. They must develop the power to do for themselves what the current system will never do to elevate them to the level of others.[52] As social and political animals, our ability to flourish and overcome adversity is strongest when involved in doing things together, rather than being exclusively concerned with private ends.[53] All decisions made with regard to what is important or worthwhile are made in the context of one's role or status in the community.

The most fundamental problem to accomplishing the common good develops out of widespread pursuit of individual interests (corruption). Working towards the common good requires replacing the current "ethic of individual rights" with an "ethic of the common good."[54] Individualism represents the most significant problem for attempts to promote the common good. Historical traditions of America place high value on individual freedom, personal rights, and allowing each person to "do their own thing." American culture views society as comprised of separate independent individuals who are free to pursue their own individual goals and interests without interference from others. In this individualistic culture it is difficult to convince people that they should sacrifice some of their freedom, personal goals, or their self-interest for the sake of others. In fact, American cultural traditions reinforce the individual who thinks that he or she should not have to contribute to the community's well-being, but should be left free to pursue their own personal ends.[55] Consequently, we face a choice between a society where people accept modest sacrifices for a common good and a more contentious society where groups selfishly protect their own benefits.

The process in which a citizen displays loyalty to the community and willingness to sacrifice individual interest for the group will look different depending on the status and conditions of the group in its original state. Meaning, the process in which the community originally establishes itself may be different; it may one of war and conquest, religion, or by the skill and contributions of labor by individual members. Despite whatever process the national community comes to establish itself, the stages in which the people come to learn the principles of contribution and obligation to the group are essentially the same. For starters, the people must be trained and educated in the knowledge of "the good"; what is good for the community and as a result, good for them as individuals. The "good" are those things that benefit the community as a whole; lead to the development, sustainment, stability, and betterment of the community overall. What is "good" for the Black community is those things that protect and sustain the shared experiences and history of that community, and thus enables it to survive attacks from the White community or the collection of different identities that make the U.S. Consequently, the "bad" is those things that lead to the detriment and decline of the standing and conditions of the Black community or causes its interests to be devalued. Members of the Black community must be educated and trained in acquiring the type of knowledge that leads to the good for the community, in addition to knowledge of what is bad for the community. Not everything done and experienced by and for Blacks is "good"; good for their development, protection, and improvement. Thus, the people must be trained in the knowledge of what is good for the whole and as a result how to avoid the things that are bad for it. Without this knowledge, members of the Black community are unable to recognize what needs to be protected, what their talents and skills should be utilized for, and what actions and behaviors are detrimental to the community's development.

Additionally, the people must be trained and educated in the importance of community values; how to put the good of the community over the good of the individual. This requires individuals to learn about team building, the significance of their shared history, culture, and heritage (those things that unite them and make them a national community). Citizens need to be trained in the things that make them a "people" in the first place. This education reestablishes the bond and affinity of what it means to be a citizen; to belong to the people of your shared history and culture, and consequently, how to preserve one's community.

Finally, the people must be trained in ways of contributing to the common good. This means people must be trained in a skill or trade, by the community and for the community; educated by members of the community in a skill or trade that will enable them to contribute to the community. Through this development it is imperative that individuals be trained in a skill that they have talent in. To have its people out of place, in jobs and occupations that they are unqualified for and incapable of doing, is the worst outcome produced by a national community. This contributes to the decline of the national community; people out of place, doing tasks they have no talent in, and are unqualified to do. The proper functioning of the community requires its members to be fully trained and qualified for the tasks in which they are assigned to contribute to the community. Each member must not only be trained in a skill, but that skill must be something they have talent in as well as a benefit to the greater society and not just their own individual aspirations. Otherwise the needs of the collective go neglected as individuals concentrate on satisfying their own self-interest. Ideally an individual's aspirations would be directed toward the community and the common good. Their trade and what they want to do with it would be aligned with the goals and objectives of the community. Meaning, what people want to do, are qualified to do, and are best at, is contributing their services to the sustainment and development of the community.

Ultimately, conceiving of citizenship as a status to be earned establishes accountability and obligation to the community. Being accountable requires that members of the community be responsible to the other members of the community for their actions. Citizens must be answerable and be able to explain their actions and behaviors to the other members of the community. This enables them to continually reinforce to the others their commitment to the good of the community and why they should continue to receive the rights and privileges associated with it. Being answerable to the other members of the community ensures that individuals will be more likely to sacrifice their own self-interest for the common good. Requiring that the rights and privileges associated with the title of citizen be earned establishes that individual members be able to explain and justify their actions that lead them to sacrifice for the common good while being responsible to other members who do the same.

The rights and privileges of citizenship provide resources that members of the community are indebted to do certain things for. An individual has to fulfill certain requirements to earn access to the rights and privileges provided by the community. Once admitted, they must demonstrate a continued commitment to the interests of the group to guarantee continued access to those rights and privileges, and the protection provided by the community. The resources provided by the community the individual cannot attain alone. Thus, access to the resources of the community establishes the foundation for which the individual's obligation rests; an obligation to actively contribute and participate in the sustainment and protection of the community in order to have continued access to the most significant resources achievable. In addition to this commitment arises a sense of duty to improve the conditions of the community to which the individual belongs. This sense of obligation also arises out of the results from customs established throughout the history of the national community. Meaning, individual members of the community feel obligated to continually contribute to the good of the community out of the history and tradition of past members who made the same sacrifice or similar contributions. Members of the national community in this sense are morally, if not legally bound, to contribute to the community, and that contribution is owed in return for the rights and privileges associated with being a member; the services for which the individual is indebted. Accountability and obligation to the community in this way establishes unity around the common goals and objectives of the Black community, objectives which in turn help establish accountability; accountable to the community to help achieve its objectives, and each individuals' contribution to those objectives. Dispersing the rights and privileges of citizenship without it being earned allows for loyalty and value in the national community to diminish. Requiring the rights and privileges to be earned creates value and limiting who receives the resources of the community makes the group more manageable.

Creating a long-term sustainable community with virtuous citizens requires exclusion or providing limited rights to a portion of the population, although this process is generally temporary; only done to get the state or people on the right path, or teach the people the fundamental values of the new system, their new privileges, and the obligations and responsibilities essential to sustain them. Fanon contends that "if you think you can perfectly govern without involving the people; if you think that by their very presence the people confuse the issue, that they are a hindrance or, through their inherent unconsciousness an undermining factor, then there should be no hesitation: the people should be excluded."[56] Blacks are known for their confusion on an issue, sometimes through no fault of their own. But through the manipulation and destruction of their culture and heritage, Blacks have become a people unconscious to the true meaning of citizenship and thus, contributing members of their community. Until Blacks stop becoming their own undermining factor, they will never be able to confront the American system successfully.

Corrupted perceptions of the meaning of citizenship are an impediment to the sustainment and betterment of the national community. The erosion in value of citizenship and belonging to the Black community opens the door for division to further impede on any potential progress by Blacks. In times when the need for unity and solidarity is so imperative to a community's development and improvement, protecting the values and access to the rights and privileges associated with its membership can best be done by excluding those people who get the issue confused, or have not demonstrated the ability or willingness to put the national community's interests and the sustainment of its values before the interests of their individual self.

What happens to those who are not citizens or going through the transition into citizenship? Those who are not citizens do not receive any of the rights, privileges, benefits, and obligations that members of the national community receive. At no point does any institution that claims to be American or benefit the Black community attempt to deny any individual the freedom of life and liberty, as idealized in liberal institutions. By excluding certain individuals from being citizens is not to deny them from the title of personhood. As in Liberal thought, there are certain inalienable rights that individuals have that cannot be taken away under any circumstances by the state or surrendered to any other person. These inalienable rights are continually recognized as those who are not citizens make the transition, or reside within the same territory with individuals who are.

Key to retaining the value of citizenship is to reinforce the fact that some people have it, and some people do not, and it is in the best interest of the community that this relationship be maintained. Maintaining this relationship is one of necessity; it ensures that those who have the title of citizenship have demonstrated and understand the significance of their contribution to the betterment of the community. Achieving the goals and objectives of the community are too important to leave in the hands of people who fail to understand the relevance of history and protect the values and interests of other members of the community, thus, sacrificing to contribute to its maintenance. Additionally, the common good can reasonably be achieved without the input of all persons. Those who fail to demonstrate the ability to put the goods of the community over their own self-interest, are incapable or unwilling to contribute to the sustainment, stability, betterment, and protection of the community and its shared history and experience, and have no knowledge of the "good" and "bad" things for that community, are not dependable enough to be considered citizens or members of that national community. It is justifiable and legitimate to exclude people who are more of a detriment and liability to the community achieving its goals from the rights and privileges of group membership until they have gone through a process in which their loyalty to achieving the goals and objectives of the community has been addressed. Those excluded from the rights and privileges associated with being a member of the national community are still protected by the inalienable rights granted to all persons, and as such, would be respected by the state or national community.

Interpreting citizenship this way sets a standard of accountability for the individual citizen. Blacks have to demonstrate that they are able to explain their behavior and be responsible to someone or something more than just themselves as individuals. There is no greater commitment to anything that an individual can make than to the sustainment and betterment of their community and assure that its history and culture is protected. Without demonstrating accountability to their own communities, Blacks cannot expect to attain any more rights or freedoms than they currently have. Those who have not learned to do for themselves and have to depend on others never obtain any more rights or privileges in the end than they had in the beginning.[57] This is a task that only Blacks can handle amongst themselves. No other group can or should be relied upon to protect the interests and values of their heritage and culture than other members of the Black community.

Correcting the corruption of citizens and the erosion of value in the Black community restores the humanity of both Blacks and Whites in the U.S. The ability of the Black community to affirm itself and protect and sustain itself speaks to the true ideals of the American dream where not just individuals, but an entire class of former slaves whose interests were dismissed and access to freedom have been denied, are realized. Blacks' ability to develop a perception of the group based on their own standards, and not the standard placed on them by another group or based on the values and beliefs of another culture, reinforces a commitment to the Black community and what it means to be American. The betterment and sustainment of the Black community, using their own methods, helps advance the greater good of the U.S. as a whole. American political culture and its ideals of freedom and equality will be fully realized once Blacks have taken the necessary steps to determine the fate of their own communities. Raising the socioeconomic bar for Blacks and improving their standing in the U.S. raises the bar and sets a brand new standard for justice and equality for everyone. Thus, solving the issues within the Black community is not just beneficial to Blacks alone, but will enable

Blacks and Whites to compromise when necessary on policies to benefit both groups from a position of mutual interdependence and strength, rather than dependence and dominance. As Freire suggests, the fight for justice for Blacks is to liberate themselves as well as their oppressors.[58]

The central problem facing Blacks that must be solved if their sustainment and betterment is to be restored is creating opportunities for themselves. Today they face the ordeal of either learning to do for the community first or witness the community die out gradually. Blacks who live in the ghettoes get far too little of the wealth and resources of American society. Waiting for the solution to be handed down from the government is the surest guarantee that there will be no effective solutions to the crisis in Black communities.[59] The Black community needs to find its voice and make a mark on the political map; they are currently treated as objects of political outcomes rather than subjects of political participation; as people to whom things are done, rather than people who can achieve things for themselves. Those who are not interested in the sustainment and betterment of the Black community and make no effort to solve it are worthless in the present struggle.[60] Restoring the commitment and value in the Black community is even more difficult to overcome if those at the top and those at the bottom are farther apart than ever.[61]

There is no way for Blacks to evade the seriousness of their responsibility to their community. Blacks must adopt an attitude that no one is free until they all are free and as a result, they are all required to participate in the production of freedom. "All or nothing" is the only possible attitude for the Black community.[62] Included in this conception of "all or nothing" is the idea that contributing to the common good of the Black community requires the kind of participation willing to do whatever it takes to preserve and protect the community. Part of the element of survival, sustainment, and stability of the community is the ability to define and assert the conditions necessary for their being in the world.[63] This can most efficiently be done by exercising whatever means Blacks deem necessary to their survival and stability. No other group can determine what is in its best interest and what is the best way to protect the shared history and experiences which make the Black community what it is to begin with. It is the obligation and responsibility of the members of the Black community to make sure that the community remains committed to that which defines its existence; the shared experiences, history, culture, and heritage.

The perception of Blacks as second class citizens and the manipulation and invasion of Black culture has influenced the corruption, erosion and devaluing of membership in the Black community. As a result of their corrupted conception of what it means to be a member of a national community, Blacks have also adopted a negative perception of their relationship to America as citizens, and conversely, members of the Black community. Adopting a conception of citizenship that reinforces the peo-

ples' commitment and obligation to the community must be institutionalized by effective leadership and thereby transform how Blacks participate in and value their advancement collectively. Thus, first, it is important to investigate how a negative conception of citizenship and one's
corrupted relationship to the community produces negative patterns of
interaction amongst members of the Black community.

NOTES

1. J. H. Carens, *Culture, Citizenship, and Community* (Oxford: Oxford University
Press, 2000).

2. Seyla Benhabib, *The Claims of Culture: Equality and Diversity in the Global Era*
(Princeton, NJ: Princeton University Press, 2002), 162.

3. Ibid.

4. Ibid., 180.

5. Ibid., 25.

6. Judith N. Shklar, *American Citizenship: The Quest for Inclusion* (Cambridge, MA:
Harvard University Press, 2001), 1.

7. Carter G. Woodson, *The Mis-Education of the Negro* (Kentucky: Tribeca Book,
2011), 105.

8. David Walker, *David Walker's Appeal* (New York: Hill and Wang, 1995), 65.

9. Frank A. Rollin, *Life and Services of Martin R. Delany* (Krause Reprints, 1969), 348.

10. Ibid., 329.

11. Kenneth M. Dolbeare, *American Political Thought* 4th ed. (Chatham House Publishers, 1998), 312.

12. Shklar, *American Citizenship*, 55.

13. Ibid., 52.

14. Ibid., 54.

15. Robert M. Goldman, *Reconstruction and Black Suffrage: Losing the Vote in Reese and
Cruikshank* (Lawrence: University Press of Kansas), 2001.

16. W. E. B. Du Bois, *Reconstruction in America* (New York: The Free Press, 1992).

17. Jack Barnes, *Malcolm X, Black Liberation & the Road to Workers Power* (New York:
Pathfinder Press), 2009.

18. Goldman, *Reconstruction and Black Suffrage*.

19. Ibid.

20. Stokely Carmichael and Charles V. Hamilton, *Black Power: The Politics of Liberation in America* (New York: Vintage Books, 1967).

21. Ibid.

22. Ibid.

23. Niccolo Machiavelli, *Discourses on Livy*. (Oxford: Oxford University Press), 1997.

24. Carter G. Woodson, "Fifty Years of Negro Citizenship as Qualified by the United States Supreme Court," *The Journal of Negro History* 6 no.1 (1921): 1–53.

25. Sellers et al., "Multidimensional Inventory of Black Identity: A Preliminary Investigation of Reliability and Construct Validity," *Journal of Personality and Social
Psychology* 3 (1997): 806.

26. Robert C. Tucker, *The Marx–Engels Reader*, 2nd ed. (New York: W. W. Norton,
1978).

27. Paulo Freire, *Pedagogy of the Oppressed* (London: Continuum, 2006), 161.

28. James Cone, *A Black Theology of Liberation* (Maryknoll, NY: Orbis Books, 1986).

29. James Cone, *Black Theology & Black Power* (Maryknoll, NY: Orbis Books, 1997),
104–5.

30. Freire, *Pedagogy of the Oppressed*, 149.

31. Ibid., 141.

32. Ibid., 36.
33. Ibid., 47.
34. Ibid., 45.
35. Ibid., 160.
36. Ibid., 153.
37. Frantz Fanon, *Black Skin, White Masks*. (New York: Grove Press, 2008).
38. Ibid.
39. Freire, *Pedagogy of the Oppressed*, 142.
40. Ibid., 141.
41. Ibid., 144–45.
42. Ibid., 74.
43. Ibid., 140.
44. Woodson, *The Mis-Education of the Negro*, 131.
45. Freire, *Pedagogy of the Oppressed*, 63.
46. Ibid.
47. Ibid., 114.
48. Ibid., 145.
49. Ibid., 104.
50. John Rawls, *Justice as Fairness*. (Cambridge, MA: Harvard University Press, 2001).
51. Cone, *A Black Theology of Liberation*, 97.
52. Woodson, *The Mis-Education of the Negro*, 99.
53. Aristotle, *Politics*, (Indianapolis: Hackett Publishing Company, 1998).
54. Manual Velasquez, Claire Andre, Thomas Shanks, S. J., and Michael J. Meyer, "The Common Good," *Issues in* Ethics 5 no.1 (Spring 1992).
55. Ibid.
56. Fanon, *Black Skin, White Masks*, 131.
57. Woodson, *The Mis-Education of the Negro*, 126.
58. Freire, *Pedagogy of the Oppressed*, 44.
59. Hadjor, *Another America*, 194.
60. Woodson, *The Mis-Education of the Negro*, 108–109.
61. Hadjor, *Another America*, 179.
62. Ibid., 57.
63. Ibid., 46.

TWO

On the Habits of Citizenship

As a result of the corrupted perception of citizenship and erosion of value in the Black community, Blacks have bad citizenship "habits." The habits of citizenship are the everyday interactions amongst the members of a national community. They are acquired patterns of behavior practiced by members of a national community that have been so regularly followed that they appear involuntary. These patterns of behavior are unconscious as they appear to be independent of individual will. Recurrent patterns of interaction are fossilized through frequent repetition. Thus, citizenship habits guide the political and social interactions of members of a national community; helping shape the public sphere and the quality of life for people in the community. The challenge is to develop habits of citizenship that can empower citizens.

A negative perception of the community or the rights and privileges of membership will produce "bad habits." Danielle Allen (2004) analyzes this perception of citizenship through the relationship of dominant versus minority groups. The Civil Rights movement amounted to a "psychic transformation of the citizenry."[1] This transformation remains incomplete because we continue to have "bad habits," that have hardened into "congealed distrust" and even "settled patterns of mutual disdain."[2] "Bad habits" stem from our political culture; our daily experiences of living amongst one other. Shaped by "deep rules" and "unspoken norms," our current political culture is one of distance and mistrust. "Bad habits" and deep rules of public interaction are learned through intuition and habit rather than education in the explicit rights and duties of citizenship.

Without committed members contributing to clearly defined group goals and objectives, producing a healthy relationship between members of a community will be difficult. Subsequently, how the people interact with one another comes to define how the group interprets the values of the community. The way Blacks interact with one another is at the root of what it means to be a member of the Black community. The quality of Black life is shaped by how Blacks treat and relate to one another. This, too, ultimately depends on the level of value placed on the Black community. The more value placed in the Black community, the higher quality of life those within the community can expect to live and share. People who hold high value in being members of the Black community will be less likely to be victims of corruption, erosion, and the "bad habits" of citizenship.

Positive elements of citizenship that should be emphasized include political friendship, trust, and sacrifice. Together, these elements contribute to the healthy relationship between citizens in order to effectively attain group desired goals. *Political friendship* means that citizens develop an intimate relationship based on affection and loyalty as allies in the fight to seek or exercise their political rights. It demands that citizens feel that they share an equitable amount of the benefits and burdens of citizenship.[3] Acts of *trust* among citizens represent the ability to rely on and be confident in another member's loyalty and commitment to the group and to the community's interests. By and large citizens analyze political problems on roughly the same conceptual turf.[4] Thus, the central problem is a lack of trust amongst citizens. Citizens must feel confident that the obligations and opportunities of society are shared equitably. Without trust, there is nothing to keep different members of the community working together. Developing habits of trust allows citizens to perceive unknown members outside of their community as friends.

Citizens have to trust that the other members are just as committed as they are, and can be relied upon continually to put the goods of the community first and share in the responsibilities and obligations concerning the common good. In the end, citizens have to trust that others are suppressing their self-interest and focusing on the goods of the community on an equal basis. Not only because the people have all made the same contribution to the community, but also because the ability to rely on such friendship and loyalty when the community's value is being tested and threatened is vital. Citizens must be able to rely on other members to come to the defense of the community, and uphold its traditions and values, and not participate in its destruction.

Lastly, *sacrifice* is the key concept that bridges citizenship and trust. Members of the community have to be reassured of the mutual surrender of something prized or desirable for the sake of something that brings greater value and resources to the community as a whole. Sacrifice is an important attribute of the good habits of citizenship in that value and loyalty in the community is reinforced over the sacrifice made by other members of the community. The only way to deal with sacrifice effectively is to build relations of trust among citizens so that they can be confident that their sacrifices will be reciprocated. Part of building trust and commitment in the community is the belief that the sacrifice made by individuals benefits the community, and that everyone in the community is sacrificing equally to all of the other members.

All the elements of positive citizenship habits are interconnected. Political friendship is innately correlated with the concepts of trust and sacrifice. Friends are more likely to understand one another, trust one another with a secret or with a prized possession, and sacrifice or give something up to another friend. Without trust, the level of political friendship that is needed to collectively fight for the rights to exercise political freedom and preserve the traditions and culture of the community cannot develop, and the amount of sacrifice needed by each citizen to contribute to the collective is lost. Without each member's contribution of sacrifice and without each person's reassurance that others have made similar or equitable sacrifices it is difficult to establish trust among members of a community. When some people make the sacrifice and others do not, one can expect the political friendship and trust to be lacking. Absent of the positive elements of citizenship, the ability for the people to produce a healthy perception of their community is diminished, and leads to negative and destructive patterns of interaction among members.

"BAD HABITS" OF CITIZENSHIP

The "bad habits" of citizenship are the result of the corrupted state of citizens and the erosion of value in the community. "Bad" habits of citizenship include distrust, suspicion, alienation, anger, and resentment. They are the reasons that interactions among citizens are unhealthy and disallow the people to build relationships of understanding that enable them to flourish collectively. Negative patterns of interaction are the reasons why Blacks have not been able to collectively improve their conditions and status in America. Together, these bad habits of citizenship contribute to the destruction of the Black community and the elimination of significant elements of their shared experiences, history, culture, and heritage. They diminish the ability of the Black community to accomplish shared goals and objectives and attain the common good.

Distrust amongst citizens and members of the Black community takes place when there is doubt and skepticism surrounding other members of the community. First is doubt as to whether individuals are making any sacrifices to the common good and have relinquished their materialistic drive for self-interest. Secondly is doubt whether other members of the community have made similar contributions and fully understand the obligations of what it means to share in the rights and privileges of citizenship. Ultimately, there is no assurance that members of the community will readily and involuntarily make sacrifices to the group and share in its fight for preservation. When citizens do not trust each other they build up barriers and organize themselves in ways that protect them from each other. Distrust leads to an element of fear whereby citizens begin to fear one another. Thus, Blacks end up protecting themselves, not from people outside of the Black community who wish to threaten the safety and value of the community, but protecting themselves from other Blacks. Fear of one another develops from this lack of trust and doubt of the actions, intentions, and motives of the other members of the Black community.

Suspicion is the tendency to doubt the trustworthiness of appearances and therefore believe that one has detected possibilities of something unreliable, unfavorable, or menacing in other members of the community. The way that Blacks are portrayed and perceived by people outside of the Black community gives the appearance that they are unreliable and produce intolerable effects on the national community overall. Such portrayals also add to the suspicion and unfavorable feeling that Blacks get when they witness other members of the Black community. Suspicion produces negative portrayals of individuals as menacing to the interests and values of the Black community as a whole. When Blacks see other members of the community acting contrarily to their beliefs and value system, this perception of individuals as a menace to the community emerges and thus the negative attitudes and feelings about the Black community are heightened.

Anger and *resentment* contribute heavily to the corrupted state of Blacks and the erosion of valuing citizenship and membership in the Black community. Members of a national community who are not friends, who are also full of suspicion and distrust, will find themselves with strong feelings of displeasure towards other members. Blacks soon begin to resent not only the individual members, but their actions, attitudes, and behaviors become intolerable. As a result, the individual attitudes Blacks feel toward other members in the community become hostile. When members of a national community resent one another and view others' actions and behaviors as hostile and detrimental to the collective interests of the community, the corruption of the citizen and the erosion of value in the community have been fully realized.

Alienation refers to the separation of things that naturally belong together, or to put antagonism between things that are properly in harmony.[5] People with shared experiences, culture, history, and heritage should not necessarily be separated; together they represent the natural "harmony" that is needed to achieve group desired goals. In the fight to preserve and sustain their community, people with such commonalities belong together and the elements essential to their community are dissolved by alienation. Communities that naturally share experiences, culture, heritage, and history are determined to be in harmony when working together for a shared objective or collective interests. As a result of alienation, individuals lose determination over their lives and destinies by being deprived of the right to conceive of themselves as the director of their actions, to determine the character of their actions, to define their relationship to others, and to use or own the value of what is produced by their actions.[6]

Karl Marx (1844) examines four elements of alienation that produce bad habits and negative patterns of interaction amongst members of the Black community. First, alienation between the individual and the product of one's labor represents the separation of the Black individual and their contribution to the collective interests of society and the common good. The products of individual labor are meant to make a contribution to the sustainment, protection, and betterment of the community. Alienation, in this sense, means that this natural connection to contribute products to the benefit of the community is lost. Instead, the products of labor are made for individual satisfaction and not the overall benefit of the community. Thus, in this stage of alienation, Blacks lose the sense of contributing goods and services to the preservation, sustainment, and betterment of the Black community; the natural allegiance between humans and the products of their labor.

Secondly, is alienation from work itself; the patterning of work into an endless sequence of discrete, repetitive, trivial, and meaningless motions, offering little, if any, intrinsic satisfaction.[7] Blacks no longer see work as a natural expression of their contribution to the community, but rather a burdensome price to pay in order to just live and survive individually within society. Work and the ability to labor is the chief and easiest way to contribute to the community and a natural or inherent part of building the commitment between individuals and the community.

Third, is alienation of the individual from himself, or from what it means to be human. For Marx, this "species being" or "essence as a species"[8] is actualized through the process of work. As political animals humans are meant to work together for collective interests and the common good. Labor, as a natural expression of human action, is not meant to be confined for the use or purpose of the individual. Our human "essence" demands that individuals work for the betterment of their community. Thus, the alienation Blacks have toward the activity and products of their labor, separates them from what it means to be human; that is, participate in the contribution to the sustainment of their race. Without this contribution, the race fails to exist in its natural condition. Working and contributing to the betterment of the Black community, through working towards the common good reconfirms their being as Blacks.

Finally, is alienation from "man to man." Rather than a social relationship between people involved in a common effort for survival or betterment, the current structure of society alienates Blacks from their mutual interest, an effect Marx called "false consciousness."[9] This false consciousness puts individuals who would rather be working together for their collective interests at odds with one another, no longer recognizing their shared experiences and objectives. Consequently, alienation from "man to man" appears to be an accumulation of all the other elements of alienation into one, or as the consequence of all the others combined. Blacks who would naturally be working together for a common purpose, under the current societal structure are left competing with one another, and working against one another and subsequently the common good. All of the bad habits of citizenship get played out in this last form of alienation, thus it is essential to the discussion of bad citizenship habits.

HISTORY AND THE DEBATE
WITH CONSERVATIVE AMERICA

The political and social habits of Blacks have been scrutinized and under investigation since the first interaction of Africans with Europeans. Before the character and behavior of Blacks were under attack by White America and conservative Republicans, the natives of Africa were declared naturally inferior, uncivilized and barbaric to the more enlightened and civilized White Europeans. Non-European people were characterized as barbarous or uncivilized, not possessing fully developed rational capacities, and incapable of fully rational function. Africans were labeled as accepting of the culture of slavery but incapable of accepting the culture of freedom. Hence they were declared to be in need of tutelage for their own good.[10] Whites, by contrast, were said to possess all the drives, talents, and predispositions to culture and civilization that make for progress.[11] Contributors to Liberalist and early American political thought, such as J. S. Mill, Thomas Jefferson, Immanuel Kant, and others, all perceived of native Africans, and ultimately American Blacks, the same way. Blacks continue to be victims of a perception of the race that has contributed nothing to the civilized world.

By 1965, Daniel Moynihan's, *The Negro Family: The Case for National Action*, again highlighted the internal deficiencies of the Black community, this time singling out the Black family as the principle source of their condition, and no longer the natural inferiority of the race. In his view, "there is now sufficiently equal opportunity for all to achieve socioeconomic success, so that failure to do so by members of any group must be due to internal deficiencies and not to external factors."[12] American Conservatives labored mightily to emphasize the progress that Blacks made since 1960,[13] largely to support their position that Blacks no longer needed assistance from the state. Blacks have been portrayed and targeted as the progenitors of a dangerous underclass culture of drugs, gangs, openly promiscuous sexual behavior and stylistic expressions in speech, dress and social mannerisms.[14] In 1995, then Speaker of the House and 2012 Republican Presidential candidate Newt Gingrich, revealed his view that the economic plight of poor Blacks was partly a result of their "habits" and that the Civil Rights Movement was more focused on grievances than on economic development. His attribution of certain "habits" to Black people extended to all Blacks, including those in the middle class. The bad "habits" based view of the reason for Blacks' status in America was typically Conservative and narrow in that it made no reference to how majority control of the American opportunity structure maintains the subordinate status of the Black community.[15]

Rev. Jesse Lee Peterson (2003) suggests what is lacking from the Black community in shaping their "habits" and attitude is a lack of good role models, personal responsibility, and moral principles. Blaming sexual immorality and drug use for the spread of AIDS and irresponsible behavior for spreading crack cocaine in inner cities, Peterson argues that Blacks have been absolved from personal responsibility for their actions by other members of the Black community.[16] For him the biggest problem facing Blacks in America is self-sabotage and an ideology of "victimology" and anti-intellectualism. The attitude within the Black community that academic achievement is a "White thing" and that Blacks must reject intellectualism in order to stay "culturally Black" are bigger reasons Blacks find themselves in the conditions they are in, rather than the racism of Whites.[17] The "lack of character" depicted by Black youth, characterized as angry, emotional, and having drug and authority problems, comes from the high volume of broken homes or homes that have been filled with violence.[18] These kids have never learned a proper work ethic or patience, nor have they seen good role models. Hence they grow up lazy, angry, and prone to violence because they live in an environment that is more like a jungle than a civilized community.[19] For Conservative America, today's generation of Black youth have no character, no moral base to live by, and no real hope for the future. Those who attempt to enter the workforce often become problems for their employers because they have an entitlement mentality that puts little emphasis on working hard to get ahead. They expect to be paid for doing little work, often show up late, and have bad attitudes while on the job.[20]

The Black family, now significantly headed by single mothers, has resulted in the extinction of the Black "father" and consequently, Black men and women have no idea how to have a normal man-woman relationship. The anger of Black women toward the incarcerated men renders them functionally incompetent to properly guide their children. Thus, the gang violence, sex, drugs, homosexuality, divorce, and lawlessness you see in the Black community are not due to racism but to absent fathers and angry mothers.[21] Black men bear much of the responsibility for the destruction of the Black family because of their sexual irresponsibility and laziness, but Black women are also at fault. As a result, Black men and women victimize each other, and the anger and rage that is produced is passed along to their offspring. The sad truth, according to Conservative America, is that Black women frequently contribute to their own children's downward spiral into welfare dependency and violence by passing on their bitterness to the children.

For Peterson, Blacks seem to care more about welfare checks and material wealth than they care about character, integrity, and personal responsibility.[22] They show no sign that they can overcome their condition and move up in the world. Lack of character, moral principles, self-responsibility, and hard work have led to the destruction of the Black community and these negative habits of interaction and citizenship are inherent problems of the Black community, and not a result of the system or the history and effects of slavery and racism. Suggesting that the Black underclass is impoverished and deprived primarily because of its own bad behavior and not because of the way society is organized is described as a "culture of poverty."[23] Problems of poverty, bad housing, and unemployment are essentially caused by the sloth of the Black communities themselves. Laziness, love of the latest fads and fashion, drug addiction and alcohol abuse, an easy attitude toward sexual relationships, and a lack of commitment to marital stability illustrate the debilitated nature of the Black community. "Dysfunctional families" of the ghetto, produced by the slack of sexual morality and lack of respect for the marital state, typifies "underclass behavior." Respect for authority, hard work, thrift and self-denial, these are the values that the "Right" claims that the "underclass" needs if it is to be saved from itself. Thus the circumstances in which poor Blacks live lead them to act in deviant ways.[24]

The debate within Conservative America is founded, at first, on the inherent inequalities and inferiorities of Blacks. Later, when the scientific evidence of inherent Black inferiority became unpopular, if not believed to be true, the focal point of Black inequality shifted to bad behavior and habits. America expects children to study hard, expects young people to refrain from having children until they can support them, expects adults to work at a steady job, and expects everyone to obey the laws. Coincidentally, if the Black poor are stuck at the bottom, it must be their own fault; a consequence of their behavior, aided and abetted by liberal "dogooders."[25]

Conservative American viewpoints regarding the habits of the Black community are inconsistent with a realistic perception of the condition, status, and history of oppression and discrimination that Blacks have faced. It is one thing to believe that Blacks are inherently inferior; another to believe that American society has advanced to the point where discrimination and racism are no longer factors. But it is something completely different to propose the laziness and dysfunction of the Black community and the Black family without acknowledging the oppressive conditions that have assisted in demonizing them. The history of slavery, racism, discrimination, and oppression has prohibited the Black community from developing and practicing similar habits as the rest of the

American community. Suggesting that the conditions of Blacks is their own fault, and has nothing to do with these societal barriers and conditions is inaccurate. To not acknowledge such a history of the Black community is to practice an advanced level of disingenuousness.

McCarthy (2009) suggests that historically disadvantaged and racially identified groups are ascribed stereotypically negative culture and character traits, which then are used to explain and legitimate the social, economic, and political inequities under which they live.[26] Conservatives obscure not only the historical roots of racially distributed disadvantages, but also the continuing role of institutionalized structures that reproduce them. Rather than attacking the massive structural inequalities of opportunity under which Blacks still suffer, the "dysfunctional culture" approach stigmatizes the victims anew, blames them for their plight, and leaves it largely to them to correct the situation.[27]

The basic institutions of American society, the institutions that structure housing, education, employment, family formation, criminal justice, and other domains, are unjust in the sense that they routinely function to the systematic disadvantage of Blacks in distributing basic opportunities and primary goods. Too few Americans are aware of the central role that New Deal programs of the 1930s played in perpetuating inequality of opportunity in labor markets, housing, and social security. Patterns of social inequality in employment, housing, and wealth have been weaved into the fabric of American life and are still visible in America today. Yet, for an overwhelming majority of Americans who came of age or immigrated after the passage of the Civil Rights Act, the elimination of *de jure* discrimination, and the gradual reduction of overt bigotry point to a lack of personal responsibility in making decisions about marriage, school, education, work, crime, and the like to explain those patterns in the Black community.[28]

In the late twentieth century, as a result of the Civil Rights Movement, there was a growing perception among White Americans that Blacks had achieved an advantage in their social, economic and political mobility at the expense of some Whites, and because of this, governmental mechanisms which fostered that advantage should be disassembled.[29] Ronald Reagan's administration alone opposed the Equal Employment Opportunity Commission's affirmative action program in employment, the Department of Education's Office of Civil Rights affirmative action program in higher education, and the minority business set-aside program of the Office of Federal Contract Compliance in the Department of Labor. The brunt of Americans' punitive approach to repeat criminal offenders falls heavily upon Blacks, suggesting that the U.S. incarceration system is also influenced by race.[30] "Three strikes" laws and mandatory minimum sentencing programs have contributed to the explosive growth in prison sentences given to young Blacks and sharply increased their incarceration rates. Associating crime, especially violent crime, with Blacks and a generalized fear of areas populated by Blacks with Black crime are becoming synonymous with Blacks.

Through the systematic rejection of court-ordered busing and the elimination of financial resources for targeted school districts, the comprehensive ideology of "school choice" turned public attention away from the challenge of developing excellence in the public school setting, with race as a strong motivating factor. The drive toward choice systems has had the effect of threatening the depletion of resources that public schools need to remain viable.[31] All of the negative depictions of the "bad habits" of citizenship practiced by Blacks, as argued by Conservatives attempt to ignore or deem as irrelevant all of the ways in which American systems and institutions have routinely attempted to restrict the access and freedoms of Blacks, and thereby contributing to the circumstances that lead to such negative behaviors. The problems that need to be addressed within the Black community are, in part, social problems dealing with the way society functions, and these social problems are often symptoms rather than causes of the biggest barriers confronting Blacks in America.[32]

The problem is not that Blacks are so dysfunctional that their community is a resemblance of their own inadequacies, rather, what needs to be addressed is what habits of interaction and participation can be developed in spite of all the constant barriers to equality and racial or social justice. Not the habits that Blacks have developed internally, but, what habits have they developed as a result of their constant battle for self-realization. The question then becomes, what are the bad habits in the Black community that are keeping them from attaining group desired goals and fully practicing their rights and duties as citizens? Not as an inherent or reoccurring problem of the Black community, but the bad habits that have developed within the Black community overtime as a result of their constant struggle for liberation.

ON THE HABITS OF CITIZENSHIP
IN THE BLACK COMMUNITY

The current habits of citizenship practiced by Blacks and the Black community—distrust, suspicion, alienation, anger, and resentment—are detrimental to the Black community and contribute to an inability to accomplish group desired goals. It is crucial not to suggest that Blacks are inherently to blame for their current conditions, or bad habits. There is nothing fundamentally flawed within Blacks' culture or heritage that makes them incapable of developing healthy relationships with one another. Although they may not be to blame for the causes of their conditions, they may have to blame themselves for not attacking the solutions head on. Since Blacks do not have the habits of citizenship to fix their conditions, it may no longer be sufficient to point the finger at the historical injustices and remaining institutional racism that currently plague American society and the structure of race relations. The most important measurement of the habits of citizenship and what it means to be a member of the Black community is how members treat one another. Thus, why Blacks in America simply do not like one another, nor value their membership and commitment to each other is the transgression of the Black community. Blacks can certainly blame White America and the structure of American institutions for creating and perpetuating the historical conditions in which Blacks currently find themselves, but certainly not for why Blacks resent one another, and consequently work to the disadvantage of their own communities.

The most important revelation concerning the bad habits of citizenship present in the Black community is the value of association(s) and membership(s) in their communities; as both members of the Black community and as U.S. citizens. W. E. B. Du Bois (1940, 2002) observed that most Blacks occupy a low status in America; both low in itself and low as compared with the national average. No matter what the true reasons are, or where the blame lies, the fact remains that among Blacks there are poverty, ignorance, bad manners, disease, and crime.[33] Du Bois' proposed solution to the problems facing Blacks, beginning with ignorance, is an inner problem of the community itself and problems with which Blacks alone would have to grapple. Woodson (1921) declared that Blacks should be angry with themselves because they have not handled their own business wisely, essentially permitting other people to determine for them the attitude that they have towards their own people. Blacks earn millions and millions every year and throw these vast sums immediately away for trifles that undermine their health, vitiate their morals, and contribute to the undoing of generations of Blacks unborn.[34] Blacks' point of view must be changed before they can reconstruct a program to bring them out of the "wilderness." If Blacks in America are to escape starvation and rise out of poverty unto comfort and ease, they must change their way of thinking and living.[35]

It is in the best interest of the Black community to be accountable and responsible for developing good habits of citizenship for two reasons: first, self-determination is a key component to strengthening the commitment and resolve of the Black community. *Self-determination* is the ability of the Black community to determine its own fate without compulsion and form its own understanding or self-consciousness. Secondly, it is unrealistic and irrational for Blacks to assume that another group would pay the price for their liberation and go beyond the granting of inclusion into the basic protections of civil liberties and protections of the state. To expect the White majority or any combination of minorities to go beyond that and also redeem the Black community from the devastating effects of slavery and racism, which may be a reasonable request, is more than unlikely. Once allowed into the pool, Blacks would have to get out there and swim on their own. Thus, the best thing that Blacks can do is to prepare and secure institutions that will sustain and protect the interests of their own community—the only thing that will maintain the interests and values of the Black community.

To do this, Blacks must develop positive habits of citizenship that will encourage them to work cooperatively to put the good of the Black community over self-interest and individualism, and develop good patterns of interaction amongst other Blacks. Blacks are solely responsible for holding their leaders and fellow members accountable to their commitment and obligations to the needs of the community and to sustaining its history, heritage, and culture. Unfortunately for Blacks, the majority have to cope with fewer jobs, worse housing, schools, hospitals, and living conditions, while what is right and in the best interest of the community overall is sacrificed because the right thing to do is not expedient, and the community has reached the point to what is not expedient is now unnecessary.

How do we know that Blacks suffer from bad habits of citizenship and negative patterns of interaction? Their everyday living conditions and the standing of the Black community display resentment, disdain, mistrust and contempt among them. The socioeconomic realities facing Blacks correspond to bad habits of citizenship because they are the manifestation of their distrust, alienation, and resentment as a community; the habits that need to be fixed to create the bonds of trust and good habits to be good citizens. Four areas where such negative interactions among Blacks can be witnessed are: economics, family and health, education, and crime. Combined, these characteristics of Blacks' conditions demonstrate the bad habits associated with membership in the Black community and their standing as U.S. citizens.

The period in America after 1968 is important for measuring the habits of citizenship among Blacks for many reasons: first, 1968 represents the beginning of Blacks access to "first class" citizenship in that they were perceived to be fully included into the rights, practices, and responsibilities as citizens. In 1964 the Civil Rights Act was signed into law. It outlawed major forms of discrimination against Blacks and women that included equal access to voting registration and the desegregation of public facilities and accommodations such as schools, jobs, hospitals, hotels, and restaurants. Additionally, the Voting Rights Act of 1965 was signed into law banning discriminatory voting practices that had been used to disenfranchise Blacks. It prohibits states from imposing any "voting qualification or prerequisite to voting, or standard, practice, or procedure . . . to deny or abridge the right of any citizen of the United States to vote on account of race or color." Lastly, Congress passed the Fair Housing Act of 1968 with the primary goal to protect home buyers and renters from discrimination. Blacks had been long-time victims of housing discrimination when it came to renting and finding suitable living conditions from Whites who did not want Blacks living in their communities, nor to rent or sell their properties to Blacks.

Looking at the status and conditions of post-1968 Black America also takes into account the death of prominent leaders Malcolm X in 1965 and Martin Luther King, Jr. in 1968. These events are important because they represent the heights and parameters of effective Black leadership. Malcolm's advocacy for Black pride and aggressive intervention among Blacks in defending their own communities spoke volumes and influenced millions of poor Blacks who agreed with his early stance on race in America, and his legacy set the stage for future leaders of Black Nationalist organizations such as Huey Newton and Stokely Carmichael of the Black Panther Party. Martin's advocacy for peace, justice, and the equality of all people under God, resonated through Black and White communities and his stance on civil disobedience gave America a glimpse into the realities of racism and discrimination, and the lengths that Blacks were willing to take to achieve equality.

Together these men ushered in a new era for advancement of Blacks' rights since Reconstruction. On one end Blacks would need to stick together under the unifying circumstances of "Blackness," be accountable to their own communities, and defend themselves. Yet, on the other hand, Blacks could not abolish a message of love that unites all people or the promises of freedom and equality that made America unique. The loss of these two prominent figures and their contributions to the advancement of the values and interests of Blacks is essential in understanding the current conditions facing Blacks in America.

Post-1968 Black America is the focal point for investigating the habits of the Black community and how Blacks currently perceive and value membership in the their community and as citizens in the U.S. because the country and Blacks may have believed that they were finally able to exercise their rights and privileges as citizens, fully included and accessible to the state and its institutions. It is widely believed that in the years since 1968, Blacks have witnessed the greatest benefits of the Civil Rights Movement and effective Black leadership, both of which paved the way for Blacks' advancement in their social, political, and economic life. Post-1968 Black America is suggested to be more free, equal, and prosperous than ever before. Thus, it is important to explore the habits and patterns of behavior that shape the interactions among Blacks, and the effectiveness of their leadership post-1968 using the four socioeconomic variables that follow.

VIOLENCE AND CRIME IN BLACK AMERICA

Violence in Black communities is one example of the bad habits of citizenship practiced by Blacks. Traditional racist thinking argues that Blacks are simply prone to violence and criminal activity, and must be held in check through rigorous surveillance and the iron hand of the incarceration system. Despite the roots of violence in Black communities, the most important component of Black violence as evidence of their corrupted state is Black on Black crime. What is more harmful to a community that is supposed to be supported by group members working together for common goals and the protection of their interests than unnecessary violence toward other members? Black on Black crime also demonstrates the lack of value Blacks have towards Black life and displays their anger and resentment towards one another. Nothing is a more selfish act contrary to the common good as the unnecessary killing of a contributing or potential contributing member of the national community; a partner in the protection and liberation of the Black community.

Blacks are more likely to live in neighborhoods with many of the hallmarks of poverty, such as lack of infrastructure and jobs; these circumstances are largely a result of the legacy of slavery and discrimination. As a result, Blacks hate their condition and hate each other for being in it, and therefore lash out brother against brother, brother against sister, and so on. Fanon (1963) interprets this notion in terms of the effects of colonization when the colonized subject, in this case Blacks, train their aggressiveness against their own people rather than Whites, who are chiefly responsible for placing them in their original condition and status in the U.S.[36]

Most crimes committed by Blacks are targeted against other Blacks. Between 1976 and 2004, 94 percent of Black murders were committed by Blacks. Homicide continues to be the leading cause of death for Black men between the ages of ten and twenty-four.[37] In 2007, 43 percent of all murder victims in America were Black and 93.1 percent of those murder victims were killed by other Blacks.[38] Since the majority of crime in America is intraracial, between members of the same race, it is important to highlight that Blacks are also victimized at a rate roughly 50 percent higher than Whites. FBI statistics show that Blacks commit half of all homicides, nearly half of all rapes, 59 percent of robberies, and 38 percent of aggravated assaults.[39]

The case for Black on Black crime and violence plaguing Black communities is even more startling when focusing directly on the state of Black men in America. Michelle Alexander (2011) highlights there are currently more Black men in prison or currently under the authority of the American justice system than were enslaved in America in 1850.[40] Since 2000 there has been a 40 percent increase in the number of Black males murdered and a 38 percent increase in that same demographic were responsible for murder during the same time period. Black males age thirty to thirty-four have the highest incarceration rate of any racial group in America (2.1 million inmates; Blacks represent 35.4 percent).[41] We have a situation in America where over the first five years of the Afghanistan and Iraq wars, fewer than five thousand Americans were killed. Over that same five years, close to twenty-seven thousand Black males were killed in America by gunfire alone. That meant that the average Black male had a better chance of surviving in the streets of Kabul or Baghdad than in the streets of their urban community.

Black on Black crime is symbol of the corrupted state of Black America—acts of violence towards other members of the community who are supposed to be working together to achieve common goals. The corrupted state of the Black community produces the condition in which violence between members, who are supposed to be united under common goals and objectives in contributing to the protection of the group, develops into a pattern. Radically transforming this negative pattern of behavior is imperative to improving the conditions of the Black community overall.

THE HABITS OF THE BLACK ECONOMY

Economic conditions in the Black community heavily influence the current status of the Black majority. How much money Blacks spend in Black communities, in Black-owned businesses, or programs that primarily benefits the Black community is another example of how Blacks' value the Black community and their contribution to it. Jawanza Kunjufu (2002) suggests that Blacks prefer to maintain a "good job" rather than own and operate their own business.[42] Overall, Black consumers only spend 3 percent of their annual income in Black businesses. Less than 2 percent of all Blacks obtain their incomes because they own a business. Thirty-five percent of Blacks work for private enterprise or corporate America. Less than 5 percent of those businesses are owned by Blacks. At the same time, Blacks account for over 40 percent of all spending in America. Blacks earn less, and spend more capital without it benefitting them in areas of employment and economic resources. They spend a larger percentage of their income on natural gas, electricity, telephone service, footwear, and a higher proportion of their money on groceries, housing, and women's and girl's clothing than any other group.[43] In 2010, Blacks earned an estimated $913 billion dollars while generating nearly $1 trillion dollars for the U.S. economy.[44] This would make the Black community the ninth wealthiest nation in the world. But to their disadvantage, 93 percent of Black income is spent outside of the Black community.

This undesirable trend results from the fact that Blacks have learned from others how to spend much more rapidly than they have learned how to earn it.[45] There can be no end to widespread drug dealing and abuse in the ghetto unless an alternative economy is created, one that can provide jobs and decent living standards for people in Black communities and not just for the small elite of the new Black middle class.[46]

HEALTH AND THE CONDITION
OF THE BLACK FAMILY

Destructive health habits are a symbol of negative patterns of behavior and the corrupt state of Blacks. A failure to value the body as the instrument of labor through which one's contribution to the community is made diminishes the quality and ability of the community to protect and sustain itself. Obesity and inactivity, disease, and unhealthy eating habits are all patterns of behavior that represent the conditions in the Black community. Taking care of the body symbolizes the value placed in the individual body as a manifestation of one's ability to contribute to society. Thus, it is a selfish act to destroy and neglect the body as an instrument of producing benefits for the protection and betterment of the group.

Multiple circumstances contribute to the racial health disparities including such socioeconomic factors as education, employment, and income; lifestyle behaviors, such as physical activity and alcohol intake; social environment, such as educational and economic opportunities, racial discrimination, and neighborhood and work conditions; and access to preventive health-care services, for example, cancer screening and vaccinations. For Blacks in the United States, health disparities can mean earlier deaths, decreased quality of life, and loss of economic opportunities. For society, these disparities translate into less than optimal productivity, higher health-care costs, and social inequity.

Blacks currently have the highest rates of obesity in America, according to the U.S. Department of Health and Human Services. Nearly 36 percent of Blacks are obese, much more than other major racial or ethnic group. In 2007, Blacks were 50 percent less likely to participate in physical activities as Whites. Black women have the highest rates of obesity in America; 79.5 percent of Black women are classified as either overweight or obese, while 37 percent of Black men fall into this category.[47] Certain populations have less access to affordable, healthful foods and safe locations for physical activity. Evidence suggests that neighborhoods with large minority populations have fewer chain supermarkets and produce stores and those healthful foods are relatively more expensive than energy-dense foods, especially in minority and low-income community.[48] Evidence also indicates that minority and low-income populations have less access to physical activity facilities and resources.

HIV/AIDS continues to have a stigmatizing effect on the Black community. According to the Center for Disease Control (CDC) statistics, of the estimated forty thousand new HIV infections each year more than 50 percent occur among Blacks. Blacks currently account for 46 percent of people in America living with HIV diagnosis and accounted for 45 percent of the new infections in 2006, a higher proportion than all other races. Intravenous drug use is fueling the AIDS epidemic in Black communities. It accounts for 43 percent of infections among Black women and 38 percent among Black men. Many women contract HIV through sex with an intravenous drug user.

Disproportionate amounts of single-Black parents and the socioeconomic conditions of Black children illustrate another negative pattern of interaction amongst Blacks and further evidence of their corrupted state. A high volume of single Black parents and poor children embodies a lack of investment and commitment in the future conditions of the Black community. Implicit in Moynihan's 1962 analysis was that marriage orients men and women toward the future, asking them not just to commit to each other but to plan, earn, save, and devote themselves to advancing their children's prospects. The family unit teaches the lessons of the community and reinforces its values and heritage to the next generation. Moynihan suspected that the familial risks were magnified in the case of Blacks, since their "matriarchal" family had the effect of abandoning men, leaving them adrift and "alienated." Families shape their children's character and ability, and by and large, adult conduct in society is learned as a child.[49] What Black children learned in the "disorganized home(s)" of the ghetto, was that Black adults do not finish school, get jobs, or, in the case of men, take care of their children or obey the law.[50] Marriage, on the other hand, provides a "stable home" for children to learn common virtues.

Overall in America, the institutions of marriage and family are dissolving; over half of all U.S. marriages result in divorce and more children are growing up in single parent homes. This leads to questions concerning the legitimacy and effectiveness of marriage as a natural relationship between men and women. In contrast to the traditionally conservative perception of women's places in the house serving a husband and children because the "family" has always existed, Evelyn Reed emphasizes how traditionally both sexes in primitive society performed "social labor." Production and child-raising were considered social functions in which both sexes were full participants.[51] The composition of today's workforce has strained the ability for both sexes to resume their role as equal participants in and out of the household.

High levels of divorce is an indication of structural issues having to do with the institutions that bear on marriage and family, an affirmation of the socially created nature of family and marriage rather than "natural" male-female relationships.[52] Maggie Trowe (2001) highlights the proportion of women in the workplace has significantly grown since the 1940s, doubling since the 1990s, plus the large amount of women in America who are primary supporters of their family.[53] One does not have to argue the merits of the "natural" order of male-female relationships to find the current composition of Black families disheartening. No society or community can find perpetual fatherlessness acceptable. The consequences of Black fathers fleeing from their children are felt inside and outside of the home. Thus, despite one's stance on the role men and women play in the household, it remains that nothing will get better in Black communities if 72.5 percent of Black children have no fathers around.

Single mothers are far more likely than married mothers to be poor, even after a post-welfare-reform decline in child poverty. Forty-three and one-half percent of single Black mother families are in poverty compared to the national average of 9.3 percent.[54] Single Black mothers also represent 25.8 percent of the total Black population. Single Black mothers are also more likely to pass that poverty on to their children. Folbre (1986) found the actual earning power of a family headed by women in the current generation influences the allocation of food, health, and educational resources to the next generation. Thus, abandonment and lack of value in the Black family unit demonstrates a lack of value in the fate of Black children and the future of Black America.

As an extension of the family unity, one's commitment to the betterment of the Black community is aided by reinforcing the values and heritage of the community and its history to the next generation. It is an act of self-interest that negatively affects the Black community overall to abandon the family structure and neglect one's investment in future generations of Blacks. Radically transforming Blacks' value in investing in the family unit and their bodies as instruments for producing goods and services to the community reverses the bad habits of citizenship within the Black community. Correcting these negative patterns goes a long way in relinquishing Blacks from their corrupted state.

BLACKS IN EDUCATION

The current state of Black education is another example of the corrupted state of Black America and its accompanying bad habits. Originally, slaves were not meant to be educated, thus the perception of education for Blacks was that they were unfit to participate in the same education system as Whites, and being educated added little value to their occupation as laborers. Beginning in the 1970s, partly as a result of integrated schools, Blacks saw increased interest in their educational attainment. Yet, today, Blacks are faced with the reality that you can be rich and successful without an education; education is perceived as unnecessary in the individual's pursuit of the good life. Conditions of Black schools, in addition to parental involvement in their child's education, demonstrate the overall lack of value in Black education.

Based on curriculum, funding, teacher-to-student ratio, and the quality of teachers in predominately Black schools, Black students are behind the rest of the nation. The Department of Education's National Center for Education Statistics reports that the high school graduation rate for Black students is 62 percent, compared with 81 percent for White students. In many large urban districts, it's even lower, according to the Schott Foundation, which also reveals that Black students have the lowest likelihood of all racial groups of attending a well-resourced, high-performing school, and the greatest likelihood of attending a poorly resourced, low-performing school.[55]

Black children tend to be concentrated in low-achieving, highly segregated schools. The proportion of Black students at majority-White schools is at a level lower than in any year since 1968.[56] Black students are more likely to come from low-income households, which mean they are more likely to attend poorly funded schools based on the patterns within the school system. Schools in lower-income districts tend to employ less qualified teachers and have fewer educational resources.[57] Additionally, Black students are often wrongly placed into lower tracks based on teachers' and administrators' expectations for minority students. Such expectations of Blacks within school systems are a form of institutional racism; students who are in these lower tracks tend to have less-qualified teachers, a less challenging curriculum, and few opportunities to advance into higher tracks. Students in lower tracks suffer from social psychological consequences of being labeled as a slower learner, which often leads to the children stop trying in school.[58]

Those Blacks who do graduate high school may be ill-prepared to tackle a college-level curriculum or attend colleges that can prepare them to compete in today's innovation-based economy, since Black students have the lowest SAT scores of any racial group. This does not exclude the children of wealthy Blacks. High-income Black students score lower on average on the SAT than low-income White students.[59] Educational inequities reduce the likelihood that U.S. schools will produce students who start companies that will create more jobs and revenues for the Black community.

Jencks and Phillips (1998) suggest that Black parents may not encourage early education in toddlers because they do not see the personal benefits of having exceptional academic skills. As a result of cultural differences, Black students tend to begin school with smaller vocabularies than their White classmates.[60] Studies show that when students have parental assistance with homework, they perform better in school, but 67 percent of Black children are in a single-parent household and students from single parent households often find it difficult to find time to receive help from their parent. Additionally, Black students may stop trying in school because they do not want to be accused of "acting White" by their peers.

The success of Blacks in college is not any more encouraging. Racial disparities in college graduation rates remain large. Throughout the nation, Black enrollment in higher education has reached an all-time high. But a more important statistical measure of the performance of Blacks in higher education is how many Black students are completing school and earning a college degree. Nationwide, the Black student college graduation rate remains at a dismally low 43 percent. Black men who attend college remains what it was in 1976, 4.3 percent.[61]

THE CONSEQUENCES OF BAD
HABITS: LOOKING FORWARD

As a result of bad citizenship habits, the majority of Blacks find themselves becoming more isolated in America today. Blacks' participation in the economy, crime, health, education, and the conditions of Black families represents the negative consequences of a people exposed to the destruction and annihilation of their culture and heritage. Such exposure manifests itself within the Black community not only culturally but economically as well, which enables the effects to cross over into all aspects of the life of the Black community,[62] including their education and how Blacks view themselves and their relationship with other members of the community. It is of no surprise that a people dispossessed of their word, their expressiveness, and culture finds it difficult to navigate in a racist society and sufficiently address their educational, economical, and behavioral interests and needs.[63]

Consequently, Blacks do not like themselves as individuals and dislike their community. Blacks lag behind both Whites and Hispanics in satisfaction with life. Only 44 percent say that they are "very satisfied" with their communities as places to live. Most say that crime, lack of good paying jobs, the number of births to unwed mothers, the high school dropout rate and the poor quality of schools are big problems in the Black community.[64] A large majority of Blacks suggest that rap and hip hop have a bad influence on society and Black communities. Fifty–three percent say that Blacks who do not get ahead are responsible for their own situation; a major shift from the primary role that discrimination played in the attitudes towards Blacks' advancement in the 1990s.[65] Ten percent of Blacks have an "unfavorable" view of Blacks—including 4 percent who have a "very unfavorable" view. Additionally, Blacks do not like how their community is depicted and valued in American society, particularly by Whites. Frustration in the Black community is partly due to the inability to fully integrate into White institutions and to gain the affinity and loyalty of Whites. The form of action that Blacks adopt is to a large extent a function of how they perceive themselves in the world.[66] How individuals feel about their membership in their community is represented in the actions that they take toward other members. Blacks' feelings about their place in the community and that community's standing and value in overall society affect how they feel and treat one another, and ultimately, their likelihood of ever achieving any group desired goals and objectives.

The Black community overall does not have the skills, behaviors, or attitudes to adequately exercise freedom and address the severity of the conditions of Black life. The negative attitudes and patterns of behavior amongst Blacks are not the product of their inherent laziness, inferiority, and incapability of behaving according to the rights, privileges, and obligations of citizenship. Yet, resentment and suspicion of individuals in the Black community and the lack of value in the Black community overall has produced conditions in which Blacks cannot develop healthy methods of interaction to enable them to unify for the purpose of confronting their conditions of disadvantage from a position of strength. As a result of these bad habits, not only are the behaviors and attitudes of positive interaction negatively affected, but the necessary attributes to fix these habits are also diminished. Low self-worth, self-respect, and negative images and feelings about the community are all consequential elements that make up the patterns of behavior in the Black community. Part of the resentment and negative feelings aimed at their own people is due to the indoctrination of Blacks to hate themselves and everything Black.

The negative habits of citizenship and the lack of value in the Black community must be addressed to fix essential elements to Black survival and prosperity in America. Unity, solidarity, and the ability to point out the inherent flaws of American society are being extinguished by the current practices of interaction and citizenship among Blacks. Developing the right virtues of character and skills to adequately address the needs of the community and advance the common good demands that Blacks utilize these elements. Without answering to these demands, any chances of promoting the common good amongst the Black community will be unsuccessful.

Unity for the Black community means *a state of oneness and agreement of particular thoughts in regards to the common good.* Although there may be differences in opinion as to what methods may be successful in achieving the common good, unity in this regard points to the obligation of contributing to society and the confirmation of the elements that are negative or detrimental to the group being recognized collectively. Blacks must be in agreement in their understanding of the seriousness of their condition and the need to address it internally. Unity within the Black community should arouse Blacks' awareness of their shared destiny, and shared history founded on the effects of slavery and the experiences of racism. A renewed value and commitment to protecting and advancing the interests of the Black community as a whole are the qualities of a unified group. The corruption of the Black individual, the erosion of value and commitment to the Black community, and the negative habits of Black citizenship and interaction amongst each other, sabotages the ability for the Black community to be unified.

Solidarity in the Black community involves *the fellowship that arises from the unification around their shared interests and commitment to common responsibilities, and interests.* Whereas unity arises from harmony and agreement of thoughts and values, solidarity embraces the common responsibility and obligations that causes members of a group to take collective action. Members of the Black community, once unified about the seriousness of their condition and the level of consciousness needed to address the problems, can apply solidarity to turn this consciousness and new-found awareness into a commitment and obligation to protect and strive to attain the values and goals of the community. Solidarity, thus, enables Blacks to mobilize to attack the systems and institutions in place that prohibit Black advancement and prosperity from a position of strength.

Finally, the bad habits of citizenship among Blacks needs to be addressed in order to point out the flaws in American society and the structure of its institutions that disproportionately affect Blacks negatively. By pointing out flaws in American society and institutions, Blacks can demonstrate that the problems plaguing America are found at the roots of how society is structured and how the institutions that are supposed to ensure equality to its members have failed. The contradictions and hypocrisies in American society and institutions must be brought to the front and addressed. Exposing the flaws in American society demonstrates that Blacks' inability to successfully achieve equality and social justice is not an inherent problem found in the community or the behavioral nature of Blacks. Part of the benefits of liberation is that it also relieves the oppressors from their own ignorance, short-sightedness, and the corruption of their individual self, and their community. America can never be the great nation of justice, fairness, and equality until it successfully addresses its historical contradictions and the inherent hypocrisies within its ideals based on its treatment of Blacks.

The bad habits of citizenship in the Black community allow for its culture to be continually under attack and questioned. Such destructive attitudes and patterns of behavior further increase the erosion and devaluing of loyalty and affinity for the Black community and its culture. Blacks who devalue their personhood and other members of the community can hold no value in the collective interests of the Black community. Those who resent themselves and others, while devaluing the values and interests of the Black community will be willing to abandon the community and its interests for another, more acceptable culture, and neglect to pass culture on to future generations. Ultimately the stories of Black history, culture, and heritage will vanish due to the failure to protect and sustain its value. Without the protection and sustainment of the culture, heritage, and history to increasingly reinforce the value and commitment needed in the Black community, the ability to successfully accomplish the goals and objectives of the community, and advocate for its collective interests is inconceivable.

Bad habits, bad leadership, and improper methods used to secure the status and standing of the Black majority are why the socioeconomic conditions of Blacks overall have not improved significantly to the point where Blacks no longer find themselves at the bottom of American society in all of the most important socioeconomic categories. Bad citizenship habits, in combination with inadequate Black leadership, whose job it is to direct the Black masses, are why socioeconomic conditions are not equal for Blacks and why they continue to practice the negative habits of citizenship that impede progress and ability to successfully accomplish group desired goals and protect the value and interests of the Black community. Methods currently employed by Blacks to secure the rights and privileges of citizenship emphasize the political process and the unfettered protection and promotion of individualism. *Real politics*, the science of government, is deeply rooted in the economic foundation of the social order. Thus, a class of people slightly lifted above poverty can never have much influence in political circles.[67] Nor can Blacks, internalizing the image of their oppressor, construct by themselves the theory of their liberating action; only in the encounter of the people with revolutionary leaders.[68] Leadership is a necessity in the radical transformation of the corrupted state of the Black community. A revolution cannot be liberating without it.

NOTES

1. Danielle Allen, *Talking With Strangers: Anxieties of Citizenship since Brown v. Board of Education* (Chicago: University of Chicago Press 2004), 3.
2. Ibid., 5.
3. Ibid.
4. Ibid.
5. Robert C. Tucker, *The Marx–Engels Reader*, 2nd ed. (New York: W. W. Norton, 1978).
6. Ibid.
7. Ibid.
8. Ibid.
9. Ibid.
10. Thomas McCarthy, *Race, Empire, and the Idea of Human Development* (New York: Cambridge University Press, 2009), 27.
11. Ibid., 51.
12. Ibid., 81.
13. Ronald Walters, *White Nationalism, Black Interests: Conservative Public Policy and the Black Community* (Detroit, MI: Wayne State University Press 2003), 31.
14. Ibid., 43.
15. Ibid., 59.

16. Jesse Peterson, *SCAM: How the Black Leadership Exploits Black America* (Nashville, TN: WND Books, 2003), 26.

17. Ibid.

18. Ibid.

19. Ibid., 39–40.

20. Ibid., 41.

21. Ibid., 154.

22. Ibid.

23. Ibid.

24. Ibid., 160.

25. Hadjor, *Another America: The Politics of Race and Blame*, 126.

26. Thomas McCarthy, *Race, Empire, and the Idea of Human Development* (New York: Cambridge University Press, 2009).

27. Ibid., 91.

28. Michael K. Brown, Martin Carnoy, Elliott Currie, et al., *Whitewashing Race: The Myth of a Color-Blind Society* (Berkeley: University of California Press), 26–30, 223–228.

29. Walters, *White Nationalism, Black Interests*, 127–34.

30. Michael Tonry, *Malign Neglect: Race, Crime and Punishment in America* (New York: Oxford University Press, 1995).

31. Walters, *White Nationalism, Black Interests*, 184–200.

32. Hadjor, *Another America*.

33. W. E. B. Du Bois, *The Souls of Black Folk* (New York: W. W. Norton, 1999), 180.

34. Ibid.

35. Woodson, *The Mis-Education of the Negro*, 111–33.

36. Fanon, *Black Skin, White Masks*.

37. Todd Smith, "Black Men, You're Headed for Self-Destruction: Report Shows Rise in Black on Black Crime," *Regal Magazine*, January 8, 2009.

38. Ibid.

39. Peterson, *SCAM*, 47.

40. Michelle Alexander, "Michelle Alexander: More Black Men In Prison Than Were Enslaved In 1850," *ColorLines*, March 30, 2011.

41. Smith, "Black Men, You're Headed for Self-Destruction."

42. Jawanza Kunjufu, *Black Economics: Solutions for Economic and Community Empowerment*. 2nd ed. (Sauk Village, IL: African American Images, 2002).

43. Selig Center for Economic Growth. *University of Georgia's Terry College of Business*, 2012.

44. U.S. Census Bureau. *U.S. Census Bureau 2015 American Community Survey*.

45. Woodson, *The Mis-Education of the Negro*, 112.

46. Hadjor, *Another America*, 110–11.

47. J. Stewart and N. E. Adler, "Reducing Obesity: Motivating Action While Not Blaming the Victim," *Milbank Q* 87 (2009): 49–70.

48. Ibid.

49. Daniel P. Moynihan, "The Negro Family: The Case For National Action," *Office of Policy Planning and Research, U.S. Department of Labor* (Washington, DC).

50. Ibid.

51. Evelyn Reed, "Women's Oppression Rooted in Class-divided Society," *The Militant*, June 8, 2009.

52. Evelyn Reed, "The Family As `Natural' Unit Is A Widespread Myth," *The Militant*, January 12, 1998.

53. Maggie Trowe, "Debate Grows on Divorce, Changes in Family," *The Militant*, February 12, 2001.

54. Nancy Folbre, "Hearts and Spades: Paradigms of Household Economics," *World Development* 14, no.2 (1986): 245–55.

55. Marcia Wade Talbert and Robin White Goode, "Black America's Education Crisis," *Black Enterprise*, September 2011.

56. Jonathan Kozol, *The Shame of the Nation: The Restoration of Apartheid Schooling in America* (New York: Three Rivers Press), 2006.

57. Martha Crowley, et al., "Education and the Inequalities of Place," *Social Forces* 84 no.4 (2006): 2121–145.

58. Jennifer Hochschild, "Social Class in Public Schools," *Journal of Social Issues* 59 no.4 (2003): 821–40.

59. Ibid.

60. Christopher Jencks and Meredith Phillips, *The Black-White Test Score Gap* (Washington, DC: Brookings Institute Press, 1998).

61. U.S. Census Bureau. *US Census Bureau 2010 American Community Survey.*

62. Freire, *Pedagogy of the Oppressed.*

63. Ibid., 138

64. Pew Research Center. "Optimism About Black Progress Declines: Blacks See Growing Values Gap Between Poor and Middle Class." *Pew Research Center: A Social & Demographic Trends Report*, Tuesday, November 13, 2007.

65. Ibid.

66. Ibid., 80.

67. Woodson, *The Mis-Education of the Negro*, 124–25.

68. Freire, *Pedagogy of the Oppressed*, 183.

THREE

On Bad Citizens, Bad Habits, and Bad Leadership

The negative perception of the citizen and the bad citizenship habits of the Black community are the product of inadequate Black leadership that has been incapable of setting a proper example and developing new methods and systems to combat problems plaguing the Black community. Black leadership, particularly "a" Black leader, has been a part of the Black American discourse throughout history. Since the passing of the Civil Rights Act of 1964 and the so-called "full inclusion" of Blacks into the mainstream, Blacks still face considerable amounts of discrimination and racism. This reinforces the perception of Blacks as second-class citizens. For as much as White racism plays a role in Blacks' inability to attain a respectable level of equality, a failure of Black leadership to properly assess the conditions of the Black community and come up with satisfactory solutions is just as significant.

Black leadership has continually failed to develop sufficient systems and institutions—such as predominately Black banks, hospitals, and health care centers—that can limit the negative effects of White racism. The inability of Black leaders to bring substantive changes that improve the lives of poor Blacks remains a salient factor in the perpetuation of negative patterns of behavior and the erosion of value of the Black community among Blacks. The longer that leadership ignores or fails to deliver antidotes to the ills of the Black community, the longer entrenched and more severe the erosion of value of the community will be, and the harder it becomes to unite the Black community or ensure its survival. In the end, leadership is important to a discussion of citizenship. The quality of leadership depends on how well the leader(s) deliver new systems and institutions capable of transforming the attitudes, habits, and behaviors of the people; thus, creating *new* citizens. Thus, problems persist in Black

America due to the incredible lack of vision and imagination of Black leaders.[1]

EVALUATING LEADERSHIP AND THE CITIZEN

Evaluating Black leadership and who qualifies as a citizen comes down to two factors: (1) one's contribution to the sustainment, protection, and improvement of the overall community and (2) what has been done to improve the lot of the masses. Blacks must evaluate their leadership, status as citizens, and other members of the Black community through the lens of sacrifice to the community and contribution to the common good. Privileges of community membership should be extended to some, and withheld from others, based on obligation and commitment to the community. The community's ability to offer rights and privileges that individuals are incapable of gaining separately, establishes the value of community membership.

The value of a community is determined by merit; that is, to be worthy of the benefits that accrue from community membership. Individuals alone cannot protect their freedom of speech, religion, or their role or status in society. They require the legitimate authority of the community or state to recognize these rights and privileges. To possess merit means to be worthy of the rights and privileges of citizenship based on accomplishments or one's contribution to the protection, sustainment, and improvement of the community. Thus, merit plays a central role in establishing and sustaining the value one places in belonging to a community.

The value placed in community membership may be high if the individual feels deserving of the rights and privileges of community membership due to one's contributions, good deeds, military service, or some other quality such as community solidarity. Many Blacks entered the military with the hope that fighting for their country would grant them in full the rights and privileges of citizenship. They felt deserving of the rights and privileges of American citizenship due to the sacrifices of military service and perceived the granting of citizenship on this basis to be a fair exchange.

Other individuals see little value in community membership due to lack of merit or due to the perception of an unequal burden or sacrifice. For example individuals may hold little value in the Black community because they have not contributed anything to its protection, sustainment, or improvement, and those whom they regard as important or significant feel the same way (Black leaders, parents, teachers, and social/cultural elites). Additionally, they may perceive little value in the Black community because they regard the sacrifice of their self-interest as an unequal exchange for the rights and privileges of group membership. This would be the case if one regards the rights and privileges of belonging to the Black community as insignificant to their overall identity and of little consequence in realizing self-interest.

To protect, sustain, and improve the value of community membership requires members to continually add to and contribute to its protection and sustainment. Citizens, leaders, and aspiring members of the community should be evaluated by contributions and commitments to the common good; in particular, one's contribution to the improvement of the condition of the Black majority. Rather than community membership being based on what a person has accomplished individually, that is, one's material well-being and position in society, the privileges of citizenship should be conferred upon those who demonstrate such commitment and sacrifice to the collective needs and goals of the community.

Black leaders must be evaluated on how well they facilitate the reduction of "bad habits" and negative patterns of behavior that prohibit unity and solidarity within the Black community. Such community solidarity is necessary to adequately address subpar socioeconomic conditions and advance the common good. The distressed socioeconomic conditions in the Black community are the most pressing issues Black leaders must address. The current negative relationships between Blacks and the economy, crime, education, and family structure and health, represent negative habits that must be addressed via radical transformations of Black collective behavior patterns. Effectiveness and efficiency of Black leadership should be measured by the ability to create new institutions that push Blacks toward positive behavior patterns that improve the well-being of the impoverished Black majority. Black leaders should focus on the creation of self-sufficient, active and meritorious citizens who advance the interests of the whole (common good). Such institutions under proper leadership should close the socioeconomic gap between Blacks and the overall U.S. population.

WHAT IS LEADERSHIP?

Leadership is the special influence that an individual exercises over others by arousing dormant attitudes, changing attitudes, or arousing new attitudes in others.[2] To arouse the dormant attitudes and become a leader is relatively easy. By being enthusiastic along traditional lines of activity, raising the cry of "danger," and the use of other cheap devices, a member of a group may shoot up into the rank of leader without much difficulty.[3] But to change human attitudes requires greater skill. To arouse entirely new attitudes and a creative type of follower is the supreme height of leadership; the ability to stimulate unsuspected possibilities and originalities in other persons makes for the greatest type of leadership. Such characteristics are often those of an individual who challenges and gives heavy responsibilities, who sets forth unique opportunities, makes the impossible seem possible, and who by deed or word arouses followers to superhuman effort.[4]

ON BLACK LEADERSHIP

The role and features of Black leadership are central to the mechanisms through which Blacks can meet the expectations of citizenship. Identifiable and efficient leadership is a recurring theme in the dialogue of Black history and the fight for equality. The most important elements of Black leadership focus on the relationship between the elites and the masses, and how well potential or active leaders meet the needs of their followers.

SLAVERY–ERA LEADERSHIP

Blacks' long-standing demands for leadership are not unique. They fall within the sociological patterns of leadership in general.[5] Leaders have generally been sought by a community to ensure its protection when survival is threatened. Thus the conditions of Blacks in America have given rise to requests for effective leadership. During slavery, Blacks were largely not organized in a manner to promote their interests, and thus were inconsequential within political institutions. The slave regime offered little opportunity for the emergence of an independent Black leadership. Most of the few Blacks of prominence during this period were free northerners who were active in anti-slavery agitation, such as Frederick Douglass.[6] Conditions of servitude on large plantations, small farms, or households provided no opportunity for leadership of the Black masses.[7] Slavery was not conducive to the development of Black leaders. Blacks comprised a large, uneducated, atomized mass living in fear of the dominant White group. It was not until 1830, when the abolitionist movement became a significant social force, that there became any generally recognized national leader of Blacks in America, in particular, Frederick Douglass.[8]

BLACK LEADERSHIP: RECONSTRUCTION TO WWII

The brief period of Black enfranchisement during Radical Reconstruction (1866–1877) brought into state offices a number of local Black politicians. During Reconstruction Blacks organized Equal Rights Leagues throughout the South and held state and local conventions to promote voting rights and disperse information following the Civil War. Additionally, Blacks organized meetings, parades, and petitions to advance equal rights and handed out campaign brochures. Widespread mass organization and leadership during Reconstruction resulted in two thousand Blacks holding elected office.[9]

After the bloody defeat of Radical Reconstruction and the solidification of Jim Crow segregation the Black community—particularly in the South—was transformed back into a politically amorphous and ineffectual mass. The shift back to organized mass Black politics begins to take place in the Black community in the early 1900s as Black leaders derived their authority from an organized membership whose support they could count on in carrying out their program. The mantle of Black leadership passed from Douglass, to Booker T. Washington and W. E. B. Du Bois. After 1930, economic crisis precipitated changes within American society. The Depression created a common economic denominator between many Whites and Blacks, resulting in a partial leveling of those social, political, and cultural barriers that emphasized differences between them. Whereas poverty, poor housing, and inadequate employment opportunities were deemed as "Black" or "minority" problems that separated them from Whites, the conditions of the Depression brought their socioeconomic conditions, as well as their living conditions in many instances, closer together. For example, during this period Black illiteracy dropped from almost 100 percent at emancipation to 16.3 percent.[10] Thus, accelerated changes in social status created a different framework in which Black leadership had to operate. Increased literacy created for Black leadership anew constituency of educated and politically sophisticated Blacks, no longer plagued by the ills of physical captivity and oppression. No longer was Black leadership needed to liberate an overwhelmingly enslaved population without any rights or freedoms. In the period after World War II in particular, the new generation of Black leaders had to address problems the Black community was facing as a result of their newfound freedoms in the workplace, in education, and in social institutions, such as public facilities, hotels, and theaters.

The changing composition of the Black population in the twentieth century, especially after 1930, created demands for leadership in areas where Blacks were previously not present. But unlike other ethnic groups, Blacks had not created a liberating cultural and political history to inspire Black unity and pride.[11] Thus after 1930, Blacks focused their collective energies and imagination on: (1) removing limitations such as segregation; (2) intergroup etiquette, that is, the rules governing the behavior between Blacks and White; (3) economic restrictions; (4) intermarriage prohibitions; (5) and political and social ostracism.[12] As Blacks strove for assimilation and developed new self-conceptions, the appeals of the early leaders had to give way to something different. The appeals of an enslaved race needing to escape to freedom and fight to be recognized as human beings were no longer the primary focus of Black leaders. As the conditions and perception in the Black community shifted the types of demands and methods used by leaders would have to change along with it. Leaders had to expand appeals to working class and elite Blacks beginning to enjoy the fruits of their labors. Without the all-encompassing issue of slavery, a multiplicity of leadership was needed to span the increasingly complex and diverse interests of the Black community. Civil rights demanded a full-time spokesperson; effort to secure jobs required another; emerging religious, political, and cultural aspirations called for others.[13] Whereas the previous leadership appealed to the moral and political ethos of a democratic America to grant enslaved Blacks freedom, the Black leadership following the Depression appealed to working class Blacks attempting to secure voting rights, fair treatment and equal pay in the workplace, safe and equal schooling for their children along with Whites, equal accommodations in public services, and fair and due process in the court of law.

POST-DEPRESSION CIVIL RIGHTS LEADERSHIP

After the Second World War, Black politicians became significant by gaining the recognition from the dominant White group and acceptance as leaders by the Black population. One major issue for Black leadership post-World War II has been a choice between non-violent direct action, or court and legislative action. Organizations like the NAACP led the legal and legislative model. Student organizations like CORE and SNCC challenged the methods of the NAACP and emphasized direct action during the early stages of the Civil Rights movement. One important characteristic has prevailed throughout the course of Black leadership in the U.S., Black leaders have directed their efforts in the struggle for full citizenship inside a framework of conformity with democratic principles. Only slight variations as a result from the need to keep pace with changes in the general pattern of leadership in America have been noticeable.[14] One variation has been the demand for Black leadership to promote a measure of antagonism toward Whites and toward the American system. In the Black community, leadership dynamics are inextricably interwoven with the general nature and character of the relationship between the two races. As the character of Black—White relationship changed, so did the nature of Black leadership.[15]

Two distinct types of leaders have prevailed in post-WWII Black America: (1) the protest and separatist or Black Nationalist model (which flourished until the late 1970s—early 1980s), for example Stokely Carmichael and the Black Panther Party, and (2) the integrationist type; the more optimistic and influential of the two. Black history is a history of the conflict between integrationist and nationalist forces in politics, economics, and culture, no matter what leaders are involved and what slogans are used.[16] After WWII, Blacks had penetrated into all aspects of general society. Conforming to democratic principles remained a salient factor in a diversifying Black population hoping to keep pace with Whites and capitalize on the progress being made. However this trend coexisted with a rise of militant Black activism and the emergence of Black Nationalism and separatist movements. The latter leadership disputed how much progress had been made.[17] The multiplicity of leadership and the emergence of Black Nationalism led to the emergence of new leaders on a national scale such as middle-class Martin Luther King, Jr. and working class Malcolm X.[18]

Black Nationalism is based on the belief that Blacks are an oppressed nation or national minority trapped inside a predominantly White society; a nation that developed its own culture, social institutions, and collective interests. Black Nationalist politics is strongly tinged by a Marxian perspective which sought not the reform of American institutions but their outright rejection.[19] Martin Delany is considered the father of American Black Nationalism and Marcus Garvey championed the term into the 1920s until Malcolm X revolutionized it into the Civil Rights era, eventually leading to platforms established by organizations such as SNCC, the Black Panther Party, and US Organization. Instead of perceiving themselves as Americans who "happened to be Black," Black Nationalists often viewed themselves as either people of African descent or Africans who happened to reside in the U.S.[20] Ontologically, the realization of critical self-awareness could be achieved only by grounding oneself in the rituals, culture, and traditions generated by and among Black people. Also central to Black Nationalism was the logical insight that an oppressed people could survive in a hostile environment only if they constructed institutions and enterprises to provide goods, services, and resources for their own group.[21]

Black Nationalism is complex, fluid, and hence multidimensional, having at least two dimensions that can be characterized as "community nationalism" and "separate nationalism." "Community nationalism" exists when Blacks control and support communities and institutions where they predominate. "Separate nationalism" rejects inclusion within the White-dominated American state and seeks the creation of a new homeland. Better-educated, middle-class Blacks support community nationalism, while younger, poorer, less-educated Blacks tend to favor separatist nationalism. Both dimensions of Black Nationalism converge around the belief that "Whites want to keep Blacks down" and that "Africa is a special homeland for Blacks."[22] Cultural nationalism has flourished among a sector of the middle class that is often on the verge of impoverishment. Black Nationalism has taken strongest root among the desperately poor.[23] Many nationalists argue that by nature White and Black interests are opposed to each other. Not only is race seen as the fundamental category for analyzing society, but America is seen as fundamentally racist.[24] Thus, core concepts of Black Nationalism include not only support for Black autonomy and self-determination, but various degrees of cultural, social, economic, and political separation from White America. Community control and the characterization of Blacks' plight as that of an internal colony are two of Malcolm X's central themes.[25]

Black Power represented a variety of reformist Black Nationalism, appealing to race group consciousness and solidarity, cultural revitalization and independent organization as means to establish Blacks as an independent force in American politics.[26] "The goal of Black self-determination and Black self-identity—Black Power—is full participation in the decision-making process affecting the lives of Black people, and recognition of the virtues in themselves as Black people.[27] The Black Power movement sparked two separate, distinct and contradictory developments in Black politics. First, it stimulated the development of a wide variety of radical, nationalist, and revolutionary organizations and leaders. The Black power movement sparked the creation of a large number of new, racially exclusive interest group organizations. From 1966 to 1969—the peak years of Black power activism—more than seventy new Black interest organizations were formed.[28] For a decade the Black freedom struggle took a sharp turn toward radicalism.[29] By 1980, as a result of factionalism and infighting within and among the groups, and political repression by the FBI, the army, and the police, the radical wing of the movement had collapsed. The second development sparked by Black power was the beginning of the integration or incorporation of Blacks into the routine of interest group structure of conventional American politics.[30] Black power contributed to an increase in Black group identification and solidarity.[31] The radical, revolutionary rhetoric of Black power, the summer urban riots from 1965 to 1968, and the revolutionary politics of the Black Panthers and other groups created a perception of crisis and showed that some Blacks were indeed willing to engage in illegitimate forms of political conflict.

Integrationists' concern for economic and political change to benefit the poverty-stricken Black masses was reformists, that is, promoting voter registration and political organizing, school boycotts, rent strikes, and community organization.[32] Many integrationists prefer building alliances between poor Blacks and poor Whites, but find the strategy difficult because poor Whites are not only unorganized but also afraid of Black competition for jobs. Integrationists want political power out of the hands of the upper-class minority in this country, and into the common people, Black and White, whose interests they conceive to be essentially the same. Thus, Black leaders have long had differences concerning both methods and goals. Despite differences in goals and strategy, Black leaders have been faced with the consistent challenge to take the disadvantaged Black community and reinvigorate it with good habits to enable full incorporation into the rights and privileges of American citizenship.

ON POST-CIVIL RIGHTS ERA BLACK
LEADERSHIP: THE 1970s

The end of the Civil Rights Movement saw the loss of Malcolm X and Martin Luther King, Jr. The collapse of the Black Power Movement saw the transition to a new era of leadership in the Black community that looked to separate itself from the activist past and concentrate more on the mainstream political and electoral aspects of leadership. After the Civil Rights Movement in the 1960s, the Black community in the 1970s witnessed the continued leadership of organizations like the NAACP, National Urban League, and the Congressional Black Caucus. Elected officials such as Charles Rangel (D-NY) and Shirley Chisholm (D-NY) gained national recognition as leaders in the Black community. As a result of the transition from social movement activism to political and elected leadership in the 1970s, today there are more Black politicians, government officials, generals, and police chiefs than ever before.[33]

The "big five" organizations of the 1960s Civil Rights era were the National Associations for the Advancement of Colored People (NAACP), National Urban League, Southern Christian Leadership Conference (SCLC), Student Nonviolent Coordinating Committee (SNCC), and Congress of Racial Equality (CORE). SNCC and CORE collapsed for essentially the same reasons: first, their turn toward nationalism and radicalism resulted in factionalism and severe internal conflicts. Second, as a result of this turn toward radicalism, White liberal philanthropic support was lost and these groups were unable to finance their operations on the basis of support generated internally in the Black community.[34] Finally, the government's repressive counterintelligence program against SNCC and other radical and nationalist organizations was factored in their demise. By the 1970s, the NAACP and the National Urban League were "without question" the most important organizations in the Black freedom struggle.[35] The other major civil rights organizations were not equipped in terms of structure and strategy to deal with post-civil rights era problems.[36]

The NAACP was founded in 1909 with the mission "to ensure the political, educational, social, and economic equality of rights of all persons and to eliminate racial hatred and racial discrimination."[37] From its inception, it emphasized effecting change by lobbying national and local legislation, educating public opinion, and securing favorable court decisions.[38] During its early stages the NAACP concentrated on using the U.S. court system to fight lynching, Jim Crow laws, and legalized racial segregation. The NAACP's Legal Department, headed by Charles Hamilton Houston and Thurgood Marshall, contested the "separate but equal" doctrine in *Plessy v Ferguson* (1896) to bring about the unanimous decision in *Brown v Board* (1954) that held that state-sponsored segregation is unconstitutional. In its basic organizational structure and its governance, the NAACP continues to resemble the NAACP of the 1960s. Like its national leadership, local chapter leaders tend to serve rather long tenures, as a result it tends to be middle aged to elderly with little opportunity for new, younger, and perhaps more aggressive leadership to emerge.[39] One of the principal limitations of the NAACP as an effective vehicle to advance the interests of Blacks is its inability to raise funds necessary to carry out its work and its continued dependence on the government and White philanthropy for financing. The NAACP keeps its donor list private, insisting it is confidential to protect its privacy and in 1950 the Courts ruled that disclosing the NAACP's donor list would infringe upon its First Amendment Rights. Yet its $14 million dollar annual budget and tax exempt status by the federal government has allowed the NAACP to receive valuable contributions from businesses such as: the Ford Foundation, Bell Atlantic, Bill and Melinda Gates Foundation, AT&T, Boeing, Tides Foundation, Carnegie Corporation of New York, and the Freddie Mac Foundation.[40] Although the NAACP's donor list is kept private, these corporations make their contributions public.

The National Urban League has not fared any better than the NAACP in improving the conditions of the Black majority in America. The very areas in which the National Urban League had been most active—the blight of segregated housing, inferior education, and persistent and pernicious discrimination in employment—has been those areas in which the virulence of racism has increased.[41] Smith (1996) argues that unlike the NAACP, the National Urban League was not conceived of as a civil rights organization but rather as a social service organization whose primary mission was to facilitate the integration of poor, rural southern Black migrants into the urban way of life.[42] It had always been more involved with the new post-civil rights issues that now go under the label of the Black underclass. Today, the National Urban League remains an organization that relies heavily on White philanthropic sources for financial support. Similar to the NAACP, the National Urban League was almost completely dependent on corporate donations to keep going. By 1991, the National Urban League had a budget close to $24 million, with 88 percent being donated by corporate or government sources.[43]

The basic problem is that while the NAACP and the National Urban League do good and useful work, they have failed to come up with a new mission, a new vision, or a new strategy to mold the mass base of Black America into an effective political force. Rather, they continue to speak and act on behalf of a Black community that is largely alienated from their middle class hierarchical model of liberal reformism and civil rights.[44] Historically the NAACP's most effective strategy was using the court system to force change; that approach is "less effective" today when key issues facing the Black community are questions of (economic) justice.[45] In the end, these organizations were "too middle-class, too scandal plagued in recent years," and "not exciting."[46]

The Congressional Black Caucus (CBC) was officially formed in 1971 by a group of Black members in the House of Representatives. Its goals are stated as "positively influencing the course of events pertinent to Blacks and others of similar experience and situation," and "achieving greater equity for persons of African descent in the design and content of domestic and international programs and services."[47] The CBC's priorities include: closing the achievement and opportunity gaps in education, assuring quality health care for every American, focusing on employment and economic security, ensuring justice for all, retirement security for all Americans, increasing welfare funds, and increasing equity in foreign policy.[48] The caucus first came to national attention as a result of its boycott of President Nixon's 1971 "State of the Union" address. As a unified liberal block within the Democratic Party, the Caucus, by threatening to withhold its vote in the House, was able throughout the 1980s to get the House majority to adopt more liberal positions on issues like welfare, crime, and the budget.

The CBC plays a symbolic role in Congress by participating in such activities as formal recommendations and testimony on judicial nominations, the presentation in floor debates of various Black agendas and "State of Black America" reports, the development and presentation of its alternative budgets, occasional meetings with the president, and its annual legislative weekend. Votes on the caucus' alternative budgets, the fate of the Humphrey-Hawkins (1976) bill, and the initiatives of the Democratic Party leadership on issues that disproportionately affect Blacks show the Congressional Black Caucus has relatively little leverage or influence in congressional decision making. Except for civil rights issues, Blacks in Congress are frequently an isolated, invisible, inconsequential minority unable to enact proposals deemed minimally necessary to meliorate the problems of joblessness, crime and dispossession that plagues its core constituency.[49] With a Republican majority, the Black caucus became a minority within a minority with little bargaining power, since the conservative Republican majority ignores the liberal minority in the House.[50]

Congressman Charles Rangel of New York was elected to the Nineteenth Congressional District in 1970. In 1974 he was appointed as the first African American to serve on the House of Representative's powerful Ways and Means Committee and also chaired the Subcommittee on Oversight and Investigations. Rangel concentrated most of his energy on the drug problem which he believed to be the curse of the Black community. Education, housing, and health were all affected by drugs, he argued, and he proposed to end economic aid to foreign countries that refused to act against the illegal drug trafficking. In January 2007 he became the Chair of the House Ways and Means Committee, the first African American to do so, although by March 2010, Rangel stepped aside as Ways and Means Chair after a series of allegations of ethics violations and failures to comply with tax laws.[51]

In 1968, two years before Rangel took his post in Congress, Shirley Chisholm became the first African American woman elected to Congress. By 1972 she ran as the first major party Black candidate for President and was the first woman to run as a Democratic nominee. Chisholm protested the amount of money being expended for the defense budget while social programs suffered. She argued that she would not agree that money should be spent for war while Americans were hungry, ill-housed, and poorly educated. In addition to her interest in civil rights for Blacks, women, and the poor, she spoke out about the judicial system in the United States, police brutality, prison reform, gun control, politician dissent, drug abuse, and numerous other topics.[52]

In the end, Black leadership during the 1970s transitioned from the marches and rallies of the Civil Rights Movement and the iconic leadership of such leaders as Malcolm X and Martin Luther King, Jr. into the emergence of national organizations and elected officials. The end of the Civil Rights Movement saw increased hope on the part of Blacks about the possibilities that newfound freedoms and increased access to the privileges of American citizenship might bring. Such privileges included increased voting rights, which enabled the influx of Black elected officials, and equal access to public facilities and education.

THE RESULTS OF BLACK LEADERSHIP IN THE 1970s

How well did Black leaders of the 1970s address socioeconomic problems facing the Black community as a whole? The Black leadership of the 1970s saw the percentage of Blacks in poverty decrease during the decade from 34 percent to 31 percent, and the median household income increase from $6,279 to $10,764.[53] Blacks making more than $100,000 per year increased from 2.4 percent to 3.4 percent, while the amount of Blacks who earned less than $15,000 increased by 1 percent,[54] yet, unemployed Blacks in America remained at twice the rate of the national average during the 1970s, similar to today.

Blacks' involvement in the criminal justice system has generally been significantly higher than the national average. While the number of offending Blacks remained consistent, the numbers in prisons, jail, paroled or on probation increased from 338,029 to 474,368 during the decade.[55] The Racial Achievement Gap in the United States refers to the educational disparities between Black and Hispanic students who are more likely to receive lower grades, score lower on standardized tests, drop out of high school, and are less likely to enter and complete college than Whites.[56] The educational achievement gap between Blacks and Whites in high school decreased nearly 6 percentage points from 23.1 percent to

Table 3.1.   Black Leadership and the Habits of Citizenship 1970–1979

	Variable	1970	1980	(+/-)	Option(s)*
Economy**	[1]Poverty	34%	31%	-3%	
	[2]Median Household Income	$6,279	$10,764	+4,485	Whites-$18,684 Gap- $7,920
	Blacks earning above $100k	2.4%	3.4%	+1%	
	Blacks earning less than $35k	61%	62%	+1%	
	Blacks earning less than $15k	28.9%	30.6%	+1.7%	
	[3]Unemployment	10%	11%	+1%	5%(national average)
Criminal Justice***	[4]Blacks in Correctional System	338,029	474,368	+136,339	
Educational Achievement**	[5]High school dropout	21.3	19.1%	-2.2%	
	High school graduates	31.4%	51.2%	+19.8%	Whites-68.6%
	College graduates	4.4%	8.4%	+4%	Whites-17.1% Gap- 9%
[6]Obesity****	Black Men	43.9%	51.3%	+7.4%	
	Black Women	59.2%	62.6%	+3.4%	

* Possible options include comparative data with white/non-Hispanic population, Hispanic population, comparison with national average, and the racial disparity gap with whites
** Source: U.S. Census Bureau. American Data Survey
*** Source: Justice Policy Institute, U.S. Department of Justice
**** Source: Health, United States, 2010, Center for Disease Control and Prevention
(1) "poverty threshold": government defined as lack of those goods and services commonly taken for granted by members of mainstream society; adjusted for inflation using consumer price index
(2) income in 2001 CPLU-RS adjusted dollars
(3) calculated by dividing the number of unemployed individuals by all individuals currently in labor force (total population of working age)
(4) population in prison, jail, probation, parole, or under the control of correctional justice system
(5) the percentage of 16 through 24 year olds who are not enrolled in school and have not earned a high school credential (either a diploma or an equivalency such as General Education Diploma [GED])
(6) Body Mass Index (BMI) greater than or equal to 25

17.1 percent by the end of the decade, while the high school dropout rate amongst Blacks decreased by 2 percent.[57] Black men graduating from high school increased from 31 percent to 51 percent,[58] influenced heavily by the new access to desegregated schools. Black college graduates increased during the 1970s from 4.4 percent to 8.4 percent of the Black population, but the gap between Blacks and Whites who graduate from college increased by 2 percent, as Whites continued to graduate from college at a higher rate than Blacks, despite Blacks' increased access to college institutions and desegregated schools (see table 3.1).[59]

In the end, the Black leadership of the 1970s benefitted from the victories of the early Civil Rights Movement which gained increased access to public education, social services, and voting rights. This enabled Blacks to increase the amount of Black elected officials, whose job it would be to protect those newly gained rights. The Black leadership of the 1970s ushered in an era with increased wealth within the Black community and greater educational achievement. On the other hand, during the same period, the Black community saw a widening gap between rich and poor Blacks. By the end of the decade, the percentage of Blacks earning above $100k increased, while Blacks earning less than $35k also increased. In particular, the percentage of Blacks earning less than $15k per year increased from 28.9 percent to 30.6 percent.[60] Similar to the national trend, the rich got richer while the poor got poorer. Additionally, more Blacks participated in the U.S. prison system or correctional facilities (an increase from 338,029 to 474, 368),[61] remained unemployed at twice the national average (10 percent vs. 5 percent)[62] and committed violent crimes at greater rates during this decade than the previous. Increasing polarization between rich and poor Blacks, unemployment at twice the national average, and relentlessly increasing crime amongst Blacks are patterns of behavior that still have not been adequately addressed today, and the majority of Blacks experience little difference between their standing today and the socioeconomic conditions of the 1970s (see table 3.1).

ON POST-CIVIL RIGHTS ERA BLACK LEADERSHIP: THE 1980s

The Black leadership of the 1980s looked to advance upon the increased access to voting rights, Black elected officials, and the newfound wealth among the Black upper-class introduced in the 1970s. During the 1980s, Blacks witnessed the election of Harold Washington as the first Black mayor of Chicago—the nation's third largest city and home to the nation's largest Black population at the time. Appointments to prominent federal positions led to General Colin Powell's rise to national recognition. Jesse Jackson ran for the Democratic nomination for the U.S. Presidency twice in 1984 and 1988 symbolizing another stage in the progression of Black leadership as it moved to make itself apart of the national political atmosphere.

In 1983, Chicago elected Harold Washington to be its first Black mayor. Washington tried to address the grievances and problems of Blacks and other constituents in the areas of housing, health care, employment, police brutality, and social services. He managed to introduce a measure of reform to city government by signing the Shakman decree, which officially outlawed patronage hiring and firing, created a freedom of information act by executive decree, and encouraged economic development in neighborhoods throughout the city instead of solely concentrating on the downtown area.[63] When vacancies occurred, Washington hired many more women, Blacks, and Hispanics for top positions and even managed to get the council to approve his nomination of an African American to be the new police chief.

In the same year America saw its first Black mayor of a major city, Colin Powell was appointed senior military assistant to the Secretary of Defense. He joined the staff of the National Security Council in 1987; in that same year President Ronald Reagan appointed him assistant to the president for national security affairs. By 1989 Powell was promoted to four-star general and became the first African American to serve as chairman of the Joint Chiefs of Staff.[64]

Powell believed that his position as the nation's foremost military leader and spokesman provided a unique opportunity to deliver a positive message to Black youth, although some Black leaders labeled him a servant of the White establishment. Because of his leadership during the Gulf War and his experience as an insider in the Washington bureaucracy, political analysts suggested Powell as a promising candidate for future political office. As a Black military leader, Powell demonstrated his commitment to helping young Black men and women succeed in the armed services. He has long contended that the military should not be criticized for putting a disproportionate number of young Black men and women in harm's way, but rather praised for its history of providing opportunities to minorities.[65]

In the 1980s Jesse Jackson became the leading national spokesman for Blacks. Jackson became involved in the Civil Rights Movement in 1965 when he went to Selma, Alabama, to march with Martin Luther King, Jr., and became a worker in King's Southern Christian Leadership Conference (SCLC). His voter-registration drive was a key factor in the election of Washington in 1983. The idea of a Black presidential candidate and/or a Black political party was aborted throughout the 1970s as a result of ideological and factional disputes. In 1980 the National Black Independent Political Party (NBIPP) was established, representing Blacks' most ambitious attempt to establish an independent third party movement.[66] It sought to develop a strategy for mounting a Black Presidential candidacy. After six years NBIPP, too, was destroyed by factional disputes. In 1984 Jackson ran for the Democratic Presidential nomination.[67] Jackson claimed this strategy would enhance Black self-esteem and the role of Blacks in shaping Democratic Party policy and programs. In what was then the strongest showing ever by a Black candidate, Jackson placed third in primary voting. After the 1984 campaign Jackson called for the institutionalization of his "Rainbow Coalition" as a permanent, multiethnic organization devoted to progressive political change that would operate not only as an electoral organization but as a broad-based social movement that included mass demonstrations, rallies, and boycotts.[68] In 1988 he staged another bid for the Democratic nomination and came in second to the party's eventual nominee, Michael Dukakis. In a poll conducted in 2006, Jesse Jackson was chosen as the most important Black leader, demonstrating his continued importance in the eyes of the Black community.[69]

The resurgence of Black voters and the presidential bids of Jesse Jackson are two developments that have shaped and influenced Black electoral behavior the most in the new Black politics era.[70] The late 1980s ushered in a new era of Black Politics. Theodore Davis (2011) identifies three eras of Black Politics: the Protest Era, Politics Era, and the current era. The current stage of Black Politics is characterized by the emergence of a new Black middle class that came of age after the Civil Rights Struggle.[71] An increase in the number of Black voters led to an increased number of Black elected officials which in turn, led to a higher sense of political efficacy within the Black community.[72] Yet, in neither 1984 nor 1988 did the major party candidates in the general election address issues raised by the Jackson candidacy. In 1984 and 1988, when Blacks had achieved their highest levels of mobilization in the Democratic Party with delegate representation, and representation on the platform committee at historically high levels, the substantive results in terms of platform language were less than in 1968 when Black representation on the platform committee and the convention were miniscule.[73] In Congress and in the Executive Branch, as nominal Black influence increased (measured by the number of office holders and delegates), substantive Black influence had remained the same or declined.[74]

The Black leadership of the 1980s struggled with a plethora of problems faced during two Ronald Reagan presidencies and one term of President George H. W. Bush, which ushered in increased attacks on social programs delivered by Democrats in previous administrations. Before Reagan, Carter appointed a number of Blacks to high-level positions on his administration and to the federal courts, supported affirmative action in the Bakke case, and reorganized the Civil Rights bureaucracy.[75] In Reagan's 1982 budget, he proposed eliminating programs through which civil rights groups had obtained funds.[76] Other Reagan proposals passed by Congress changed eligibility requirements for cash assistance to the poor through Aid to Families with Dependent Children (AFDC) and lowered its budget by 1 percent, reduced the food stamp budget by 6 percent and delayed the adjustment for inflation, and severely lowered the low income housing assistance budget, and lowered the budget for school lunch programs by 4 percent.[77] Those social programs heavily contributed to increased access to better education, housing, and capital in Black communities. "Reaganomics" produced legislation that stripped many of the gains of the Civil Rights Movement and decreased support from the justice system in the appointment of conservative Supreme Court Justices. In 1990, George H. W. Bush vetoed the Civil Rights Act designed to overturn several Supreme Court decisions that made it difficult to enforce employment discrimination laws, calling it a "quota bill."[78] The progress made by Blacks since the Civil Rights era left many Whites feeling resentment and convinced that the progress made by the Black community came at the detriment of Whites, reinvigorating what Ronald Walters calls "White nationalism."[79]

THE RESULTS OF BLACK LEADERSHIP IN THE 1980s

The Black leadership of the 1980s was faced with the difficult task of confronting the increased need of providing assistance to its impoverished majority with less aid and assistance from the national legislature. Economically, the median household income for Blacks grew in the 1980s, although it remained well below the American population overall. Nationally, the median household income was $31,435 for Whites and $19,758 for Blacks. Black households typically brought in 63 cents for every $1 that went to a White household; it was 62 cents for every $1 a decade earlier.[80] The percentage of Blacks in poverty increased from the previous decade to 31 percent, peaking at 36 percent between 1983 and 1985.[81] Blacks earning above $100,000 increased 3 percentage points to 6.4 percent during the 1980s, while those Blacks earning less than $35,000 declined from 62 to 56 percent.[82] Educational attainment in the Black community continued to improve during the 1980s as the high school dropout rate continued to decline from 19.1 percent the previous decade to 13.2 percent by the end of the 1980s. Black men enjoyed a 9 percent drop in high school drop-outs alone.[83] Overall high school attainment rose from 51 percent to 66 percent, and college attainment rose 3 percent. The educational achievement gap in high school between Blacks and Whites closed to 13 percent, but again increased by 2 percent for college graduates. Finally, the 1980s saw the amount of Black homicide offenders decline from 51 percent to 46 percent (see table 3.2).[84]

On the other hand, the unemployment rate for Blacks during the 1980s remained twice the national average, peaking between the years 1983–1985 at 17 percent.[85] Despite an increasing number of Blacks gradu-

Table 3.2. Black Leadership and the Habits of Citizenship 1980–1989

	Variable	1980	1990	(+/-)	Option(s)*
Economy**	[1]Poverty	31%	32%	+1	
	[2]Median Household Income	$10,764	$18,676	+$7,912	Whites-$31,231 Gap-$12,555 Hispanics-+$13,651
	Blacks earning above $100k	3.4%	6.4%	+3%	
	Blacks earning less than $35k	62%	56.4%	-5.6	
	Blacks earning less than $15k	30.6%	29.1%	-1.5	
	[3]Unemployment	11%	13%	+2	5.6% (national average)
Criminal Justice***	[4]Blacks in Correctional System	474,368	1,614,195	+1,139,827	
Educational Achievement**	[5]High school dropout	19.1%	13.2	-5.9	
	High school graduates	51%	66.2	+15.2	Whites-79.1%
	College graduates	8.4%	11.7	+2	Whites-22% Gap-10.7%
[6]Obesity****	Black Men	51.3%	58.2	+6.9	
	Black Women	62.6%	68.5	+5.9	

* Possible options include comparative data with white/non-Hispanic population, Hispanic population, comparison with national average, and the racial disparity gap with whites
** Source: U.S. Census Bureau. American Data Survey
*** Source: Justice Policy Institute, U.S. Department of Justice
**** Source: Health, United States, 2010, Center for Disease Control and Prevention
(1) "poverty threshold": government defined as lack of those goods and services commonly taken for granted by members of mainstream society; adjusted for inflation using consumer price index
(2) income in 2001 CPLU-RS adjusted dollars
(3) calculated by dividing the number of unemployed individuals by all individuals currently in labor force (total population of working age)
(4) population in prison, jail, probation, parole, or under the control of correctional justice system
(5) the percentage of 16 through 24 year olds who are not enrolled in school and have not earned a high school credential (either a diploma or an equivalency such as General Education Diploma [GED])
(6) Body Mass Index (BMI) greater than or equal to 25

ating high school, they continued to comprise 50 percent of those convicted of crimes.[86] The number of Blacks in prison or otherwise under the supervision of the justice system increased by the end of the decade to 1,148,702, and the Black male homicide rate increased from 28 to 65 per 100,000 (1/29 for Black men compared to 1/186 for White men).[87] A decrease in social programs and access to adequate social services put increased pressure on Black families. Consequently, the number of single-parent Black households with children increased to 31 percent for Blacks compared to just 10 percent for Whites and the level of divorce and separation of Black families rose at twice the rate of Whites.[88] Additionally, Black life expectancy remained six years shorter than the national average. Overall, a similar pattern in behavior was present in the 1980s as in the previous decade: Blacks continued to earn just over half the proportion of wealth as Whites, their poverty was 3.5 times higher, and unemployment in the Black community was twice as high as the national average (see table 3.2).

ON POST-CIVIL RIGHTS ERA BLACK LEADERSHIP: THE 1990s

At the end of Jesse Jackson's presidential run in 1988, the transition to electoral politics as the main avenue Blacks would utilize in their quest for racial equality continued. Leaders such as Jesse Jackson and Colin Powell continued to have an influence on the pulse of Black America. The appointment of Clarence Thomas to the U.S. Supreme Court symbolized the potential fulfillment of Blacks' rightful standing in American society. Meanwhile local and regional elected officials such as Maxine Waters, Douglas Wilder, and James Clyburn also received national attention for their influence in representing Black interests nationally. Finally, grassroots organizers and spiritual leaders like Al Sharpton and Louis Farrakhan arrived on the scene as representative of Blacks' national interests with varying levels of success.

At the beginning of 1990, Black elected officials continued to infiltrate the American political system. In Virginia, Douglas Wilder became the first African American elected governor of any state in the U.S. As a *Washington Post* correspondent wrote shortly before Wilder's gubernatorial inauguration, "Willingly or not, Wilder becomes a symbol of the changing climate of politics in the South and the nation as a whole, the aspirations of American Blacks to assume an equal place in society, and the uncertainties that confront any public leader as a new century looms."[89] After only two years in the governor's mansion, Wilder announced on September 13, 1991, his intention to seek the 1992 Democratic presidential nomination but withdrew it six months later pointing to financial problems in the state of Virginia.[90] Wilder left office in 1994, but by 2004 ran for and was elected the mayor of Richmond, Virginia.

Some Blacks complained that Wilder refused to pay enough attention to their concerns. Wilder came out against proposals to create a Black-majority congressional district in Virginia after the 1990 census. Wilder declared that his election proved Blacks did not need special treatment to win office. His administration saw no major increase in the number of Black appointees as most of his key advisers were Whites who were personally loyal to him. Wilders election to governor of Virginia in 1990 illustrates two political realities of the post-civil rights period: first, with the end of racial segregation, the Black community lacks structures of accountability that would modify or effectively check the public or political behavior of its own elected officials. Second, growing numbers of Blacks in government and in political parties are trying to transcend their own racial designation of "Black" in order to further their own careers.[91]

At the same time Wilder was getting elected as the first Black governor in Virginia, Maxine Waters was elected to the U.S. Representatives by Californians. Representative Waters continually fought for legislation promoting aid to poor and minority neighborhoods. Waters was instrumental in the formation of the National Political Congress of Black Women in August of 1984. Due to the frustration of Black women leaders, the organization emphasized mainstream electoral politics as a way to focus on what they felt were unique and neglected problems facing women. The organization's goal was to encourage every Black woman in America to become involved in political activity.[92] Waters succeeded in passing an affirmative action bill that required California to set aside 15 percent of all state contracts for companies owned by members of minority groups and 5 percent for companies owned by women.[93] The bill was acclaimed as landmark legislation because it was the first major statewide bill to mandate such programs.

Waters was Jesse Jackson's most vocal backer in the 1984 and 1988 presidential races but later advocated breaking away from the Democratic Party and possibly creating a third party that would be responsive to the concerns of Blacks and other people of color. In *the Nation* she commented: "When I look at what is currently happening to the masses of Black people, to America's poor in general and the entire nation, I am angry and frustrated. But we cannot yield to feelings of helplessness; we must transform anger and frustration into bold and direct action. As for the Democratic Party, it must prove itself in these critical times or stand, like the Republicans, as just another instrument for betrayal and suppression of the people."[94]

Waters emerged on the national scene during the Los Angeles riots following the "not guilty" verdict of the policemen involved in the Rodney King beating. Much of the destruction and mayhem took place in Waters' district. In 1992 she introduced a bill which would have provided

$10 billion to fight urban decay. In defending her proposed legislation she claimed that America's cities deserve the same consideration as Russia and Israel, both recipients of massive U.S. foreign aid.[95] Waters also called for job training for Black males aged seventeen to thirty, increased Black ownership of small businesses, and tougher anti-discrimination banking laws.[96]

Al Sharpton gained national prominence with his tactics in the 1986 Howard Beach racial killing in which three Black men leaving a pizza parlor were assaulted by a group of bat-wielding White youths.[97] One man died when he was chased into traffic and run over by a car. Sharpton led a "Days of Outrage" protest that shut down traffic on the Brooklyn Bridge and halted subway service in Brooklyn and Manhattan. He used his exposure protesting against police brutality and racial injustice to run for a United States Senate seat from New York in 1988, 1992, and 1994. In 1997, he unsuccessfully ran for Mayor of New York City.

On January 5, 2003, Sharpton followed the path of Chisholm and Jackson before him and announced his candidacy for the 2004 presidential election as a member of the Democratic Party. The stated purpose of his candidacy was, first, to raise issues of concern to Blacks, the poor, and other minorities; issues the other candidates might ignore. A second stated purpose was to win sufficient votes in primaries, caucuses, and delegates at the Convention so that he might be able to exercise some influence on the eventual nominee, the party platform, and the campaign strategy in the general election.[98] In addition to his "name recognition" problem, Sharpton waged an ineffective campaign due to his inability to raise money, which resulted in lackluster showings in New York and southern primaries where the Black vote was important. Finally, Sharpton did not use the campaign debates to raise issues of importance to Blacks, minorities, or the poor.[99] Sharpton's campaign was therefore a failure in both its stated and unstated objectives; he did not successfully raise issues of special concern to Blacks during the campaign, he did not get enough votes and delegates to have influence on the nominee or platform, and he did not displace Jackson as the nation's preeminent Black leader.[100]

Louis Farrakhan is the longtime head of the Black religious organization the Nation of Islam (NOI). Farrakhan is known as a powerful speaker who has promoted Black separatism and self-reliance. After the death of Elijah Muhammad in 1978 he has been the prominent figure making the Nation of Islam a force in Black urban communities. Farrakhan's loyal following was evident by his ability to call upon at least one million Black men to converge on the nation's capital on October 16, 1995. The "Million Man March" was meant to create solidarity amongst the Black community. Farrakhan received support from the likes of Maya Angelou, Jesse Jackson, Stevie Wonder, and a host of other notable personalities from the Black community. The march surprised many, not only because of the sheer force of attendance, but because Farrakhan was able to not only promote, but deliver a non-violent protest in Washington, DC. In a language both spiritual and visionary Farrakhan exhorted Black men to transform their lives, protect their families, to give their time and financial support to Black institutions.[101]

Farrakhan's entire program presumed the permanent boundaries of race and racial antagonisms and the need to construct racial institutions that promote order, social stability, and patriarchal households within the Black community.[102] In the immediate aftermath of the Million Man March, many Black organizations reported significant increases in membership. Marable (1999) argued that Farrakhan and the Million Man March become reactionary and akin to Booker T. Washington's program of Black petty entrepreneurship and political cooperation with White conservatives.[103]

THE RESULTS OF BLACK LEADERSHIP IN THE 1990s

The Black leadership of the 1990s ushered in perhaps the most compelling increases in the economic, educational, and criminal patterns of Black life. First, Blacks earning above $100,000 increased to its highest levels to date from 6.4 percent to 11 percent while Blacks earning less than $35,000 dropped to an all-time low of 42 percent.[104] Those who earned under $15,000 were cut in half to only 24 percent.[105] Although unemployment in the Black community peaked at 14 percent in 1992–1993, by the end of the 1990s unemployment fell to 7 percent and the percentage of Blacks in poverty fell from 31 percent to 24 percent (see table 3.3).[106]

The Black community also saw its highest levels of educational attainment during the 1990s. High school graduation rates rose 12 percent to 78 percent total, closing the racial achievement gap down to 6 percent.[107] Black college level graduates increased by 5 percent to an all-time high of 16 percent, although, the achievement gap between White and Black college graduates remained the same at 10 percent. High school dropouts between the ages of sixteen to twenty-four remained constant at about 13 percent, while there was an increase in the number of young Black male dropouts from 11.9 percent to 15.3 percent. Yet, the 1990s saw Black women surpassing their male counterparts in likelihood to graduate high school 42 to 37 percent and the proportion of Black men college students remained 4.3 percent, the same as in 1976 (see table 3.3).[108]

By the end of the 1990s, there appeared to be significant decreases in criminal activity within Black America. Black homicide victimization declined by 45 percent, and since murder is primarily intraracial, meaning Blacks tend to kill Blacks and Whites tend to kill Whites, the amount of Blacks who committed homicide offenses also fell by 45 percent in the

Table 3.3. Black Leadership and the Habits of Citizenship 1990–1999

	Variable	1990	2000	(+/-)	Option(s)*
Economy**	(1)Poverty	32%	24%	-8	
	(2)Median Household Income	$18,676	$29,667	+10,991	Whites-$43,916 Gap-$14,249 Hispanics-$33,556
	Blacks earning above $100k	6.4%	11%	+4.6	
	Blacks earning less than $35k	56.4%	42%	-14.4	
	Blacks earning less than $15k	29.1%	14%	-15.1	
	(3)Unemployment	13%	9%	-4	4% (national average)
Criminal Justice***	(4)Blacks in Correctional System	1,614,195	2,347,066	+732,871	
Educational Achievement**	(5)High school dropout	13.2%	13%	-0.2	
	High school graduates	66.2%	78.5%	+12.3	Whites-84.9%
	College graduates	11.7%	16.5%	+5.8	Whites-26.1% Gap-10%
(6)Obesity****	Black Men	58.2%	-	-	
	Black Women	68.5%	-	-	

* Possible options include comparative data with white/non-Hispanic population, Hispanic population, comparison with national average, and the racial disparity gap with whites
** Source: U.S. Census Bureau. American Data Survey
*** Source: Justice Policy Institute, U.S. Department of Justice
**** Source: Health, United States, 2010, Center for Disease Control and Prevention
(1) "poverty threshold": government defined as lack of those goods and services commonly taken for granted by members of mainstream society; adjusted for inflation using consumer price index
(2) income in 2001 CPLU-RS adjusted dollars
(3) calculated by dividing the number of unemployed individuals by all individuals currently in labor force (total population of working age)
(4) population in prison, jail, probation, parole, or under the control of correctional justice system
(5) the percentage of 16 through 24 year olds who are not enrolled in school and have not earned a high school credential (either a diploma or an equivalency such as General Education Diploma [GED])
(6) Body Mass Index (BMI) greater than or equal to 25

1990s. Blacks who were victims of non-homicidal crimes, primarily rape, robbery, and aggravated assault, declined by 49 percent during the 1990s and arrest rates for Blacks involved in violent crimes other than murder dropped by 53 percent.[109] Increased wealth and education contributed to the improvement in living conditions of Black families. Blacks experienced significant improvements in life expectancy and the infant mortality rate dropped from 18 percent to 14 percent during the 1990s, although, still relatively high compared to Whites (5.7 percent) (see table 3.3).[110]

Despite the statistical improvements made by the Black community in the 1990s, it remains unclear just how much improvement was actually made, if any. Darity Jr. and Myers Jr. (2000) argue that by the end of the 1990s, Blacks were actually worst off than the beginning of the decade. Although the mean Black income started at $26,000 between 1990–1993 and reached $38,000 by 1999, the ratio of Black to White incomes fell during the same period.[111] While Blacks' income had reached a high of $38,000, Whites' mean income, which started at $43,000, had reached $65,000 by the end of the decade.[112] Additionally, married Black couples had earned 25 percent less income than married White couples during the same period. Thus, the ratio to Black and White incomes fell because Whites were still earning income faster than Blacks, despite gains in overall income made by Blacks (see table 3.3).[113]

Black violent crime and violent offenses remained disproportionately above any other racial or ethnic group in the 1990s. Although Blacks were 12 percent of the population, they comprised 55 percent of those convicted for murder.[114] Barry Litzer (2008) suggests that part of the decline in criminal activity is possibly due to Blacks' movement away from some of America's most troubled and crime ridden cities. Additionally, he points out that some of the most crime-ridden Blacks may have been "taken off the street" due to changes in the judicial systems such as "Three strike laws."[115] From 1990 to 2000 the total number of sentenced inmates rose 77 percent and 10 percent of young, Black males between the ages of fifteen to twenty-nine were in prison compared to only 1 percent of Whites within the same category. In fact, urban, Black, lower-class young mean saw an increase in crime and victimization by 2 percent.[116] Finally, the ever-growing HIV/AIDS epidemic caused unprecedented consequences and disadvantages for the Black community since gaining notoriety as a serious, life-threatening illness in the 1980s. The proportion of Blacks living with HIV/AIDS in America increased from 30 percent in 1990 to 44 percent by the year 2000, and Blacks continued to be the majority of new diagnoses (see table 3.3).[117]

ON POST-CIVIL RIGHTS ERA BLACK
LEADERSHIP: 2000 TO PRESENT

The Black leadership of the past decade has increased its representation and influence in the American political system, including, most importantly, the election of America's first Black President. The Black community currently enjoys more Black mayors, judges, CEOs, and principle decision makers in major U.S. corporations and governments than ever. The number of Black elected officials (BEOs) has increased from 1,469 in 1970 to over 10,500 today.[118] As a result, Black leaders during the past decade are as diverse and insubstantial as they have ever been. Blacks' newfound accessibility into key institutions of American society includes sports, the military, journalism, education, law enforcement, politics, and big business. As Black access increased, so did the varying interests and priorities within the Black community. Greater access to more institutions in American society resulted in not only more diversity; Blacks also earned more money and received greater power than previously experienced. As a result, they sought to protect and sustain their position and newfound wealth and power rather than continue to fight for the interests of the Black poor. In the fight to protect their accomplishments, these leaders have opted out of the fight to change the conditions found in the Black community.[119] Fighting to change the conditions of the impoverished Black community can come into conflict with sponsors and other leaders in their professions, donors, and philanthropists. For example, in the height of his career and popularity, Michael Jordan refused to take a strong political stance on issues facing the Black community, stating that "Republicans buy shoes too." From the continued influence of elected officials, to the introduction of professional athletes such as Michael Jordan and Tiger Woods, musical moguls such as Russell Simmons, and TV personalities such as Oprah Winfrey and Tavis Smiley, today's Black community has a plethora of individuals assuming leadership roles in the Black community.

Organizations such as the NAACP and the National Urban League still participate in the racial dialogue concerning Black interests, but with less impact, visibility, and participation from the Black masses, especially the youth. Elected officials in the Congressional Black Caucus (CBC) go largely ignored by the general public, the Black masses, and by the principle decision makers in their own party. Most notably, the CBC has been in disputes with President Obama, the nation's first Black President, over the disproportionate number of Blacks affected by unemployment and home foreclosures. Notable figures like Jesse Jackson and Al Sharpton have remained visible in the Black community, if not as visible on the national stage, over the past decade. Most notably, Al Sharpton has transformed himself from a Civil Rights activist to nightly talk show host on MSNBC.

Prominent figures in government such as Condoleezza Rice and Colin Powell have remained important figures in Black America. After being Secretary of State and leaving his post in the State Department, Powell was visible during the 2008 Presidential election where he endorsed Democratic nominee Barack Obama after donating the maximum amount to John McCain's campaign. After serving as the Secretary of State from 2005 to 2009, Condoleezza Rice returned to Stanford University as a political science professor. In addition to Powell and Rice, Conservative Black leadership gained visibility since 2000 with newly elected Tea Party representative Allen West, former Chairman of the Republican National Committee Michael Steele, and one-time candidate for the Republican Party Presidential nominee Herman Cain.

From 2003 to 2007, Michael Steele served as the Lieutenant Governor of Maryland where he chaired the Minority Business Enterprise Taskforce that actively promoted an expansion of affirmative action in the business world. From 2009 to 2011 he served as the first Black chairman of the Republican National Committee but after four rounds of voting dropped out of the race for reelection. Similar to Sharpton, Steele has now made his way around the political talk show circuit as a contributor on MSNBC, Fox News, and CNN.

Allen West is the first Republican to join the Congressional Black Caucus since 1997. Along with newly elected Tim Scott, they represent the first Black Republicans in Congress since J. C. Watts retired in 2003.[120] As one of thirty-two Black Republican candidates for Congress in 2010, West said he supported the Tea Party movement and dismissed the notion that the movement was motivated by racism as a creation of liberal critics and the news media.[121] West believes he is "the modern day Harriet Tubman" leading people away from the plantation, which is overseen by "perceived leaders in the black community" like Jesse Jackson who bow to the wishes of White liberals.[122] West argues Black Democrats have consistently failed to address high unemployment in the Black community and, in the meantime, continue to take Black votes for granted come election time.

Herman Cain used his business success as chairman and CEO of Godfather's Pizza to be a front-runner in the Republican Party Presidential nomination in 2011. His proposed "9-9-9" tax plan made him the most covered candidate in 2011.[123] Although race played a significant role in the coverage of Cain's campaign, he insisted that race played no role in his policies as a candidate or in his ideology as a politician. While campaigning on CNN's "State of the Union" Cain stated that Blacks "weren't held back because of racism." Cain told CNN's Wolf Blitzer that Blacks had been "brainwashed" into not considering a conservative point of view. Cain has insisted that his race has played little factor in his life in compared to hard-work, and a belief in the American dream. He resists being called African-American, preferring American instead and has consistently defended the Tea Party over allegations of racism. [124]

Perhaps the most significant symbols of the progressive Black leadership of today and representation of how far Blacks have come in America are the elections of Corey Booker in New Jersey and President Barack Obama. Booker became the Mayor of Newark, New Jersey in 2006 after losing a controversial and well-documented race in 2002 against Sharpe James. After his first week in office Booker announced a 100-day plan to implement reforms in Newark including adding police officers, ending background checks for many city jobs, an effort to help former offenders find employment in the city, refurbishing police stations, improving city services, and expanding summer youth programs. [125] One of the mayor's first priorities was to reduce the city's crime rate. Crime reduction has been such a central concern that Booker, along with his security team, were known to personally patrol the streets of Newark until times as late as 4 a.m. early in his first term. [126] Crime has dropped significantly in the city of Newark, which currently leads the nation in violent crime reduction. From 2006 to 2008 murders were down 36 percent, shooting incidents 41 percent, rapes 30 percent, and auto thefts down 26 percent. [127] In 2008, Newark had its lowest murder rate since 1959. In addition to lowering crime, Booker has both doubled the amount of affordable housing under development and confidence in his abilities to bring about substantive changes to Newark resulted in the donation of $100 million dollars to the Newark school system from Facebook founder Mark Zuckerberg. [128] Lastly, Booker has expanded the awareness of his programs and politics through the Sundance Channel's *BRICK CITY*, which follows Booker, Police Director Garry McCarthy, and Newark citizens from across the socioeconomic spectrum to tell the story of Newark's continuing transformation.

President Barack Obama made a historic rise from a Senator in Illinois to the highest office in the U.S. Obama's campaign of "hope" and "change" led to record setting numbers for fundraising. Obama sought and received the Black vote at record numbers receiving 96 percent of Black votes in his 2008 Presidential election. President Obama faced numerous questions during his campaign about his role in the Black struggle and as a leader of the Black community. Obama emphasized that it was his duty to lead not only Blacks, but everyone in the nation and that he was unable to promote the agenda of Blacks alone. Controversial remarks made by Reverend Jeremiah Wright, an outspoken leader of Obama's church in Chicago who has been heard articulating hateful and insensitive rhetoric about Whites and Jews in America, led to Obama's "A More Perfect Union" speech to address the much broader topic of race in America on May 18, 2008. His speech closed with a plea to move beyond America's "racial stalemate" and address shared social problems. [129]

President Obama's legacy as the first Black President for some is a symbol of how far Blacks have come and the new atmosphere of progressive race relations in America. With the election of President Obama, Blacks were assumed to have unprecedented access to the highest office in the U.S. His campaign and election received remarkable support from all facets of the Black community, Democrat and Republican, young and old. Support and endorsements poured in from TV personalities like Oprah Winfrey, Conservatives like Colin Powell, former Civil Rights leaders like Al Sharpton and Jesse Jackson, and every rapper young and old claiming that their "President is Black." If Black progress was to be achieved nationally, it could be assumed that they would find no more sympathetic figure with the power and ability to affect such changes than with President Obama in the White House. Blacks could exhale; their time to witness the types of changes that they had long envisioned for themselves as a people had finally arrived.

Obama is Black, but not a "race man." This position has made him "painfully safe" and thus unlikely to affect real change in American race relations.[130] Obama's career is full of confusing and conflicting views on racial and personal responsibility, greed, and ambition versus social justice. His avoidance of discussions of race until the Reverend Wright episode, fit neatly into a paradigm that says that race and racism are concerns of the past. As a result, Black politics has degenerated from debate about the efficacy of a Talented Tenth to the money-grubbing preaching of prosperity churches and growing divisions among class lines.[131] Unfortunately, a lot of Blacks have pinned their hopes on President Obama. Yet, President Obama is not a Black leader; he is president of the United States, not the president of Black America.[132] Therein lies the great irony of Obama being the first black president of the United States. There is great expectation that President Obama will be that liberator for Blacks; the modern-day Malcolm meets Dr. King. Part of the reason why some Blacks have been so hard on President Obama for not being Black enough for their tastes, is because of the huge vacuum in visionary Black leadership for so long that they expect Obama to tell it like it is on race and racism.[133] Such a tendency speaks of the desperation for leadership that has never existed in the White House.

THE RESULTS OF BLACK LEADERSHIP: 2000 TO PRESENT

What effect has the new, progressive leadership and the ascendancy of President Obama had on the state of Black America? First, economically, Black households have experienced three consecutive annual declines in income and the largest household income percentage decline in America. The poverty rate amongst Blacks (26 percent) has grown by 2 percent over the past decade while the number of Blacks earning above $100,000 a year increased by 0.9 percent.[134] Blacks earning less than $35,000 increased by 8.4 percent and those earning under $15,000 per year decreased by 1.1 percent since 2000.[135] In the end, the Black leadership over the past decade has watched as Blacks have gotten poorer, and remained at more than double the poverty rate of Whites, increasing the earnings gap between the two races. Nationally, in the year 2000, 57.9 percent of Black households had an annual income above $35,000 compared to just 38.2 percent in 1970, but by 2009 that number had dropped by 10 percent.[136] Historically speaking, in 1973 the income of Black families was 63 percent of that of Whites but by 2004 the income of Black families had dropped to 58 percent of that of Whites. In addition to the increase in the wage gap despite the overall increase in earnings, the unemployment rate for Blacks has more than doubled over the past decade and unemployment for Black men under the age of twenty is over three times the national average. Since 2000, Black home ownership has also declined (see table 3.4).

The condition of the Black family has taken a significant hit over the past decade. Female householders without a spouse now make up 46 percent of the Black population in America, while the national average remains 19.2 percent.[137] Those women also earn $25,034 per year, over $4,000 less than their White counterparts and over $13,000 dollars per year less than the mean earnings for women in America annually.[138] Women already have the burden of earning less than men, while single parents who are women have the additional burden of earning less than even single women. For Black women who are disproportionately living as single parents, the burden of raising and providing for a family becomes even more challenging. Subsequently, 43.5 percent of these families headed by single Black mothers live in poverty and receive cash assistance and food stamps at over twice the national average; coincidentally, 30 percent of all Black children are in poverty.[139] Meanwhile, the income of Black men has declined overall the last decade, as women have entered the work force quicker and more effectively (see table 3.4).

The past decade has seen moderate changes and accomplishments in regards to the quality and success of Blacks in education. Educational attainment in the Black community grew over the past decade by 6 percent to 84 percent of Blacks receiving a high school diploma or an equivalent, and a 5.5 percent increase in college graduates.[140] Subsequently, the high school achievement gap closed by 3 percent, but the college graduate gap between Whites and Blacks increased to 22 percent. Overall there still appears to be a significant problem with the level of achievement between Whites and minorities, in particular, Blacks. Over the past forty-five years, students in the United States have made notable gains in academic achievement, although the racial achievement gap remains because not all groups of students are advancing by the same intervals (see table 3.4).[141]

Table 3.4. Black Leadership and the Habits of Citizenship 2000–Present

	Variable	2000	2010-14	(+/-)	Option(s)*
Economy**	(1)Poverty	24%	26%	+2	
	(2)Median Household Income	$29,667	$35,398	+5,731	Whites-$60,256 Gap-$24,858
	Blacks earning above $100k	11%	11.9%	+.9	
	Blacks earning less than $35k	42%	50.4%	+8.4	
	Blacks earning less than $15k	24%	22.9%	-1.1	
	(3)Unemployment	9%	11%	+2	6.3% (national average)
Criminal Justice***	(4)Blacks in Correctional System	2,347,066	2,553,000	+205,934	
Educational Achievement**	(5)High school dropout	13%	7.3%	-5.8%	
	High school graduates	78.5%	84%	+5.5	Whites-87.1%
	College graduates	16.5%	22%	+5.5	Whites- 44% Gap- 22%
(6)Obesity****	Black Men	62.9	69%	+7.9%	
	Black Women	77.2	82%	+5.2%	

* Possible options include comparative data with white/non-Hispanic population, Hispanic population, comparison with national average, and the racial disparity gap with whites
** Source: U.S. Census Bureau. American Data Survey (2015)
*** Source: Justice Policy Institute, U.S. Department of Justice
**** Source: Health, United States, 2010, Center for Disease Control and Prevention
(1) "poverty threshold": government defined as lack of those goods and services commonly taken for granted by members of mainstream society; adjusted for inflation using consumer price index
(2) income in 2001 CPLU-RS adjusted dollars
(3) calculated by dividing the number of unemployed individuals by all individuals currently in labor force (total population of working age)
(4) population in prison, jail, probation, parole, or under the control of correctional justice system
(5) the percentage of 16 through 24 year olds who are not enrolled in school and have not earned a high school credential (either a diploma or an equivalency such as General Education Diploma [GED])
(6) Body Mass Index (BMI) greater than or equal to 25

As the Black community faced economic disadvantages during the past decade, the effects have led to crime remaining a pivotal hindrance to Black advancement in America. Murder among Black males has drastically increased since 2000, while homicide continues to be the leading cause of death among Black males fifteen to thirty-four.[142] The Justice Policy Institute, a Washington, DC-based think tank, disclosed that there are currently more Black men in jail or prison than in college.[143] Coincidentally, unemployment and low educational attainment are also conditions plaguing Black men and contributing to their entry into the criminal justice system. The past decade has seen an unprecedented rate of Black men being incarcerated, a 6.3 percent increase since 2000, while the female incarceration rate has declined by 0.5 percent (see table 3.4).[144]

Overall, the Black leadership has done nothing to curb the increase of Black on Black crime on the national level. The propensity of Black men being victims of murder, most likely at the hand of another Black male, and the number of Blacks in the jail or prison system has increased since the year 2000. Thus, it is difficult to justify any allegiance and loyalty to the current leadership within the Black community based on the current condition of the majority of Blacks despite greater access to Black elected officials and representatives. The Black community has seen little improvement to their condition, status, and standing in the U.S. with little accountability from Black leadership, 1968 to present (see table 3.4).

NOTES

1. Kevin Powell, "Black Leadership is Dead," *Ebony* 65 no.12 (2010): 85–87.
2. Emory S. Bogardus, "Leadership and Attitudes," *Sociology and Social Research* 13 no. 4 (1929): 377–81.
3. Ibid.
4. Ibid.
5. Hugh H. Smythe, "Changing Patterns in Negro Leadership," *Social Forces* 29 no.2 (1950): 191–97.
6. T. G. Standing, "Nationalism in Negro Leadership," *The American Journal of Sociology* 40 no.2 (1934): 180–92.
7. Ibid.
8. Ibid.
9. Ibid.
10. Ibid.
11. Smythe, "Changing Patterns in Negro Leadership."
12. Ibid.
13. Ibid.
14. Ibid.
15. Tilman C. Cothran and William Phillips, Jr., "Negro Leadership in a Crisis Situation," *Phylon (1960–)* 22 no.2 (1961): 107–18.
16. Harold Cruse, *The Crisis of the Negro Intellectual* (New York: New York Review Classics, 2005).
17. Ibid.
18. Donald Cunnigen, "Black Leadership in the Twenty-First Century," *Society* (July/August) 43 no.5 (2006): 25–29.

19. Arch Puddington, "The Question of Black Leadership," *Commentary* 91 no.1 (1991): 22–29.

20. Michael Dawson, *Black Visions: The Roots of Contemporary African American Political Ideologies* (Chicago: University of Chicago Press, 2001).

21. Manning Marable, *Black Leadership: Four Great American Leaders and the Struggle for Civil Rights* (New York: Penguin Books, 1999), 166.

22. Hanes Walton Jr. and Robert C. Smith, *American Politics and the African American Quest for Universal Freedom,* 3rd ed. (New York: Pearson/ Longman, 2006), 72.

23. Dawson, *Black Visions,* 48.

24. Ibid., 87.

25. Ibid., 97.

26. Robert C. Smith, *We Have No Leaders: African Americans in the Post-Civil Rights Era* (New York: SUNY Press, 1996), 29.

27. Stokely Carmichael and Charles V. Hamilton. *Black Power: The Politics of Liberation in America,* 47.

28. Ibid.

29. Ibid., 103.

30. Ibid.

31. Ibid., 105.

32. Carleton Mabee, "The Crisis in Negro Leadership," *The Antioch Review* 24 no.3 (1964): 365–78.

33. Hadjor, *Another America,* 177.

34. Smith, *We Have No Leaders,* 80.

35. Gunnar Myrdal, *The American Dilemma: The Negro Problem and Modern Democracy.* (New Jersey: Transaction Publishers), 1999.

36. Ibid., 90.

37. NAACP.org/history.

38. John White *Black Leadership in America: From Booker T. Washington to Jesse Jackson.* 2nd ed. (New York: Longman, 1990), 50–51.

39. Smith, *We Have No Leaders,* 91.

40. Steve Miller and Jerry Seper, "NAACP Tax Status Questioned." *The Washington Times,* February 4, 2001.

41. Smith, *We Have No Leaders,* 94–95.

42. Ibid.

43. Ibid., 90.

44. Ibid., 98.

45. Rodney Hurst, *It Was Never About A Hot Dog and A Coke!* (Livermore, CA: WingSpan Press), 2008.

46. Smith, *We Have No Leaders,* 94–98.

47. Robert Sing, *The Congressional Black Caucus: Racial Politics in the U.S. Congress* (California: Sage Publications, 1997).

48. Ibid.

49. Smith, *We Have No Leaders.*

50. Hanes Walton Jr. and Robert Smith, *American Politics and the African American Quest for Universal Freedom,* 172.

51. Carl Hulse and David M. Herszenhorn, "Rangel Steps Aside From Post During Ethics Inquiry," *The New York Times,* March 3, 2010.

52. Lenna K. Itkowitz, *Shirley Chisholm for President* (New York: Random House, 1974).

53. U.S. Census Bureau. *US Census Bureau 2015 American Community Survey.*

54. Ibid.

55. Justice Policy Institute, U.S. Department of Justice. www.justice.gov. Accessed October 17, 2015.

56. U.S. Census Bureau. *US Census Bureau 2015 American Community Survey.*

57. Ibid.

58. Ibid.

59. Ibid.

60. Ibid.

61. Ibid.

62. Ibid.

63. Marable, *Black Leadership.*

64. Ibid.

65. Karen DeYoung, *Soldier: The Life of Colin Powell* (New York: Knopf, 2006).

66. Smith, *We Have No Leaders*, 75.

67. Ibid., 229.

68. Ibid., 250.

69. Sean Alfino, "Poll: Jesse Jackson, Rice Top Blacks," *CBSNews*, February 15, 2006.

70. Katherine Tate, *From Protest to Politics: The New Black Voters in American Elections* (New York: Russell Sage Foundation, 1994).

71. Theodore J. Davis, *Black Politics Today.* (New York: Routledge, 2011).

72. Ibid.

73. Smith, *We Have No Leaders.*

74. Ibid., 239.

75. Walton Jr. and Smith, *American Politics and the African American Quest for Universal Freedom*, 208.

76. Walters, *White Nationalism/ Black Interests*, 69.

77. Ibid., 73.

78. Ibid.

79. Ibid.

80. Felicity Barringer, "White-Black Disparity in Income Narrowed in 80s," *The New York Times*, July 24, 1992.

81. U.S. Census Bureau. *US Census Bureau 2015 American Community Survey.*

82. Ibid.

83. Ibid.

84. Ibid.

85. Ibid.

86. Ibid.

87. Ibid.

88. Ibid.

89. Glen Macnaw and Tom Pendergast, *Wilder, L. Douglas, Contemporary Blacks Biography*, (2005).

90. Ibid.

91. Manning Marable, *Black Leadership: Four Great American Leaders and the Struggle for Civil Rights* (New York: Penguin Books, 1990), 157.

92. Vitnia Zwaykin, "Maxine Waters." *Encyclopedia World Biography* 16: 1313.

93. Juliana Malveaux, "Maxine Waters: Woman of the House," *Essence* no.1 (1990): 55.

94. *Contemporary Black Biography*, 67, Gale Research, (2008): 159.

95. Zwaykin, "Maxine Waters."

96. Ibid.

97. Lynn S. Chancer, *High Profile Crimes: When Legal Issues Become Social Causes* (Chicago: University of Chicago Press, 2005).

98. Smith, *We Have No Leaders*, 135.

99. Ibid., 138.

100. Ibid., 139.

101. Ibid., 161.

102. Ibid., 165.

103. Manning Marable, *Black Leadership: Four Great American Leaders and the Struggle for Civil Rights* (New York: Penguin Books), 1999.

104. U.S. Census Bureau. *US Census Bureau 2015 American Community Survey.*

105. Ibid.

106. Ibid.

107. Ibid.

108. Ibid.

109. Justice Policy Institute, U.S. Department of Justice. www.justice.gov. Accessed October 17, 2015.

110. U.S. Census Bureau. *US Census Bureau 2015 American Community Survey* .

111. Samuel Darity and Samuel L. Myers, Jr., "The Relative Decline in Black Family Income During the 1990s." Presentation at the Southern Economic Association Annual meetings (Washington, DC: November 9–12, 2000).

112. Ibid.

113. Ibid.

114. Justice Policy Institute, U.S. Department of Justice. www.justice.gov. Accessed October 17, 2015.

115. Barry Litzer, "The Great Black Hope," *Claremont Review of Books*, Winter (2009).

116. Ibid.

117. U.S. Census Bureau. *US Census Bureau 2015 American Community Survey* .

118. Joint Center for Political and Economic Studies, "National Roster of Black Elected Officials," November, 2011.

119. Cunnigen, "Black Leadership in the Twenty-First Century," 27.

120. Frank James, "It's All Politics: Black GOP Lawmakers Face Tricky Relations With Democrats," *National Public Radio*, January 4, 2011.

121. Jennifer Steinhauer, "Black Hopefuls Pick This Year in G.O.P. Races," *The New York Times*, May 4, 2010.

122. Jennifer Bendary, "Allen West: I Am the Modern Day Harriet Tubman," *The Huffington Post*, August 18, 2011.

123. Pew Research Center. "The Year in the News 2011: Top Newsmakers," *Project for Excellence in Journalism: Pew Research Center*, December 21, 2011.

124. Hermain Cain, *They Think You're Stupid* (Atlanta, GA: Stroud & Hall Publishers), 2005.

125. Ryan Smothers, "Booker Has 100-Day Plan for Newark's Reorganization," *New York Times*, July 11, 2006.

126. Sean Gregory, "Cory Booker (Still) Optimistic He Can Save Newark," *Time*, Monday, July 27, 2009.

127. Ibid.

128. Richard Perez-Pena, "Facebook Founder to Donate $100 million to Help Remake Newark Schools," *The New York Times*, Sept. 23, 2010.

129. Matt Apuzzo, "Obama Confronts Racial Division," *Huntington Post,* March 18, 2008.

130. Rick L. Jones, *What's Wrong with Obamamania?: Black America, Black Leadership, and the Death of Political Imagination* (New York: SUNY Press), 2008.

131. Ibid.

132. Powell, "Black Leadership is Dead."

133. Ibid.

134. U.S. Census Bureau. *US Census Bureau 2015 American Community Survey*.

135. Ibid.

136. Ibid.

137. Ibid.

138. Ibid.

139. Ibid.

140. Ibid.

141. Richard Rothstein, Class and Schools: Using Social, Economic, and Educational Reform to Close the Black White Achievement Gap," *Economic Policy Institute*.

142. U.S. Census Bureau. *US Census Bureau 2015 American Community Survey*.

143. Ibid.

144. Ibid.

FOUR

On The Failures of Black Leadership

Applying Machiavelli's framework for effective leadership to Black leaders suggests that leaders must develop new political systems or institutions to reinvigorate the Black community with good habits. Using a variety of political tools, leaders develop new followers, or citizens, equipped with the ability and willingness to sacrifice their self-interest for the interests of the national community, or "common good." Leaders take the people to unsuspected possibilities, rather than using their influence to advance the interest of a few over the many. Black leadership has allowed conditions and standing of the Black community overall to decline. Thus, based on Machiavelli's standard for effective leadership, the Black community has had inefficient and ineffective post-civil rights leadership.

Blacks are earning more income annually than in 1970, a median increase over $20,000 annually, yet during that same period the income gap between Blacks' and Whites' earnings has increased, and the gap in earnings between Blacks and all other races have increased, including Hispanics who now out-earn Blacks in America. In every decade the gap in annual income between Blacks and Whites has increased, and since 1980 the income gap between Blacks and Hispanics has increased. All other racial groups have not only out-earned Blacks, they have generated higher incomes faster than Blacks during the same time period.

Blacks are earning more money than before, but (1) not at the same rate as the rest of the country, and (2) despite their gains in income, Blacks now have the lowest annual income of all races in America. Over 50 percent of all Black households still earn less than $35,000 per year, and more of those are being heading by single-mothers. Since 1970, another clear distinction can be made; there has been a significant increase in the number of Blacks earning above $100,000, over five times as many

Table 4.1.   U.S. Median Household Income By Race 2014*

Race	Median Household Income**	+/- Since 1980
Asians	$74,297	
Whites	$60,256	+41,527
Hispanics	$42,491	+28,841
Blacks	$35,398	+24,634

* Source: U.S. Census Bureau. American Data Survey (2015)
** Income in 2001 CPLU-RS adjusted dollars

as there were in 1970. Similar to the national trend, the rich got richer, while poor Blacks have seen mediocre progress at best. Average after-tax income for the top 1 percent of U.S. households almost quadrupled, up 275 percent, from 1979 to 2007. For people in the middle of the economic scale, after-tax income grew by just 40 percent. Those at the bottom experienced an 18 percent increase.[1] It is also important to note that the U.S. economy grew overall, increasing in GDP from $1,237.9 billion dollars in 1970 to $14,523.5 billion in 2010.[2] Thus, improvement in Black wealth can be reasonably perceived as having no result of changes made by Black leaders or the Black community itself. The fact is that there was more money and wealth in the country overall and the Black community has been along for the ride with a few Blacks receiving the benefits of this "new" economy and Blacks' greater participation and access to it.

Blacks have seen a 6 percent increase in unemployment since 1970, the highest of all races. Despite the current economic conditions, Blacks' unemployment has consistently been twice the national average. They continue to have a more difficult time finding work, and there are more Blacks out of work now than in 1970. Blacks are graduating from high school and college at greater proportions than previously experienced, but even with greater access to higher education Blacks are 22 percentage points behind Whites in college graduation rates, a wider gap than in 1970. Increased educational attainment and greater access to higher education has not led to significantly better conditions for the majority of members of Blacks because they have not translated into better jobs and resources back into the Black community. Blacks' participation in the correctional system is higher now than it has ever been, and here too, they have seen greater gain than any other race in America. More importantly, Black leaders have developed no strategy to address Black on Black crime and the violence taking place disproportionately in predominately Black neighborhoods.

Overall, Black leaders have been unable to come up with institutions to combat the poor conditions of Blacks; the facts are, Blacks earn less and earn it slower, while also committing crime and representing the greatest proportion of the correctional system of any other race in America. Blacks have become worst off in economic standing now that Hispanics earn more than Blacks. Thus, the question is, where has the post-civil rights leadership taken the Black community? What public good or service have they provided to the masses of the Black community to make them feel like more than second-class citizens? Blacks need to think of leaders as people who accomplish great things for others; change peoples' lives, behaviors, and possibilities, rather than those who accomplish great things for themselves or for a few. The fact that Blacks' median household income has increased overall may not be a resemblance of the leadership; overall more wealth was generated and all races saw increases in earnings. What the Black community has experienced in the post-civil rights era are people who attain to lead the Black community who do a good job of taking care of the few, but not so good at improving the conditions and standing of the majority of Blacks.

THE TRANSFER OF HABITS

The key to successful Black leadership is to shake the impoverished Black majority out of their comfort zone and the negative habits associated with their patterns of behavior and interactions with one another. These negative habits and patterns of interaction with one another are a result of their corrupted perception of citizenship. In order to change these negative habits of interaction into positive ones through radical, drastic change in how the Black community perceives themselves and their involvement in the status quo, a Black leader must instill in the impoverished Black community the same habits and attributes that are in the leadership. Just as the effective leader is capable of leading and directing the masses in productive, positive behavior, so too must the Black individual learn to be capable of leading and directing their own individual behavior into disciplined, community-building activities that contribute to the betterment of the group.

The positive habits that a Black leader must transfer over to the masses or lead to their reemergence within their already existing character include sacrifice, courage, self-respect, dedication to hard work, and self-determination, in addition to the habits of moral character. Such habits of moral character include knowledge of the proper rules of conduct and principles of right and wrong patterns of behavior and interaction amongst members of the community. There is a right and a wrong way in which Blacks can develop and thrive under healthy arrangements of communication and cooperation, and knowledge of these ways is of vital importance. Any Black leader would be wise to study and investigate these ways.

To sacrifice one's own personal self-interest for the common good of the Black community as a whole is an essential element of an effective Black leader and thus, an important attribute that all members of the Black community must adopt to raise the status of their most disadvantage members. If all members of the Black community are willing and devoted to surrendering a portion of their self-interest and contribute to the overall sustainment and health of the community as a whole instead, sufficient progress can be made in improving the conditions of the Black community. It is crucial that all members of the Black community make equal sacrifices to the sustainment of the community and promote commitment to community's values by renouncing certain aspects of their self-interest that are contrary to the betterment of the community as a whole such as uninhibited materialism.

To be comfortable making that sacrifice and confront the system of oppression that members of the impoverished Black community face takes courage to face difficult times and yet proceed on. Not having the ability to selfishly seek personal satisfaction and self-aggrandizement is certainly contrary to the traditional practices in society and it will take confidence to act accordingly with conviction that the sacrifice being made will ultimately be successful. It will take courage to act upon those convictions in the face of a society that promotes corrupted values and has corrupted perceptions of success and what individuals should aspire to. Members of the Black community must have courage in their convictions that their sacrifice will pay off when times get difficult, and the strength to continually perform selfless acts.

A Black leader must instill in the Black community a sense of self-respect with a dedication to hard work. One fundamental component associated with negative habits of citizens and the detrimental patterns of interaction amongst Blacks are the consequences of a mistrusting group, with little commitment and respect for one another and the group as a whole. Black on Black crime and the condition of the Black family are a few examples of the inherent lack of respect that Blacks have for themselves and for their community. Not that African Americans hold no esteem or regard for their character, only that they do not hold high enough esteem and sufficient value in their attitude towards one another to effectively institute change.

CORRUPTION AND BLACK LEADERSHIP

A failure of Black leadership enables the persistence of the bad habits of citizenship and contributes to the reasons why the conditions for Blacks have not improved and why Blacks still find themselves at the bottom of American standing and social status. Blacks have integrated into government and taken leadership positions in many industries, and yet Blacks remain worst off in America based on the widening economic gap between Blacks and the rest of the nation, and twice the unemployment and participation in the correctional system than any other race. It is the role and duty of Black leadership to shake the corrupted spirit of the Black community and develop unsuspected possibilities and entirely new attitudes among them. Black leaders are to blame for the condition of today's Black majority because they have failed in their role to lead the people into a proper understanding and conception of themselves as Blacks and thus, their role, duties, and obligations as members of the Black community. The Black leadership has failed in its responsibility to the advancement of the poor and defining their role and responsibilities as U.S. citizens.

The corruption of Black leadership is equivalent to the corruption of the Black community; the inability and unwillingness to put the good of the community over self-interest and advocate for the poor and serve the Black majority. Once the people have entered into a corrupt state, a state of putting one's self interest over the needs of the community, leaders need to come forth with creative, innovative ideas to shake the people out of their corrupt state. The corruption of Black citizens and the community is manifested by Black leaders' inability and unwillingness to put the good of the community over self-interest and self-aggrandizement. Leaders must be the vigorous spokesperson and the incorruptible defender of the masses; a direct expression of their will, interests, and aspirations. Today's Black leaders are not willing to sacrifice their individual "self" to accomplish the goals of the community at-large. In particular, many of the members of the Black "middle-class," which has grown in the post-civil rights era, have gone out of their way to distance themselves from the Black poor. Thus, corruption is measured by the conditions and standing of those supposed to be led. It takes place when leaders act in the interest of the individual self, or a few elites, over the people. For example, a corrupt king may tax his citizens heavily for his personal wealth and entertainment while they remain poor; as he gets richer, they remain in the same condition or worst.

The corruption of the Black leader renders their methods of achieving the objectives of the Black masses useless due to their inability to develop innovative and creative institutions which can stimulate new attitudes among the Black majority. Corruption takes place when the individual asserts their self-interest over that of the community by lacking contribution and responsibility to the protection, sustainment, and improvement of the Black community, through labor and positive patterns of interaction, in particular. Lack of jobs and high unemployment means many Blacks are not physically contributing to the Black community positively through labor, or are unable to contribute their labor, thus money and other resources. Blacks' spending the majority of their money outside of Black communities demonstrates lack of value and resources in Black communities created by its leadership. High crime in Black communities and increasing numbers of crimes committed by Blacks, predominately against other Blacks, indicates low value in Black life and negative feelings towards the Black community overall; a bad habit and symbol of erosion, or lack or diminishing value in the Black community. Increased access to education has been one achievement shared by the Black community overall, and has resulted in increased educational attainment, following *Brown v Board* (1954), but Blacks have no structure or system in place to take full advantage of Blacks' increased access to education.

The incipient incorporation of Black leadership into systemic institutions and processes has had the predictable consequence of further isolating them from the community they intended to lead.[3] Instead of pursuing leadership, organization, and mobilization within its core community, Black leaders in America have instead pursued integration into systemic institutions which they generally have very limited power to control and make widespread changes inherently needed in the Black community. This is partly the result of Black leaders being largely middle class in origin and orientation, and consequently is in danger of losing its claim to speak for the Black masses, and control over the dynamics of the Black struggle.[4]

The great issue with Black leadership is that it has reached a historical moment in which it no longer seeks to liberate the people or transform the world, but often languishes in vulgar careerism and selfishness which reinforces, rather than opposes, American peripheralization.[5] The only remedy to such a situation is an intellectual, social, and political revolt of the oppressed masses against those who have abandoned the suffering populations. Leadership will only be effective and liberatory if people are seriously committed to forming oppositional movements to capitalist exploitations; a call for the identification, rejection, and replacement of Black leadership which is not committed to challenging permanent American hegemony.[6] Only if committed Black leadership is present can functional alternative paradigms be examined, constructed, and implemented. The central purpose must be the merger of leadership with everyday people into cadres of local, regional, and a national united front which addresses the struggles of race as well as class confronting Black America. Leadership which is committed to struggle against marginalization must work diligently, along with the people, to form seamless units in which they work together for the needs of the collective. In such a model, leaders submit to the will of the people, not vice-versa.[7]

Leaders must address the habits of negative interaction, or harmful actions or influence directed at members of the Black community, and resentment, or feeling displeasure or indignation at some act or person in the group. A feeling of displeasure at being Black, or poor Black identification leads to less value in the Black community, and thus, whether or not individuals contribute to its maintenance or not. Blacks holding a negative perception of their history and socioeconomic conditions and standing in American society, move away from the Black community and hold little value in its sustainment. An effective Black leader is one who changes the patterns of behavior of Blacks and makes positive changes in these areas that demonstrate "bad habits" of citizenship; to take the oppressed and dominated Black community and reinvigorate them with good habits.

BLACK LEADERS AND
THE DEVELOPMENT OF INSTITUTIONS

To change the patterns of behavior among members of the Black community and reinvigorate them with good habits requires the development of innovative political systems and institutions. Institutions are organizations or system of practices devoted to promoting a particular cause which establishes new laws or customs. Leaders of the Black community have failed to develop innovative and creative institutions to stimulate good habits of citizenship among Blacks. Increasing Black crime, unemployment, and diminishing economic standing are signs of negative patterns of behavior and corruption within members of the Black community, in addition to its leadership. Not valuing the Black community or Black life is a bad habit; illustrated by Black on Black crime being at over 90 percent. They are also demonstrations of the corruption of the Black citizenry and erosion of value in the Black community because positive contributions to the conditions of the Black masses are lacking. Black leaders must transform these bad habits, or negative patterns of interaction among members of the Black community. This has not been done for the majority of Blacks, based on the economic, criminal, educational, and familial structure of the Black community. Contemporary Black leaders have demonstrated the inability to fix these problems with innovative systems and institutions that reinforce contribution and responsibility to the community in these key areas. The fact that Blacks' economic standing and employment opportunities have worsened, and crime in Black communities have increased, demonstrates bad or ineffective leadership and the need for new institutions in the Black community.

To adequately guide the Black community towards unsuspected possibilities and new habits of citizenship, Black leaders must create institutions that unite and create solidarity amongst the members of the community. Unity and solidarity from the Black community will enable them to challenge the American social and political system from a position of strength. Black leaders need to establish organizations that are devoted entirely to the promotion of building unity, commitment to the community, and restoring pride and value in the Black community. Black-led institutions should focus primarily on the objectives of social uplift, public welfare, and dependable and sustainable economic practices. They can be a part of preexisting cultural systems such as schools, churches, and other social programs, taking into account the possible contribution of developing healthy habits and positive patterns of behavior that cultivates a new commitment to the common good of the Black community. Rather than organizations built to promote and advance middle-class values, institutions capable of improving the conditions of the Black majority must be focused on building the knowledge-base, commitment, and attitudes of the Black poor and in predominately Black neighborhoods. Thus, Black leaders would be wise to develop institutions that pay attention to the specific needs and interests of lower class Blacks, while promoting healthy attitudes and commitment to the community as a whole.

By creating self-help, nation-building political systems, and institutions Blacks leadership will be able to produce good habits among members of the Black community that reflects community solidarity and improved socioeconomic status of the Black community. Additionally, these institutions must reinforce accountability and responsibility to the group. The conditions and resources present in predominate Black communities demonstrates no value in contributing economically to the Black community, no obligation or commitment to contribute one's labor to the community, and no responsibility for valuing Black life and not harming one another. These are the times when leaders are needed the most; to develop and cultivate new habits and positive patterns of behavior amongst members of the Black community through systems and institutions that combat these negative habits. Black leaders must develop institutions that encourage Blacks to value their community and reinforce obligation to protect, sustain, and improve the conditions of Black life.

Institutions that can address the bad habits, or negative patterns of interaction amongst members of the Black community must be self-helping, in that they produce the conditions in which the Black community and its members are able to provide certain goods and services internally. The most important goods and resources that the Black community can provide must be discovered and addressed within the Black community, thus the importance of participating in activities as members. Those goods and resources must be those that are in most need of being addressed or the issues that produce the most negative effects or consequences to the Black community. The creation of such institutions lessens dependence on others groups and the government. If Blacks are receiving inadequate health treatment and facilities and employment opportunities they must identify leaders who can develop and bring these much needed resources to the community through new institutions. This enables the Black community to determine its own fate by providing their own resources. Being self-sufficient in these areas will put the Black community in a position of strength in that they can choose to participate in government and ally with other groups when it is mutually beneficial. The ability to provide the goods and resources for one's own community and solve the conditions facing the Black community internally, challenges corruption and reestablishes value in the Black community.

To accomplish this task Black leaders need to be innovative and creative. It appears as though those aspiring to the mantle of leadership have run out of creative ideas to reach and inspire the Black masses in a positive, community-reinforcing way. This requires leaders to bring something new to the table; introduce the Black community to new ways of looking at their community and themselves as individuals, their history, standing, and what it means to be a member of the Black community. An important attribute of effective leadership that fosters one's ability to accomplish these tasks requires them to lead by example. This means that Black leaders must demonstrate through their actions personal sacrifice and giving back directly to the Black community, not just random philanthropy that is multiracial or diverse. The Black community needs Blacks to give back directly to Blacks. This requires institutions and programs that are targeted directly to impact the Black community.

Another attribute that contributes to a leader's ability to accomplish the goals of the community at-large is responsibility. Black leaders have to develop institutions that reinforce accountability to other members of the group. Leaders cannot be afraid to hold Blacks responsible for their commitment and contribution to other members of the Black community. Ultimately, the conditions present in the Black community require political and social institutions that employ elite Blacks, in predominately Black communities, although they may be able to receive higher pay and better living conditions in other organizations or parts of the country. To do this, the people, as well as its leadership, have to be committed to sacrificing their self-interest and put the good of the community first. This will encourage the Black community to contribute to its own protection, sustainment, and improvement. For example, Black schools and educational facilities, hospitals and medical centers, rehabilitation centers and resources for newly released criminals, and parenting centers, all funded and employed by elite, powerful, and influential Blacks in each respective field. Conversely, today many elite Blacks lead, teach, or work in professions outside of the Black community or in predominately White institutions.

Post-civil rights Black leaders have failed because they have spent too much time chasing racial and political integration into electoral politics and mainstream social institutions rather than creating top-notch Black institutions. Integration in all too many instances has resulted in the decline or destruction of a number of important institutions that thrived under segregation, including neighborhoods where all social classes lived in relative proximity, as well as independent businesses, schools, and cultural institutions directed by the voice of Blacks.[8] Rather than creating top Black medical facilities, schools, and employment opportunities through businesses, and so forth, Blacks fought to be included in White schools, have access to White jobs, and be able to be seen in White hospitals. Elite Black teachers and lawyers fought to teach and work in top White schools and law firms rather than developing equal facilities that are directly tied to the interests of the Black community. This was a big misguided consequence of the Civil Rights movement. The majority of Blacks would have benefitted more from the creation and development of top-tier Black facilities, with top Black professionals from each field. Because there was little value placed in the Black community, success meant leaving the Black community, or working for Whites, a higher valued group.

One example of alternative leadership, that may not necessarily fit the model described above, but has shown its effectiveness in changing the patterns of behavior within Harlem's Black community, is represented by Geoffrey Canada's *Harlem's Children Zone* (HCZ). Canada's *Harlem's Children Zone* is a non-profit organization for poverty-stricken children and families living in Harlem, New York. The organization provides free support for the children and families in the form of parenting workshops, a pre-school program, three public charter schools, and health programs. Its mission is "aimed at doing nothing less than breaking the cycle of generational poverty for the thousands of children and families it serves."[9] Thus, Canada hopes to keep children on track from as early on in their history as possible, through college, and into the job market. HCZ designs, funds, and operates a holistic system of education, social services, and community-building programs within Harlem to counter what Canada perceives to be the negative influences of crime, drugs, and poverty, and to help children complete college "no matter the costs" and enter the job market competitively.

Components of HCZ's program include a Baby College (a series of workshops for parents with children between the ages of zero to three), all-day pre-kindergarten, and it's *Promise Academy*, which functions as an extended day charter school. The *Promise Academy* operates from the hours of 8 a.m. to 4 p.m., 210 days out of the year, which goes beyond the 180 days required by law, and includes a twenty to twenty-five day mandatory summer program. Other important aspects of the program include the creation of a critical mass of adults around the children who understand what it takes to help them succeed. This is typically done through parenting classes and requirements that parents attend educational meetings and conferences with instructors and counselors, and participate in academic and social activities with their child. This model represents the type of accountability and changes in the behavior that potential Black leaders can follow.

Ultimately, Black leaders have not been successful in achieving the objectives of the Black masses because they have been unable to build sustainable national organizations to deal with the internal problems of Blacks and their relationship to American society. Predominately Black organizations have increasingly in the post-civil rights era resorted to ritual political posturing as a means to cover up or disguise their inability to develop a realistic program of action to deal with the problems of its core constituency of the inner city poor.[10] Civil Rights organizations like the NAACP and Urban League have been ineffective in maintaining viable and effective strategies to remain relevant to poor, young Blacks because they have accommodated their message to the concerns of an emerging Black elite and middle class and to the organizations that provide their funding. Rather than seriously address the problems of the Black poor, these organizations have used the problems of poor Blacks as leverage to gain benefits from White, political elites.

The basic problem with organizations such as the NAACP and the Urban League is that while they do good and useful work, they have failed to come up with a new mission, a new vision, or a new strategy to mold the mass base of Blacks into an effective political force. Rather, they continue to speak and act on behalf of a Black community that is largely alienated from their middle class, hierarchical model of liberal reformism and civil rights.[11] On the other hand, groups like the Congressional Black Caucus are mechanisms for pursuing largely middle class or professional interests in the context or under the umbrella of racial interests. Except for their race, Black congresspersons resemble their White colleagues in terms of social background. They are largely middle-aged, middle-class men with considerable educational and occupational attainments, while relying heavily on PAC contributions, largely from trade unions although corporate connected PACs contribute substantially to several caucus members.[12]

This points to an important constraint in post-civil rights era Black politics. In an era when PACs have become increasingly important in financing increasingly expensive campaigns, Blacks, despite several efforts, have been unable to develop a viable PAC to finance their own campaigns and contribute to the campaigns of others. Often Blacks fail to raise money to establish institutions which they might control, but they readily contribute large sums for institutions which segregate and disadvantage Blacks. Black politicians at all levels—city, state, and local—like the traditional civil rights organizations are heavily dependent on Whites and their institutions to sustain themselves.[13] The creation of Black PACs should advance the interests of the Black majority. If the goal of PACs was to lead and improve the conditions of the Black community, they should promote the interests of the Black community and its constituency. Any Black PAC that contributed to the demise of the Black community and acting against its own interest would be an example of its corruption, even if they are used to finance Black candidates who fail to advocate for the interests of the Black majority. What would be the point of a Black PAC that did not further and promote the interests of the Black masses?

An important aspect of leadership is the ability for institutions to be maintained after the death of leaders. The inadequacy of Black leadership continues to be displayed by their inability to develop institutions that are bigger than the individual leader who creates it. Once the leader was no longer present, organizations and institutions developed by such Black leaders as Washington and Du Bois, Malcolm X, Martin Luther King Jr., and Marcus Garvey were not able to successfully maintain the tenacity and political success of the institutions. For President Barack Obama and other contemporary Black leaders, the excellence of their leadership will be determined by their ability to establish new political institutions and systems that can be sustained, protected, and improved by the members of the Black community.

Developing Black institutions aimed at promoting community values and commitment to the common good of all Blacks, including the poor and underrepresented, will enable the Black community to make demands on an American political, economic, and justice system that has traditionally left the Black masses behind and treated the majority of Blacks as second-class citizens. Black-led institutions can call into question and insist on an explanation and justification for the current condition and distribution of resources to Black communities, the treatment of poor Blacks, and the rules that currently govern the American political and economic system.

In the end, the need for Black political and social institutions that promote sacrifice, take place in predominately Black communities, and emphasize nation-building and contribution to fixing problems in the Black community are still badly needed in Black America. Black leadership will continue to be dead if Blacks do not rise up to the challenge of holding its leadership and other members of the community accountable. The new model of Black leadership in the twenty-first century must concentrate on building or maintaining institutions that serve Black communities not exploit them. It must change the direction of their conversation once and for all, and being on the frontlines with the people as much as possible.

BLACK ELECTED OFFICIALS: CIVIL RIGHTS AND THE PROBLEMS OF INTEGRATION

The transition from protest to electoral politics elevated Black elected officials to the forefront of Black leaders, signaling a preference for institutional rather than non-institutional strategies. In the end, disruptive protest demonstrations gave way to conventional methods for pursuing public policy. Since 1968 Black political leaders have become incorporated into an electoral system which has rendered them largely ineffective in addressing the problems of urban decay and Blacks entrenched in poverty.[14] Many times, Black elected officials become so consumed with the office and the bid for reelection that serving the poor Black community becomes impossible. Blacks seeking election or reelection have a fear of being a "Black candidate," or one that cadres to the Black community. The Black leader, in this instance forgets the "delinquents of his race" and the result is a core Black community that is increasingly poor, dispossessed and alienated.[15] Rather than advocate for the Black poor, who at times play a significant role in their election, once elected, Black officials have done little to further the progress of America's most disadvantaged group. Simultaneously, Black leaders have spent too much time pursuing racial and political integration, which may have benefitted middle-class Blacks but left poor Blacks marginalized. The conditions of the Black community today show that "undeveloped Blacks" have been abandoned by those who should help them.[16]

Black mayors, congresspersons, cabinet officers and the rest are unable to deliver on promises and programs to meliorate conditions in the Black communities, and increasingly even consider themselves leaders of American institutions who just happen to be Black. Throughout the post-civil rights era Blacks have controlled several big city governments such as, Newark, Gary, Detroit, Atlanta, and Chicago including the mayor's office and a majority of city council seats. In many of these cities the conditions of the Black underclass has not improved in the last twenty years, if anything they have gotten worse. Big-city Black governments have generally pursued policies and programs of minority appointments and employment, contracts to minority businesses and efforts to restrain police misconduct in minority communities, but little in the way of policies that might affect the underlying problems of ghetto poverty and dispossession.[17] Finally, local governments find it all but impossible to undertake programs that would deal with the problems of joblessness and poverty in predominately Black neighborhoods and communities.[18] The current structure and process of Black participation in electoral politics and the performance of Black elected officials has resulted in a model of Black leadership that threatens to render the mass base of the Black community leaderless or, in the worst case, the creation of a leadership group opportunistically working against the collective interests of the race in pursuit of narrow personal or political advantages.

Among Black politicians, the fight against oppression is frustrated by their co-optation into the very political positions that marginalize the masses.[19] The over-arching problem which plagues Black leadership, political or otherwise, that supposedly addresses the discrepancies with Liberalism and capitalism is that many of them are, or aspire to be, members of the capitalist bourgeois elite themselves.[20] Consequently, they balk when faced with the reality that the only course of actions which may alleviate Black suffering is the dismantling of hegemonic capitalist structures. One clear reason why Black elites, inside and out of politics, resist serious challenges to capitalism is because they have positioned themselves to be the members of the Black community who are most likely to enjoy its fruits.[21] Black capitalists conveniently suffer from selective amnesia when loyalty to the struggle of the masses does not benefit them economically. After economic benefits are garnered at the expenses of the Black masses, Black capitalists desert the people as well as the projects which may benefit them, but are not sufficiently profitable.

In the midst of this fray of greed, Black leadership often engages in political and economic competition to determine who has the "right" to become "sub-oppressors." This only further commodifies and exploits the masses. The failure of Black leaders to distinguish between ethnicity and race has made it difficult for them to address the subordination of Blacks in a capitalist society that commodifies Black culture and supports an expanding Black middle class at the same time that larger numbers of Blacks become poor. To counter or reverse this trend, a strong voice must be found for the poor, Black, and scapegoated members of the society.[22]

The "waning of Black leadership," which Nelson (2003) attributed to the period of the 1970s and 1980s, heralded the triumph of the conservative movement among Whites and a retrenchment on civil rights. "Waning" is correlated with the rise of Black conservatives, anti-government rhetoric, and Black elected officials. New office-holding elites began to overshadow the traditional civil rights leadership class and "unlike Black leaders of the previous century who devoted themselves to ending racial discrimination and creating opportunity for African-Americans, high-profile Blacks on the eve of the twenty-first century acted to help the White establishment maintain hegemony in the judicial, executive, and legislative affairs of the nation."[23] As a result, a new White "anointed" Black leadership defined by its ability to "carry the White folks' water," in government and political and cultural debates has resurfaced. This new group has only a temporary connection to the Black masses. This new leadership group does not appear to really care what the great "unwashed masses" think about its actions, even when they show indifference to the needs of the community. When mere survival requires confronting a gauntlet of "specially designated authentic community leaders"[24] who denigrate their middle-class Blackness as a non-Black perspective, and facing a hostile White community that views their modest accomplishments as proof positive that all is right with the world, many potential middle-class Black leaders opt out of the fight to change the conditions found in the Black community.[25]

Contemporary Black leaders suffer from less clearly articulated purposes, and lack of clarity of goals. The lack of clarity may be a direct consequence of the rightward turn of the American body politics and the inability of a powerless and predominantly left-leaning Black leadership to find a method to engage Blacks as they embark on political agendas.[26] The belief in the efficacy of Black politicians still permeates Black political discourse. The fact that some of those elected officials are interested in self-aggrandizement rather than the best interests of their constituents has not been a deterrent to their election and re-election.[27]

Incorporation may be viewed as co-optation, or "selling out," when it results in relatively few substantive gains for the group and when it has the tendency to decrease or undermine the capacity of the group to press its demands for gains in the future. Incorporation and integration are viewed positively by many Blacks because it is believed to result in substantive gains for the group and, more important, by "working with the system" it increases the capacity of the group to press effectively for further gains.[28] But Black leaders have not really been fighting against the system, but against being left out of the system. Consequently, they participate all too readily in the grand design of the deception of the Black community in America.[29] Although the Black community is divided into classes, and not homogenous, there remains inseparable history, experiences, and conditions that unite members of the Black community. The thought of "irreconcilable differences" amongst members of a national community, in this case the Black community, are the result of continued susceptibility to manipulation and self-deprecating practices and perceptions of division based on lack of trust among members of the Black community, in addition to the idea that there is something wrong or inherently negative with "Blackness" and the attributes of Black culture in the Black community.

One of the priorities and elements of effective Black leadership is the ability to reinforce the issues and experiences that unite members of the Black community. Rather poor, working class, a student, small farmer, or a small entrepreneur, as a member of the Black community you are either still poor, once was poor, parents were poor, have experienced or been a victim of racism, been negatively influenced or effected by White racism, discrimination, and oppression, and share the history of slavery and the experiences of disenfranchisement. It should be the aim of Black leaders to reinforce the elements and characteristics that produces the Black community in the first place; afterwards, protect, sustain, and improve upon those circumstances. If the intention of elite Blacks was never to promote the interests of the Black majority, this would not qualify as leadership; the measuring stick for leadership is the improved conditions and opportunities of the many, not the few.

As a result, incorporation has failed for three reasons: (1) the Black community has not been effectively mobilized, (2) the progressive coalition of Whites and other ethnic minorities has not materialized,[30] and (3) the political party that supports Blacks, on the rare occasion that it has control of the national government as President Obama did during the first year of his term where Democrats held a majority in both the Senate and House of Representatives, has tended to ignore Black demands or respond with symbols. In the post-Civil Rights era, virtually all of the talent and resources of Black leaders has been devoted to integration or incorporation into the general institutions of American society. The work of the traditional Civil Rights Movement, although changed laws, essentially appealed to the conscience of White America. It asked for Blacks to be included in the total American social and political structure of the White American way.[31] Meanwhile, the core of the Black community has become increasingly isolated, and segregated.[32] Protests in the post-civil rights era have become institutionalized and those that have occurred in America over the last twenty-five years have been largely symbolic or ceremonial.[33]

The methods of post-civil rights era Black leadership have been unsuccessful in achieving the objectives of the Black community due to an unwillingness to practice political virtue and hold Blacks responsible for their own liberation. Virtues are those personal qualities that are needed for the attainment of one's own ends. Every action a leader takes must be considered in light of its effect on the community, not in terms of its intrinsic moral value. Virtue requires the leader to be willing to do whatever it takes, by any means necessary, to achieve their vision.[34] Part of the dilemma, and a central concern for contemporary Black leaders, is embracing certain aspects of political character that, although they can be useful for the leader in attaining his vision, violate moral practices the majority expects. This means that Black leaders have difficulty displaying certain traits that may help accomplish the task of transforming the habits and patterns of behavior in the Black community, but in its current corrupt condition, the Black community might not anticipate or understand. Part of the responsibility of shaking the people out of their corrupt state involves certain conduct the Black community might find uncomfortable, such as the appearance or perception of being mean, revengeful, or merciless.

Political virtue in regards to the Black community means to employ any means possible to achieve their goals, including violence and protest as a mechanism to produce change. Many advocates of nonviolence as the only possible American response of Black people to White domination are also the most ardent defenders of the right of the police to put down Black rebellion through violence.[35] Yet, the violence and brutality of the authorities at Selma during the demonstrations led by Martin Luther King resulted in earlier-than-planned submission of stronger and speedier passage of Civil Rights legislation by Congress.[36] The 1968 Fair Housing Act appeared stalled in Congress until the violent rebellions in the aftermath of Dr. King's murder resulted in its expected quick passage. The American system responded substantively only when protests, violence and disorders threatened or at least were perceived by national elites to threaten system maintenance or stability.[37]

No one disputes that since the 1960s the Black movement has shifted from protest to participation in politics. Prior to the violent rebellions in the aftermath of Dr. King, Rustin (1965) argued that legislation that directly benefit Blacks, such as full employment and other social reforms could only be achieved through "political power," since the passage of the Voting Rights Act of 1965 provided the tools for millions of potential Black voters to advocate for Black interests. By the early 1970s this position had become dominant, displacing strategies of protest and violent rebellion.[38] While Black leaders are integrated into American political organizations and institutions, their core community is segregated, impoverished, and increasingly in the post-civil rights era, marginalized, denigrated, and criminalized.[39]

This is the crux of the problem of post-Civil Rights era Black Politics. Since the late 1960s, a bewildering series of conventions, meeting, leadership summits, assemblies, congresses, institutes and so forth have replaced rallies, marches, demonstrations, and lawsuits as the principle routine activity of the Black leadership establishment. Consequently, the Black leadership establishment is set on trying to achieve non-systemic demands by routine, systemic methods. The predictable response based on such a program in today's American society is neglect, or at best, symbolism.[40] On the one hand they seek to play leadership roles in mainstream American politics but on the other, they try to lead and not lose touch with the Black masses, in which Black Nationalism and radicalism are integral components.[41] As a result, the Black leadership has proven susceptible to political cooptation, "the process of absorbing new elements into the leadership-determining structure of an organization as a means of avoiding threats to its stability."[42] American political institutions and organizations are more than willing to include the right type of Black leaders, easily corruptible and interested in personal gain, which can respectfully be absorbed into mainstream institutions and organizations without little effect to the status and standing of Whites.

There is a significant inability of today's generation of Black leadership to seriously counteract the moral, social, and political onslaught against their people.[43] Spoonfuls of moral uplift cannot fight the cancer of public policies that reward corporations and the super-rich through tax giveaways and punish the Black poor and working class for their "moral" shortcomings.[44] Thus, Black leaders should be just as concerned with specific political problems and policies that harm the Black community, as they are in trying to solve the moral ills of the people. The current Black leadership's ineptitude and impotence emanates not only from the widening of the White-Black divide, but the increased differentiation between the treatments meted out to different sections of the Black population. Although a lucky few in the middle-class are offered visible and lucrative positions in Washington and elsewhere, the vast majority of the

Black community is being pushed further and further into poverty and marginalization.[45]

Black leadership has been unsuccessful since the end of the civil rights era because they have not prepared the Black masses to assume responsibility for their own uplift. The Black community in America remains organizationally ill prepared to take part effectively in institutional politics or to address the problems of the Black underclass. Effective participation in institutional politics requires a national capacity to mobilize and use in a disciplined fashion the limited resources of the Black community in a way that will transform it into an effective pressure group with the capacity to sustain innovative and effective Black institutions.[46] A devotion to self-help, community-building on a national level, and a commitment to the impoverished Black community are key elements missing among Black leadership.

To conclude, in the post-civil rights era Blacks have gained considerable access to elected officials and the institutions of government through the passage of the Civil Rights and Voting Rights Act. Although Blacks are earning more today, the actual gap in earnings between Whites and Blacks has increased. Blacks are attaining education at greater rates and levels of accomplishment than ever before and yet the academic achievement gap remains. The numbers of Black men in college is being dwarfed by their participation in the criminal justice system. Blacks have been victims and offenders of more violent crimes in their own community since the civil rights era. Typically deemed a step in the progression towards higher income and greater opportunities, the increase in Black educational attainment has not proven to close the socioeconomic standing of the majority of Blacks in America. Lastly, Blacks have an increasingly lower likelihood of having health insurance, have a lower life expectancy than the national average, and remain the most obese group in the U.S. All of these attributes illustrate the negative habits of citizenship that produce the destructive patterns of behavior and cooperation that renders the Black community incapable of mobilizing around their interests to advance their objectives and improve their daily lives and conditions. Most importantly, they illustrate just how little value and commitment there is towards the Black community and the protection, sustainment, and improvement of their lives.

The post-civil right era Black leadership has done little to address the negative habits of citizenship and improve the status of the Black majority. Similarly to the corruption of the Black individual and community, the corruption of Black leaders reinforces the inability and unwillingness to put the good of the community over their own self-interest. As a result, Black elites have received considerable advantages and those aspiring to the mantle of leadership have gained remarkable personal and professional benefits, but have not seen those advantages extended to the Black majority. In the end, the methods of today's Black leadership has been unsuccessful in achieving the objectives of the Black masses because they have spent too much time chasing racial and political integration, have abandoned violence and protest as a potential mechanism to produce change for strict systemic politics, and their inability to build sustainable national organizations and institutions that can stimulate new attitudes and patterns of behavior among their constituency. Because the methods practiced by Black leaders in the post-civil rights era have been unsuccessful in achieving the objectives of the Black masses, a new type of leader is needed.

NOTES

1. Andrew Taylor, "Rich Got Richer, Outpace Middle-class," *USA Today*, October 27, 2011.

2. U.S. Census Bureau. *US Census Bureau 2015 American Community Survey.*

3. Smith, *We Have No Leaders: African Americans in the Post-Civil Rights Era*, 137.

4. Ibid.

5. Rick Jones, "Permanent American Hegemony: Liberalism, Domination, and the Continuing Crisis of Black Leadership," *Black Scholar* 31 no. 2 (2001): 38–48.

6. Ibid., 45.

7. Vincent H. Nelson, *The Rise and Fall of Modern Black Leadership*. (Lanham, MD: University Press of America, 2003).

8. Smith, *We Have No Leaders: African Americans in the Post-Civil Rights Era*, 133.

9. Harlem Children's Zone. http://hcz.org/.

10. Smith, *We Have No Leaders: African Americans in the Post-Civil Rights Era*, 84.

11. Ibid.

12. Ibid.

13. Ibid., 109.

14. Ibid.

15. Cathy Cohen and Michael Dawson, "Neighborhood Poverty and African American Politics," *The American Political Science Review* 87 (1993): 286–302.

16. Carter G. Woodson, *The Mis-Education of the Negro*, 68.

17. Ibid.

18. Paul Peterson, *City Limits*. (Chicago: University of Chicago Press, 1981).

19. Jones, "Permanent American Hegemony: Liberalism, Domination, and the Continuing Crisis of Black Leadership."

20. Marable, *Black Leadership: Four Great American Leaders and the Struggle for Civil Rights*, 44.

21. Ibid.

22. Ibid.

23. Ibid., 311.

24. Nelson, *The Rise and Fall of Modern Black Leadership*.

25. Ibid.

26. Ibid.

27. Ibid., 27.

28. Smith, *We Have No Leaders: African Americans in the Post-Civil Rights Era*, 21.

29. Harold Cruse, *The Crisis of the Negro Intellectual* (New York: New York Review Classics, 2005).

30. Bayard Rustin, "From Protest to Politics: The Future of the Civil Rights Movement," Reprinted from *Commentary*, February, 1965.

31. Cone, *Black Theology & Black Power*, 136.

32. Smith, *We Have No Leaders: African Americans in the Post-Civil Rights Era*.

33. Rufus P. Browning, Dale Rogers Marshall, and David H. Tabb, *Protest is Not Enough: The Struggle of Blacks and Hispanics in Urban Politics* (Berkeley: University of California Press, 1986).

34. Machiavelli, *The Prince*.

35. Cone, *Black Theology & Black Power*, 138–39.

36. Smith, *We Have No Leaders: African Americans in the Post-Civil Rights Era.*

37. Ibid., 16–17.

38. Ibid., 22.

39. Ibid., 279.

40. Ibid., 23–24.

41. Ibid.

42. Ibid., 9.

43. Hadjor, *Another America: The Politics of Race and Blame.*

44. Frederick C. Harris, "Black Leadership and the Second Redemption," *Society* July/August 43 no.5 (2006): 22–29.

45. Ibid.

46. Ibid., 122.

FIVE

On Black Leadership

Black leaders must protect and preserve the interests and values of the Black community. They should be the executioners of justice within the community; entrusted by the people to execute justice and care for and manage their affairs. Leaders guide and inspire people by setting an example of excellence. The transformed public in turn instills the same virtues in the community. Leaders are people who *do* things. The most important and recognizable acts by leaders improve the daily lives of the public. For a Black leader to meet the criteria for excellent leadership this transformation must create a new political system in America where the political institutions are founded on racial justice and equality, and Blacks no longer find themselves at the bottom of the socioeconomic ladder. Thus, a leader turns previously oppressed or dominated people into citizens; a unit committed to work together for the protection, sustainment and improvement of all.

Effective Black leadership will mold a new creative type of follower with unrevealed capabilities. The standard for Black leadership that should be applied is the ability to alter Blacks' patterns of behavior in order to make positive changes by reversing "bad habits" of citizenship (economics, education, crime, health, and family structure). Through work and example, a new leader can guide the Black community to new values and attitudes that enable Blacks to mobilize and achieve collective interests.

The greatest achievements of leaders are those done to benefit the community and make the nation better. Accomplishing great tasks means taking people out of their comfort zone and instituting radical changes in attitudes and behaviors. To institute radical changes in the negative habits of the Black community a leader must shake the people up so they can realize new, unrecognized opportunities. These transformations require

117

new institutions that radically reorganize how the conditions of the Black community are perceived. Changing the level of consciousness and political and social behavior in the Black community is imperative. This involves a fundamental transition of Blacks out of lifestyles in which they feel comfortable. The comfort zone in Black America is one rampant with unchecked individualism and self-centeredness. Some Blacks are perfectly content with the current conditions as long as their advantage over and exploitation of the Black masses endures. Many Blacks have the potential and opportunity to better themselves and their families but the transition to such a lifestyle is too drastic a change. Here is where effective leadership comes in: to guide the Black community through the shock and discomfort associated with change, to be an example of character worthy of being followed, and, finally, to be responsible and accountable to the fears and needs of those struggling with the transformation the most.

Establishing institutions that develop new habits of interaction among Blacks should create a self-sufficient, respectful, dignified, and knowledgeable people able to confront the American system from a position of strength. This will enable Blacks to attain their collective goals with self-determination; telling their own story, recognizing their connection with their ancestry, and determining the fate of their own communities. Blacks must learn to take care of themselves, love each other, take pride in what it means to be a member of the Black community and protect its value and interests. Developing new, positive habits in the Black community will create necessary solidarity and unity to push America to fulfill the promises and expectations of American idealism. To be effective, a Black leader must lead the people into a unified, self-respecting community, capable of reaching levels of equality and justice never seen before in America.

ON REVOLUTIONARY LEADERSHIP

It requires a revolutionary Black leader to guide the Black community into tomorrow. The current attitudes and accepted patterns of behavior are unacceptable because they are incapable of enabling Blacks to achieve new heights of racial equality. Revolutionary leaders actively engage in radically new and innovative practices outside of established norms. Revolutionary Black leadership actively participates in and advocates radical changes in the politics and social realities of the Black community. Radical change is marked by sudden or profound changes in the habits, attitudes, and patterns of behavior in the Black community. To be revolutionary is not to expect to improve the conditions of Blacks and change the current structure of America by promoting the status quo. Revolutionary Black leadership requires a transition from the current system of affairs within the Black community. Extant methods of pursuing racial equality and the Black community's improvement are insufficient and counterproductive.

There are two elements associated with the concept of revolutionary leadership. First, the outcomes that revolutionary leaders propose are contrary to the status quo and demand a change in ideology amongst the people. Many times, revolutionary leaders ask the people to perceive their current conditions or understanding of reality differently, and that a change in ideas will ultimately lead to changes in their behavior and actions. Secondly, the method of change utilized by revolutionary leaders is contrary to societal beliefs and expectations of order and stability. Revolutionary leaders generally advocate all options on the table in order to achieve their desired outcomes, including political violence as a tool for change and liberation. A "by any means necessary" approach to accomplishing the goals of the Black community was made popular by Malcolm X and the Black Power Movement during the Civil Rights era. Both factions advocated changes in Black self-perceptions, changes in the American political and social order, and changes in Blacks' collective behavior that were contrary to the status quo. Revolutionary leaders will seek to transform the state of Black America and develop institutions for changing the attitudes and behavior. They introduce radical changes in the theory and praxis with which the Black community fights and advocates for equality and social justice. The spirit of struggle, courage, and the capacity to love the oppressed and disadvantaged are required of revolutionary leaders.[1] A revolutionary Black leader undoubtedly requires the adherence of the people.[2]

ON THE FUTURE OF BLACK LEADERSHIP

Role and Duty of Tomorrow's Leaders

A Black leader plays a significant role in effectively arousing new attitudes within the Black community and setting out towards the old goal of racial equality with new vigor. First, the most important thing that a leader must do is lead, or guide the people. Second, a Black leader must inspire the people to live more abundantly, to learn to begin with life as they find it and make it better.[3] To lead means to not only influence, but to transform. The most important transformation instilled by a Black leader is a new Black-perception that facilitates: (1) higher socioeconomic status and living conditions; (2) healthy community centric attitudes and; (3) a renewed commitment to the value of membership in the Black community.

One roadblock to transformation is community susceptibility to corrupted leadership. Corrupt leaders damage the Black community's pursuit of common goals. Corrupted leadership creates faction and dishar-

mony and promotes negative habits and injustice in the Black community. Alternatively, exceptional leadership takes those with little or no
hope and gives them a new sense of direction and purpose.

The fundamental duty of Black leadership is to fight alongside the
people. Leaders of the people must adopt the worldview of the disadvantaged—their concerns, doubts, hopes, their way of seeing the leaders,
their perceptions of themselves and of the oppressors, their beliefs, and
their rebellious reactions.[4] In order for Black leaders to be revolutionary
and guide the Black community into new habits of citizenship, they must
be accountable to the most disadvantaged and underrepresented groups,
and speak frankly to them about the reality of their condition, the
achievements of the community throughout history. Leadership requires
public admission of mistakes and failures, miscalculations, and difficul-
ties in the struggle for justice and equality.[5]

An effective leader sees leadership as service. A servant of the Black
masses must live among them, think with them, feel for them, die for
them, and essentially commit oneself to identifying with the impoverished Black majority. Such a position can require that a Black leader
renounce the class to which they belong and join the oppressed in an act
of solidarity. Fannie Lou Hamer used her contacts with elites to help the
least advantaged members of the Black community. With no career to
advance, Hamer had an uncompromising commitment to eliminating
conditions that kept poor Black people impoverished and enslaved.[6] Her
loyalty demonstrates how leadership and service aim to enhance the
rights and personhood of the least privileged.[7]

Joining with the oppressed requires going to them and communicating with them. Patient, respectful dialogue between the leader and the
people—who often have a naïve worldview—is essential. Leadership
does not entail wholesale adaptation of the people's worldview.[8]
Through joint political action with the community, leaders show the ap-
propriateness of their program and strategy, thereby winning the respect
and confidence of the people. The people must find themselves in the
emerging leader, and the leader must be found in the people.[9] Perhaps,
no other leader during the Civil Rights Movement was more acquainted
with the deprivations, seductive pleasures, and repressed potential of
ghetto life than Malcolm X. Malcolm gave incendiary voice to the discon-
tents of the urban Black underclass.[10] His first-hand knowledge and un-
canny ability to diagnose the wounded psyche of the urban Black community earned him tremendous support among poor Blacks. Malcolm
aimed his fierce rhetoric toward the urban underclass in order to mobilize fellow wounded souls to claim their personhood.[11]

To adequately serve the impoverished Black majority, a Black leader
must respect and have affection for the disadvantaged and commit to the
advancement of their interests and improvement of their conditions. If
Black leaders would fall in love with their own people and sacrifice for

their uplift—if the wise and educated class of Blacks would do these things—they could begin to solve problems facing Black America. Love is a commitment to others. No matter where the oppressed are found, the act of love is a commitment to their cause.[12] This commitment creates new, or untapped opportunities to improve the status of the Black majority. To love and respect the people, to be willing to sacrifice for the interests of the Black community as a whole, exemplifies the courage of Black leadership.[13]

The ability of a leader to trust the people is indispensable for creating an atmosphere of love and commitment to the interests of the poor and instituting revolutionary change. According to Freire, if the people cannot be trusted there is no reason for liberation. Thus, leaders are critical to the process because although it is in the power of individuals to create and transform, in a situation of alienation, individuals may be impaired in the use of that power.[14] Black leaders cannot believe they have all of the answers and are thus justified in ignoring the voice of the disadvantaged Black majority. Black leaders cannot believe that only they know anything because this means that they doubt the capabilities of the people. Liberation requires a relation of mutual understanding and trust. Trust is the foundation of credibility, effective sustained political action, and institution building. Rumors of back-room deals and duplicitous relationships with colleagues shadowed half of Adam Clayton Powell Jr.'s tenure in public office and gradually eroded the trust of his constituents.[15] The trust of the people in the leader reflects the confidence of the leader in the people.

A Black leader must believe that the people are capable of participating in pursuit of their own liberation, yet at the same time, must always mistrust the ambiguity of oppressed people; that is, mistrust the oppressor "housed" in the Black community.[16] Mistrust within the community does not mean the leader lacks confidence in the people, only that they are realistic and knowledgeable of what can reasonably be expected from an oppressed group that still has elements of the oppressor's values residing in their consciousness. As long as the oppressor within the consciousness of the oppressed is stronger than the commitment for liberation, the impoverished Black community's natural fear may lead them to denounce a revolutionary Black leader.[17]

Transforming the attitudes and behaviors of the Black majority is most authentic when it is derived from the core of the Black majority. Authentic organization will not be promoted by the benefactors of oppression and alienation within the Black community. They regard dialogue between the oppressed Black poor and the revolutionary leadership as a real danger to be avoided.[18] Authentic organization is challenged by the elite strategy of integration and political cooptation. This limits the advancement and revolutionary capacity of Black leaders by attempting to include them in the status quo as advocates of middle-class values. By seeking to include and assimilate wealthy, educated Blacks into the American political system as currently constructed, the benefactors of racial discrimination and oppression build a gap between the needs of the most disadvantaged people to whom Black leaders should be most directly accountable to, and makes Black transformation via revolutionary ideas impossible.

It is up to revolutionary Black leadership to organize the Black community around a system of shared goals and principles that is going to sufficiently address the roots of their condition and also offer viable solutions to the negative habits of citizenship in the Black community. Transformative leadership must develop within the poor Black community the power and confidence to elevate itself from current conditions. One way a Black leader can do this is by reflecting mass aspirations. Leaders must create, coordinate and direct organizations that create harmonious interactions amongst members of the Black community. To achieve their aspirations, Black leaders cannot treat poor Blacks as passive subjects. Leaders guide by example and show the masses why they must and how they can actively participate in their own struggle for equality.

A Black leader must concentrate on creating harmonious interactions amongst members of the Black community rather than integrate the Black community, in particular the Black poor, into the preexisting structures of oppression. They must transform the current system so that the Black community can become "being for themselves."[19] This includes altering the way the Black community finds solutions to poor living conditions, lack of value in their community, and in the overall American polity. Whereas Black leaders have sought integration and assimilation into mainstream American institutions and organizations as a principle method of achieving racial justice and equality, it is essential that revolutionary leadership in Black America attempt to foster the spirit of change and a newfound value in the Black community within the core of the Black community itself.

To effectively uplift itself, the Black community must create authentic, organic organizations within the core of its most disadvantaged and underrepresented groups. Without it an organization cannot survive, and revolutionary action is thereby diluted.[20] The Black community should be seen as one that takes care of its most disadvantaged and underrepresented people, who are mobilized and unified to fight all forms of oppression and discrimination, and place the highest value and commitment as members of the Black community to its protection, sustainment, and improvement. Self-determination of this sort requires that the Black community be able to sustain itself and the majority of its population through its own institutions and organizations. To control its own destiny, the Black community will need to develop institutions that not only build up the esteem and value in the Black community, but also provide essential resources that improve daily lives. Booker T. Washington urged

Blacks to voluntarily segregate from Whites for the purpose of building a separate economically strong Black community.[21] Malcolm X advocated for the Black community's control of education, specifically tailored to the psychological needs of the urban Black poor.[22] The Black Power Movement in California provided members of the community with training and education, meals to kids, and other resources aimed at alleviating problems concerning Blacks in poor neighborhoods, succeeded in offering the Black community an opportunity to do for self. Thus, it is up to revolutionary Black leadership to organize the Black community around a system of shared goals and principles that is going to sufficiently address the roots of their condition and also offer viable solutions to the negative habits of membership in the Black community.

Today the Black community needs a leader who can avoid both contemporary traps—conservatism and victim politics—and create a culture of Black people standing up for themselves to change a system that keeps them down.[23] Through unity and a commitment to the interests of the Black community, especially the Black poor, institutions developed by Black leaders can put the type of pressure on the system that would force the attention of the American political hierarchy to adequately address the relationship between the state and the Black community. Black leaders must dedicate themselves to an untiring effort for *unity among the oppressed*—and unity of leadership with the oppressed—in order to successfully achieve the goals and aspirations of the impoverished Black majority.

Black leadership must seek to help Black people help themselves, to consider seriously, even as they act, the reasons for mistrust on the part of the people, and to seek out avenues of communion with them.[24] To cure the negative citizenship habits of mistrust and mutual disdain prevalent within the Black community, Black leaders must work diligently to seek out ways to cure the seeds of doubt among members of the Black community and develop significant means of union instead. Through the unity of the group, a Black leader may help the members of the Black community help themselves critically perceive the reality of their condition and the sources of their oppression. Ultimately, they must assist in removing the barriers that prohibit the Black masses from critically evaluating the effectiveness of their leadership and assessing the value and commitment of other members in the Black community in addressing the interests of the entire group.

Finally, a Black leader today must develop methods to validate the bitter experiences of the Black poor and disadvantaged, in such a way that it evokes the rest of the community to take action. The key for a Black leader to be effective is to emphasize the commonalities in the Black community, in particular the shared history and experiences with racism and discrimination. Rather than searching for differences, a leader must reinforce similarities and commitment to their most disadvantaged members. It is imperative for a Black leader to focus on large issues that all members of the Black community face and that all members of the community can benefit from rather than factional battles that distract the community and diminish from its potential for solidarity. There are certain problems within the Black community that can be solved regardless of sex, class, religion, and education—certain basic rights from which all members of the Black community can benefit. Thus, effective Black leaders will use their resources and talents to promote issues and establish institutions that encourage Blacks to focus on those shared benefits and discourage factions that lessen the value and commitment to the disadvantaged. A leader's pursuit of unity is an attempt to organize the people, requiring witness to the fact that the struggle for liberation is a common task.

ISSUES FACING BLACK LEADERS TODAY

There is a plethora of issues facing contemporary Black leaders: classism, sexism, whether Blacks want or need leaders, and the various methods to achieving the goals of the community at-large. With all the division in the Black community there is little surprise that there has been difficulty in achieving their group desired goals. This section will focus on the issues facing contemporary Black leaders, and how the leaders of tomorrow can overcome them.

Classism

Classism is a biased or discriminatory attitude based on distinctions made between social or economic classes. One of the most pressing issues of concern, with the rising number of Blacks entering the upper-class, is the separation between wealthy and poor Blacks. Abigail and Stephan Thernstrom (1997) suggest the serious inequality that remains between Blacks and Whites is less a function of White racism than of class disparities between Blacks and Whites, and amongst Blacks internally, for example, the racial gap in levels of educational attainment, the structure of the Black family, and the rise in Black crime.[25] As Blacks gain in wealth and education their interests differ from the Black poor and become more aligned with those of middle-class White Americans. The ability to empathize and trust in the pursuits of the impoverished Black community is diminished as interests shift towards middle-class White America.

Intra-racial class distinctions tend to polarize Blacks, with growing and increasingly secure middle-class Blacks at one pole and an expanding and progressively alienated underclass at the other.[26] The problem with class distinctions for Wilson (1978) is that it undermines solidarity. Differences in income and educational attainment militates against the development by racial movements of a high degree of consensus on specific goals, the means of their attainment, and casts doubt on the ability of Black leaders to speak to Blacks as a group. Booker T. Washington stressed that education not be an avenue for individual gratification or passage away from one's community. Instead education should instill a sense of social connectedness to others that would manifest itself in serving the least advantaged members of the Black community.[27] According to Wilson, classism diminishes solidarity because it prompts Blacks to develop perceptions of themselves as members of different socioeconomic classes with non-complementary, if not conflicting, interests, rather than as members of an oppressed minority with a shared past and common future.[28] In the end, emerging Black class structure resembles a burgeoning middle-class of talented, educated Blacks who benefit from the expanding corporate and government sectors, and a large Black under-class increasingly concentrated in unskilled, low-paying, dead-end jobs.

On the other hand, Michael Dawson (1994) suggests that race continues to be the decisive factor in political outlooks of Blacks as opposed to class. Measured by income and educational attainment, class does differentiate some political attitude amongst Blacks; higher income Blacks are less likely than low income Blacks to support economic redistribution policies and less likely to express a commitment to Black political autonomy, and measured of perceived racial group interests.[29] Yet, these incipient class differences are muted by the widespread perception of linked or common fate among Blacks. Evaluations of Black economic class status in relation to Whites and perceptions of linked fate serve to suppress the effects of class. The terms of party identification among Blacks are more significantly shaped by the perceptions of racial group interests, over class. Thus, despite great changes in Black class structure and growth of the Black middle class, race is still a potent influence due to a shared sense of common fate or perceived group interests which lends coherence to Black political behavior on a range of issues.[30]

Solutions to perceived class differences are an important aspect in need of address by Black leaders. A constant theme in Black radical ideology is the belief that capitalism systematically disadvantages Blacks. West (2001) argues that any analysis of Black oppression must analytically place capitalism at its center.[31] According to this view, the intersection of race and class often serves to place Blacks at the bottom of the socioeconomic ladder. The profits from the super-exploitation of Black workers have been used historically to buy off sectors of the White working and middle class.[32]

Black leaders now labor to frame an agenda that will generate interest and build solidarity across income and class levels.[33] A Black leader must emphasize that one's class does not change the Black experience in America. The Black experience in America only changes when there are transformations in the collective standing of Blacks; how the people interact and are treated by the state. One's social class does not change the shared history and experiences of racism that generally affect all Blacks despite of class. Regardless of class, race remains to be the most determining factor of an individual's success and potential in the U.S.[34]

Wealthy Blacks should have just as much interest in racial economic equality, better education, and housing options for Blacks as poor and disadvantaged Blacks. Both groups feel the weight of racial discrimination in social settings; being the only Black person in the office or in the classroom, or having trouble getting a cab in New York City. Many of the wealthiest Black Americans grew up in humble middle or lower class surroundings, and have experienced the hardships of poor Blacks firsthand. It is, in part, this firsthand experience of poverty and desperation that leads one to renounce and separate completely from one's former existence and why many elite Blacks find themselves at odds with poor Blacks; hoping to escape and ignore their past history and former self.

Improving the condition of the impoverished Black poor improves the status and standing of all Blacks; how they are perceived as a race and how members of the race generally feel about one another. Bridging the gap and working across social classes improves the levels of trust and sacrifice among members of the Black community. Thus, a Black leader must lead the way in a newfound commitment to the Black poor and regaining their trust that they will not be left behind as collateral damage as a few wealthy and privileged Blacks acquire all the benefits.

It is important for a leader of the Black community to reject unregulated capitalism and unchecked economic self-interest. Unrestrained self-interest and excessive wealth and materialism are at the root of corruption. Together, they inevitably put the wants and interests of the individual over that of the collective. In their pursuit to radically transform the state of the Black community, leaders may have to renounce those elements of capitalism that enslave the consciousness and prohibit chances of liberation. Malcolm X shared Marx's contempt for bourgeois capitalism and repudiated the Black man's attempt to emulate and surpass the White man in economic rationality.[35] He routinely criticized Muhammad for wearing $200 suits while his followers struggled to make ends meet.[36] That is not to say that the leader cannot have nice things or be a wealthy individual. In fact, some level of wealth will be beneficial for the leader to have in order to demonstrate to the Black community the possibility of attaining material wealth; through working to improve the standing of the Black community collectively.

In no way does material wealth exclude a lower class leader without material wealth from leading the Black community. As a victim of poverty, a Black leader will inherit a considerable amount of credibility and access to the members of the Black community they are attempting to help. A Black leader who has been a victim of poverty and has the experience of living amongst the poor, but makes the transition into wealth through means the Black community feels admirable will enable a leader to promote ideas of collective wealth. Such a transition helps when wealth is acquired in such a way that not only encourages Blacks to work together, but gives back resources to their community as well. This may include professions that not many Blacks get into, or positions of authority that brings the community credibility. If the leader is going to have a considerable amount of wealth, it is even more imperative that they live in or work in a predominately Black community. As an advocate for the poor, the leader must speak to the conditions and heart-ache that poor Blacks experience, and the poor services and quality of education in predominately Black communities. Nothing brings the leader more credibility than personal experience and such personal experience that the rest of the Black community can relate to will make them more likely to follow. It is difficult to lead the Black poor from a distance.

The Black leader must emphasize to elite Blacks the benefits of improving the conditions of their poor brethren. They must tap into the psyche of those with success and remind them of their journey and shared experiences as members of the Black community. Topics of common concern include: the miseducation of Black youngsters and the commensurately soaring school dropout rate; lack of employment and technical job training; poor quality housing; inadequate health care; the self-destructive behavior of Black youth; the growing rate, and accompanying problems, of low-income, single-parent families; teen pregnancy, lack of economic power, and Black on Black violence. It is important for the Black leader to stress unity amongst Blacks of all economic classes and levels of education. But it is imperative that they mobilize and unify poor and working class Blacks who comprise the majority of the population.

Blacks' participation in the American economic system may not follow the same path as Whites or the rest of the country. This is one area where revolutionary leadership is essential; to get Blacks to reevaluate and change their economic habits. Washington's idea of self-imposed segregation, although sounds like a step-back to pre-civil rights conditions for Blacks, such a stance may actually benefit the majority of Blacks. Effective leaders will create institutions that reinforce economic unity while encouraging elite Blacks to commit resources to creating economically sufficient Black communities. Leadership must find new ways for Blacks to participate in the current economic system that is more favorable to their conditions and promotes community values, investments, and contributions.

Sexism

Sexism (discrimination or devaluation based on a person's sex) remains a salient factor in determining the methods and progress within the Black community. The idea of Black liberation and progress follows a similar path of the American patriarchal system that challenges the relationship between Black men and women. Black women after slavery were outraged at the idea that men, with whom they shared the horrors of slavery and discrimination, would be given the right to vote and not them. To give "Blacks" the right to vote, meant giving men the right to vote.[37] In the transition from the Civil Rights Movement of the early 1960s, to the Black Panther Party and Black consciousness, the aim of the Black political movement became the "pursuit of manhood" and the open denigration of Black women was its consequence.[38]

Frederick Douglass, the only nationally recognized Black leader of the time, once stated, "as soon as the women are brutally beaten, murdered and ostracized just for being Black men, then they could argue for their right to vote."[39] He saw the entire racial dilemma in America as the struggle between White men and Black men. Douglass was a supporter of women's rights and participated in many meetings for women's suffrage, but he ultimately supported the Fifteenth Amendment giving Black men the right to vote before women. Where Black men had the opportunity to completely overhaul the system by making women partners in the fight for liberation of the Black community as a whole, they reverted back to traditional American patriarchal stereotypes.

Elaine Brown, who in 1974 became the chair of the Black Panther Party after Huey Newton was arrested for the murder of a seventeen-year-old Black prostitute, soon learned that "pulling together" was men's work, and that women were supposed to be helpers and supporters in the Black liberation struggle. As the leader of the Panthers, her first obstacle was to smash the anti-woman barrier that existed within the party. Until Brown had become chair, women were only allowed to cook and make love to their "warriors." They were surprised to be told "sisters did not challenge the brothers. Sisters stood by their Black men, supported their men, and respected them."[40] It was not only "unsisterly" to want to eat with their Black brothers, but it was a punishable offense. A woman in the Black Panther movement was considered, at best, irrelevant; if she asserted herself she was a pariah, an enemy of the Black people.[41] If a Black woman assumed a role of leadership, she was said to be eroding Black manhood and hindering the progress of the Black race.

Under her leadership, Black women began taking on more official roles with greater responsibility. While this did not sit well with many of the male members, Brown gave them little room to disagree. When Newton was acquitted of his crime, his return signaled a change once again in the party. He was more interested in supporting the "brothers" in the organization than in dealing with the party's political activities. Women were once again treated as irrelevant sexual objects and became the focus of years of frustration and anger by the "brothers" who had seen them rise to power. Those leaders who had thrown their support to Brown during Newton's absence quickly withdrew that support from her. She knew it was only a matter of time before she would have to face party chastisement to appease the "brothers." [42] Believing it was the only thing that she could do, Brown left Oakland with her daughter in 1977 and immigrated to France.

If racial equality is the ultimate goal of the Black community then it is necessary to shed itself from its masculine frame. Black men cannot confuse liberation with the ability to dominate Black women as White men have historically done. It is essential for a Black leader to emphasize the sacrifice and contribution made by both sexes—that both are responsible for their commitment to the good of the community. Through the creation of new institutions and systems a leader must establish new methods and practices of interaction between Black men and women. A lot of the issues facing the Black community start with mistrust and the inability to communicate between the sexes, thus, transferring healthy habits of interaction to future generations becomes futile.

A Black leader must change the current attitudes and behaviors between the sexes, and one important way to do so is by setting a fine example. With a disproportionate amount of single-Black mothers, the Black community needs a leader to emphasize and recommit Blacks to positive familial structures. Thus, a leader must reinforce the perception of a great husband and father—an example for other men and young boys to aspire to and a standard of expectations to meet. Through this communion and mutual understanding, the Black community can produce healthy relations and an environment for both sexes to thrive, unlike today where Black women have out-achieved their male counterparts in educational attainment and employment opportunities, if not in income. Improving the conditions for the majority of Blacks depends on mutual understanding of the pressures placed on both sexes and their renewed commitment to trust in one another to fix it together.

A Black leader must emphasize the partnership between men and women of color to work together in the fight for racial equality. Black women can help transform the habits and patterns of behavior of Black men and Black men can participate in the transformation of habits of Black women. When a man sets an example of excellence, he not only affects men, but they also set a standard by which women respond to measure potential mates. Similarly, a woman may transform the habits of men by setting a standard of excellence that thereby transforms the habits of men based on newfound standards that women are willing to accept. Ultimately, men and women working together to achieve common goals changes the perception that they have towards one another in addition to how to meet each other's expectations.

It is imperative not to deny the past and continuing contributions and involvement of Black women in the Black struggle for justice and equality. Black men must be equal partners and advocate for women's rights and their interests, just as Black women must be advocates for the issues plaguing Black men. Male leadership can appoint women to positions of authority and leadership within their organizations and vice versa. Black men can stand with Black women at the forefront on issues of pay equality and worker's rights, as women can stand in support of Black men in avoiding the justice system and disproportional disparities in education and employment. Only together can the Black community advance the interests of the Black community as a whole. Not with one sex attempting to achieve their interests alone. It is up to the leadership to create the systems in which they can work together and create the positive patterns of behavior between Black men and women.

One way that they can demonstrate being a positive example of male and female relationships is through their own marital or professional relationships. A reputation for positive relationships with the opposite sex is desirable. As a husband or wife, it is imperative to demonstrate healthy patterns for the rest of the community to follow. President Obama and the First Lady Michelle Obama, represents one example that demonstrates a healthy, positive relationship between husband and wife that Blacks find admirable and can be an example for other members of the Black community of partnerships that work together and familial responsibility and accountability. Establishing a relationship as law students that transitioned into the moments of fist-bumping, presidential support demonstrates the love, commitment, and teamwork that Black men and women can learn from. Leadership must reinforce the commitment to each other as members of the opposite sex working together as a unit to accomplish the goals and interests of the Black community and repair the relationship between Black men and women.

Religious Differences

The ability to lead the Black community spiritually is important to a successful pattern of Black leadership. Blacks are markedly more religious than the U.S. population as a whole, including their level of affiliation with religion, attendance at religious services, frequency of prayer and religious importance in life.[43] Demographically, over 80 percent of Blacks identify with a sect of Christianity, 45 percent of those being Baptist; 12 percent identify as "non-religious," and 4 percent identifying as Muslim.[44] More than half of Blacks reportedly attend church regularly. The average church attendance in Black churches is 50 percent greater than a White church. Additionally, 82 percent of Blacks versus 55 percent of Whites say that religion is very important in their lives, and 86 percent of Blacks believe that religion "can answer all or most of today's problems."[45]

Michael Battle (2006) explains that spirituality displays Blacks' communal practices of the divine life, even in the face of the harshest oppression.[46] In its origins, the Black churches in America were concerned with a full range of human needs, both spiritual renewal and demands for a comfortable life. They encompassed Blacks' history and incorporated within it religious doctrine, worship, and community outreach.[47] Worship promoted survival and resistance, thus, making the orientation of Black spirituality communal. From the debate over slavery to the civil rights movement, Black religious centers and ministries have shaped the way that political figures and the public viewed race relations.[48]

The Black church must reclaim its traditional values and teachings, such as the importance of the community and family. There is a passionate quest for something deeper and more authentic than what often passes for religion in the current generation.[49] Big, stadium churches, fancy suits, nice cars, and material wealth are often perceived as success and evidence of God's favor. It is important to balance individual and communal need. This means that Black leaders must address the real, deep-seeded needs of the individual soul, but also be an agent of change in the Black community. This requires them to comfort, confront, challenge, and invite people into a closer relationship between their faith and spirituality and their output back into the Black community; to answer the call of poverty and despair, giving, and communal responsibility.[50] To bridge the gap between the early Black church and the contemporary needs of the Black community, a leader's imagination and knowledge of its history, as well compassion for the impoverished Black majority is imperative.

Differences of religious faith should not be a barrier to an effective Black leader in accomplishing the will of the Black masses. Martin Luther King, Jr. believed moral persons should be concerned not only with the state of their own bodies and souls but also with the moral hygiene of the community.[51] Specifically, the church represented the conscience of the community. In response to religious differences that were present, in particular the strength of Malcolm X and the platform of the Nation of Islam, King introduced a formula of "unity without uniformity." He urged for Blacks, regardless of religious affiliation, to concentrate on the unity of their circumstances rather than accentuating their differences.[52] Emphasizing commonalities, a Black leader can demonstrate and articulate a clear program that allows members of all faiths to contribute to the common good and serve the interests of the Black community. Despite religious differences, there is an unquestionable obligation to sacrifice and be accountable to serving the needs of the Black masses and it is the responsibility of a Black leader to continually demonstrate and charge all members of the community with the same responsibility.

Since a good portion of the Black community holds some religious or spiritual belief it is imperative that in order to transform the attitudes of the Black majority, that a leader be able to demonstrate positive moral character. How can one effectively promote the values of good character to the Black community while violating the same terms you want them to accept and integrate into their lives? Such hypocrisy and contradictory behavior is why there has been very little trust in the current Black leadership, and the declination or shift away from the pastor as the *de facto* leader of Black communities today. Additionally, their persistence for self-gratification and wealth while paying little attention to the majority of Blacks leads to mistrust among members of the Black community who believe pastors and church leaders are genuinely interested in protecting their flock.

It is essential that through the process of transforming the commitment and values of the Black community that the leadership set the proper example and demonstrate the proper relationship individuals should have with their community. To develop and transfer the positive habits and attitudes of citizenship, the leader must continually practice and display these characteristics themselves; otherwise there would be no lead for the masses to follow. If we are to expect the people within the Black community to be self-respecting, high character citizens, then they are going to need good examples from a leader to demonstrate that they can hold such esteem for themselves and their community and be successful contributors to the common good at the same time.

One does not have to prescribe to one specific religion, as long as the leader practices a strong commitment to honoring faith and spirituality by practicing good deeds. Despite religious affiliation, a leader must have a strong commitment to follow some religious doctrine, if not, one must still acquire the virtues of spirituality since the majority of the Black community holds some religious or spiritual framework. The Black community must feel as though a leader has equal stake and commitment to being a good, moral person, although no one may meet religious expectations fully. This means that the leader must exercise strong moral character and be an example for other believers or members of faith to follow. Since Blacks are predominately religious, as a leader one must demonstrate strong moral character and its importance and relevance in their daily life and successes. Express to the community how faith and values enable and further one's ability to work for the interests of the Black community; how faith and commitment to moral character have improved one's life and can improve the conditions of the Black community as a whole. This means that the leadership must put their faith in practice.

There appears to be a disconnect between the Black community's religious aspirations and beliefs and the output of their actions, meaning, their habits and patterns of behavior may not match their religiosity; it is up to the Black leader to reconcile the two. One important way that this can be done is through the power of testimony; leaders must reveal and illustrate religion and spirituality's value and influence on the leader's platform and personal life. Share one's story of suffering and triumph.

Reconcile and unite your personal story with themes and stories of the Bible and other religious doctrine. Make connections clear and explicit for the Black community the relationship between their religious beliefs, faith, and the improvement and conditions of the Black community and the fight for racial and social equality. Stories of personal struggle and spiritual triumph may easily translate or be easily relatable to the rest of the community, and as a result, reinforce the Black community's ability to transform their faith into practice.

Multiplicity

The multiplicity of leadership has brought a consciousness of group disunity on the part of Blacks. Blacks complain of the need for a great leader, yet after the Civil Rights Movement it became questionable whether they wanted or really needed one. Even before the Civil Rights Movement it was common among Blacks to attribute their racial problems to lack of competent leadership.[53] The Montgomery Bus Boycott of 1955–1956, the sit-ins conducted by SNCC and the SCLC, and freedom rides of 1960–1961 represent Blacks' criticism of their leaders in the sense that these movements bypassed established Black organizations, particularly the NAACP.[54] Leader factions develop around intergenerational differentials, views of the proper militant stance regarding the total community, and around different expectations of change.[55]

A single recognized leader makes for speed and efficient progress, where masses are ignorant and docile and leaders are wise and honest. When the community is sophisticated and the issues are complex, having a large variety of leaders is beneficial.[56] The multiple pattern of leadership has prevented the rise of any monopolistic tendency to which any potential leader is no longer vulnerable under a standard of "great man" leadership.[57] In this new framework, numerous individual leaders bring into play a check-and-balances factor. A variety of leadership involves association with other minority group leadership, which brings with it new problems. Questions of what techniques to employ on given issues, the problem of pace and timing in pushing for civil rights and social integration, and where to attack first, face each leader and met with different reactions. Such questions are even more significant since nationally accepted Black leaders live and operate all over the country, rather than as historically concentrated in the South.[58]

To be an efficient leader of the Black community, one should not be concerned with attempting to be all things to all people or lead every possible faction or aspect of the Black community. This does not mean that you cannot be influential or make an impact in multiple spheres of the Black community, for example, one can have political, artistic, educational, and economic impact at the same time, and not necessarily be the one leader in every category. The key for you as the leader is to be a standard of excellence and create habits that infiltrate different aspects of the Black community. Most importantly, is that the leader be capable of uniting multiple factions and groups within the Black community to see and then accomplish common goals and interests. This is one area where the leadership's advising and who leaders keep around them is important. Although the leader does not have to be all things to all Black people in order to lead them, it is necessary to have quality people around them from different backgrounds and fields of specialization that can be trusted. Regardless of the different groups and sects within the Black community, as a leader one must ultimately find themselves accountable to the group as a whole. The leader must bring all the needs and interests of the different sects of the Black community together into a unified, mobilized group.

METHODS

The principles that should organize the conduct that Black leaders should take, creates another dilemma facing contemporary Black leaders. Accommodation and increased integration into mainstream political, social, and cultural institutions versus protest and solitary or isolationist programs that emphasize Black autonomy remain significant areas of division regarding the methods Blacks should take to improve their conditions. Interracial communication is essential in either type of leadership. These forms of leadership differ on the perception of how much progress Blacks have made.

The accommodation type of leadership accepts the White community's definition of "Blacks' place," thus, the extent to which the accommodation leader can be said to exercise power is dependent upon tenuous support from the White community.[59] As the "accommodation" leader moves closer to the characteristics of the protest leader, his measure of influence increases. In situations where accommodation leadership prevails, changes in race relations are gradual and are initiated by negotiation, compromise, and the impersonal forces of the market, such as technology, urbanization, and international relations.[60] This optimistic school says that Blacks have made splendid progress in the years since slavery. Although they have not caught up to Whites, yet, it is hardly fair to expect them to so soon. As long as more and more Blacks are voting, going to college, finding jobs toward the top, and being welcomed in social settings like hotels and theaters, reasonable individuals can acknowledge that significant progress in the Black community has been made. Prior to the ascendancy of the protest leader, the "accommodation" type leader gained his position of prominence and prestige through the acceptance and support of the White community.

In protest leadership, the greatest source of power is located at the refusal to cooperate with the process of segregation and discrimination in the social system. When protest leadership prevails, changes in race relations occur through the manipulation of judicial, political, economic, and moral power. According to the protest or pessimistic view, Blacks in America were placed in an inferior position during colonial times and are still there. The major device by which Blacks have been kept inferior is segregation. Essentially segregation survives in all aspects of the Black political and social life, including, schools, housing, and churches. Despite considerable success in improving upper-class job opportunity for Blacks, the decline in jobs for the unskilled Black worker is being wiped out.

The protest leader gains prestige and status through acceptance in the Black community and rejection by a considerable part of the White community.[61] Failure to cooperate with racial super-ordination and subordination through the utilization of negative sanctions, "non-violent" resistance, legal attacks on segregation in federal courts, and sit-in demonstrations, question the legitimacy of the application of power by the White community to maintain the existing system of race relations. Protest leaders are more willing to sacrifice themselves personally; to use instruments of pressure to accomplish their purposes, and to recognize that the function of the Black revolt is not merely to overturn legal segregation, but to overturn segregation whether legal or "extra" legal, North or South.[62]

Different perspectives on the proper methods Blacks should use to achieve their objectives remain vital in explaining different factions within the Black community. It is in no greater aspect of the Black struggle that effective leadership is highly important; it is here that a leader exercises political skill upon the masses. It is important to emphasize outcomes over methods; accommodate when it is successful in protecting and promoting the interests and values of the Black community, in particular the Black poor, and protest and separate from mainstream society when necessary to let the Black masses know you still have their best interests at heart and have not been corrupted by the "establishment." Use a variety of methods but never forget your base constituency—the impoverished Black majority. The significance of Black Nationalism in the Black community cannot be forgotten, nor should it be left stagnant. The tenets of unity, solidarity, and the concepts of shared history and linked fate remains prevalent among a significant portion of the Black community. At the same time, upper and middle-class Blacks' interests in having access to mainstream American institutions should not be ignored. Regardless of the method, racism must be condemned at every level.

Part of an effective leaders skill set requires the ability to pursue any and all means in providing the resources necessary to improve the conditions of the Black masses. The disadvantaged members of the Black community will pledge their allegiance to the leader who guides them to newfound possibilities and opportunities, regardless of the methods; they will accept the method that brings out the desired outcome. But this outcome must result from the mutual understanding of what is in the best interest of the community as a whole. The willingness to explore and employ all options, while being realistic in the time frame and what outcomes can reasonably be achieved is an important task and takes extraordinary commitment of a Black leader.

LEADERS OF THE NEW SCHOOL:
A GUIDE FOR TOMORROW'S BLACK LEADER

Black leaders capable of transforming attitudes and behaviors within the Black community should preferably be victims of poverty, lower-class intellectuals willing to sacrifice financial success or fame for the good of community. They recognize the corruption of today's citizen that is mainly money motivated and selfish. Anyone aspiring to the mantle of an effective twenty-first century Black leader, capable of producing radical transformation to Blacks' habits, can expect to be shunned and rejected by the Black community initially because of the responsibility and high level of expectation that they have for members of the Black community. The new habits and institutions that must be established will appear foreign and controversial to the Black community, even "Uncle Tom-ish" and conservative in the aspects of controversial, conservative thinking that suggests Blacks forego certain constitutionally guaranteed rights of citizenship in the immediate interest of racial harmony.[63] Booker T. Washington urged Blacks to consider economic instead of explicitly political means for supporting their claims for equal opportunity. Washington was convinced that all were not ready for full political responsibility, as he surveyed the conditions of the Southern Black masses following the demise of Reconstruction. The poor or irresponsible exercise of political rights might produce resentment and hurt the cause.[64] Thus, he suggested that Blacks subsume their immediate political goals under long term, economic benefits.[65]

By his willingness to entertain particular stances within the oppressive majority to attain his vision of Black development, Washington was able to acquire substantial funding from Whites in both the North and South. Ultimately, the role of the leader is to shake the bad habits from the public by any means necessary, regardless if they are liked or not, and using a variety of tools. The next step in the investigation of Black leadership is to explore the essential characteristics capable of developing such institutions capable of leading the Black community into a new era and perception of themselves as citizens.

ELEMENTS REQUIRED OF BLACK LEADERSHIP TODAY

Drive

To be successful as a Black leader today requires a strong work ethic and will to overcome adversity. A demonstration of one's drive (strength of will; a strong motivating tendency or instinct, especially of aggressive origin, that prompts activity toward a particular end) is represented by the actions the individual takes when faced with adversity. Adversity is fundamental to the experiences of Black leaders and the Black community, thus, it is essential that Black leaders not get dismayed easily when confronted with difficult tasks or unfavorable conditions. When things get difficult or the situation gets worse is when it is time for a leader to work even harder and demonstrate commitment to see the accomplishment of the task all the way through. The leader must get better and stronger, even more focused the more impossible and unlikely the circumstances appear; when thing get bad, you as the leader, must be at your best.

A leader should vigorously and aggressively pursue their plan to accomplish the common good in the Black community. Booker T. Washington put enthusiasm and unlimited drive into his plan to further the cause and platform of Tuskegee Institute. His steady persistence in pursuit of Black economic development despite racial limitations led to increased enrollment and curriculum at Tuskegee. This enabled him to garner unmatched support for his programs from White and Black philanthropists alike. Ultimately, the leader must demonstrate to the Black community the hard work and dedication it takes to accomplish great and memorable tasks worthy of admiration by other members of the Black community, while simultaneously providing a public good or service.

Vision

To be an effective leader and accomplish a public good or service worthy of Black community admiration requires vision (ambition to succeed, comes alive in big moments or most crucial times, tenacity and ferociousness in which one attacks their dreams and goals.) It is imperative to think big; have a strong ambition to succeed and make your plans or goals for the community a reality. The greatest accomplishments are those done to improve the conditions of the lowliest and serve the common good. Thus, one should have a vision to improve public welfare and the conditions of the lowliest or most disadvantaged members of the community. Fannie Lou Hamer believed that she, as an individual, could make a difference, and thus, envisioned what might be for Black Mississippians. Her vision was to remove the obstacles to Black voter registration, first in Sunflower County, then in Mississippi.[66] As her horizons broadened with exposure to the wider world, her vision also expanded and encompassed economic development, day care, and health and nutrition education.[67] Hamer was known to trust her inner voice that housed her vision of the Black community. As a result, certain principles were simply inviolable, even if it harmed her circle of influence. Hamer was uncompromising when it came to empowering working-class and poor Blacks in Mississippi. This enabled her vision for the community to come into fruition.

Hamer's experience demonstrates the importance of advocating one's dreams and goals with aggressiveness and tenacity. To be successful one must have a "don't take no for an answer" framework in which you attack your vision. Be uncompromising and narrowly-focused on accomplishing your goals for the community that you are attempting to serve. In this case, to lead the Black community into the successful transfer of positive habits and patterns of interaction will require an earnest desire to see the Black community transform itself and achieve the common good.

Intelligence

Perhaps there is no greater element to successful and efficient leadership than the ability to exercise wisdom and knowledge. Intelligence (use of new tools, a source of good judgment, study enemies and the conditions of the environment, wisdom) is an important element of effective revolutionary leadership in the Black community. Intellectual ability includes, first of all, knowledge of "good," or the common good. The common good refers to the ways and practices that assure the sustainment, protection, and improvement of the Black community. Thus, a leader's knowledge in this regard refers to knowledge in the most efficient ways that Blacks can achieve their desired outcomes, and the roles that each person is best suited to play in the coming system of liberation. This knowledge is important because it enables the leadership to have a better perception on the reality of the situation of the community, the severity of Blacks' condition, and the most efficient ways to do the most good. With the knowledge and wisdom of how to sustain, protect, and improve the conditions within the Black community comes an ability to also better assess the root causes of the disadvantaged, and see through the symbolism and other tools of manipulation.

It is imperative that the leader of the Black community acquire knowledge of what methods and tools have been politically successful and which have been failures and why. One must study the conditions and behavior of the Black community and the environment and attitudes of mainstream American society. W. E. B. Du Bois' knowledge of Black history enabled him to master the essential arguments made against Blacks, in addition to the development of a greater appreciation for the home continent of Africa. Nineteenth century scholars presented Blacks in the most unfavorable light. Whites had argued that Blacks had not improved upon their conditions for thousands of years. It was vital to slaveholding interests that Blacks were deemed inherently inferior, and thus, the natural subjects to more sophisticated and civilized Whites. Du Bois used the resources provided to him to learn of Black history and the accomplishments of native Africans to have knowledge of the self-hatred that was present within Blacks' consciousness.

Knowledge is more than just learned in school. Fannie Lou Hamer had limited formal education, but absorbed lessons from people she met on her journey and through her own experiences.[68] Thurgood Marshall mastered constitutional law and used it to outmaneuver Whites seeking to deny Blacks rights and privileges accorded to other citizens.[69] One of the greatest attributes of an effective leader is to be a rapid learner; the ability to pick up new tools and methods quickly. Martin Luther King, Jr. successfully used David Thoreau's *Civil Disobedience* to use nonviolent resistance to achieve social change and learned Mahatma Gandhi's nonviolent civil disobedience campaign used successfully against British rule in India.[70] Nonviolent direct action did not originate in America, although it found a natural home here where refusal to cooperate with injustice was an ancient and honorable tradition.[71] By 1963, Martin Luther King Jr. had turned nonviolent resistance into a force in mass-action strategy for freedom.

To be an effective Black leader today, one must have the ability to discern what tools and methods to utilize and when. The education from which one can acquire this knowledge can be gained from books, experience, and connections and relationships with others. Leaders should use access to education to study and learn new tools that may be used to help liberate and uplift the impoverished Black community, regardless of their source; the key is that they work. Lastly, it is important to articulate the importance of education in the struggle for the Black community to attain the common good. As a lover of wisdom, the ability to transfer the value of education to other members of the community, and engage others to want to further their education and be smarter and see education as important is an essential requirement of tomorrow's leadership. Leaders should emphasize and demonstrate the value of education and knowledge and the significance that education and the acquisition of knowledge plays in their person life and their ability to succeed.

Innovation/Creativity

One of the most important elements of effective Black leadership needed to improve the conditions of the Black community is innovation/creativity (the introduction of new or original thoughts, methods, or strategies). The Black community needs new methods and practices, and new ideas on how to accomplish its goals. This includes the ability to attack the same old problems within the Black community for decades in new, more effective ways, and at the same time be aware of the possible effectiveness of old solutions to new problems. What is most lacking from the Black community today and from its leadership is fresh ideas and new ways to attack the ills that are currently plaguing Black communities, in addition to very little knowledge of the old ways that Blacks were able to address their needs despite being considered second-class citizens.. Thus, the Black community needs a leader with advanced, modern ways and methods of solving the issues facing the Black community in a changing world and changing national demographics in the U.S. which will present new challenges and a new role for the members of the Black community.

What was innovative about Booker T. Washington's program was that he indissolubly linked enthusiasm, unlimited energy, and perfect faith into his program, and changed it from a by-path into a veritable "way of life."[72] Washington turned Black's accommodation of White southerners for employment purposes into a uniform way of life that encompassed their entire racial interaction. W. E. B. Du Bois' innovative way of diagnosing Blacks' way of life presented the Black community with new ways of perceiving themselves in America. Additionally, the use of literary, music, and the arts to express Black life became significant to the Black community's quest for equality. For Blacks to think of themselves in new ways, transcending the imposed blinders of inferiority and self-doubt, Du Bois believed culture must be seized as a creative, reconstructive tool. Thus, Du Bois promoted a permanent cultural revolution among Blacks. Although never attaining his vision of global African liberation, Du Bois utilized a multitude of political skills to reintroduce Blacks to their heritage and create a cultural revolution.

Many of the problems within the Black community are not new, thus it is essential to attack old problems such as racism and inadequate housing options in new ways. To be an effective leader one must provide new solutions to old problems. Additionally, one may show how old solutions may solve contemporary problems, perhaps with some adjustments or variations as a result of modernization, such as technology, for example. Strategies used by the Civil Rights Movement or abolition may still be relevant and useful tools for contemporary Blacks to use in their fight for racial equality today. To be an effective Black leader today, it is imperative to bring something new to the Black community; present new ideas, new methods, or new strategies to attain shared goals and interests.

Sacrifice

The hardest virtue for potential leaders of the Black community to display is the ability to surrender personal happiness, satisfaction, or aggrandizement for the good of others or the community overall. To successfully lead the Black community requires of the individual the potential to sacrifice (the surrender of something prized or desirable for the sake of something considered as having a higher or more pressing claim) income, opportunities, friends and other relationships, in the name of the common good and setting a fine example for other members of the Black community to follow. It may be required of them to sacrifice popularity and fame, two things that are highly prioritized and contribute greatly to the corruption of potential Black leaders. Thus, as a leader one must be willing to be made fun of, made to look a fool, or not be very well liked because the steps taken in order to elevate and lead a corrupted society will not be very well-received.

One of the many virtues Du Bois sought to embody and inculcate was self-sacrifice. Without it, leaders would not be able to serve the community. By sacrifice, Du Bois meant:

> real and definite surrender of personal ease and satisfaction. . . . To increase abiding satisfaction for the mass of our people, and for all people, someone must sacrifice something of his own happiness. . . . With the death of your happiness may easily come increased happiness and satisfaction and fulfillment for other people—strangers, unborn babies, and uncreated worlds.[73]

Thurgood Marshall and A. Philip Randolph had pitifully low salaries throughout their respectively lengthy tenures at the NAACP Legal Defense and Educational Fund and the Brotherhood of Sleeping Car Porters. A Philip Randolph made tremendous financial, emotional, and physical sacrifices in founding the Brotherhood of Sleeping Car Porters in 1925. Randolph never earned more than $15,000 a year. He argued that Blacks refrain as workers and as a race which did not enjoy democracy at home from participating in the war efforts and as a result led to clashes with the organized labor movement in developing the first predominately Black labor union.[74] In 1949, Marshall who was leading the greatest legal movement in America earned a salary of $8,500 a year. Nearly, a decade later, in 1958, Marshall's salary was only $15,000. Three years later, when President Kennedy appointed him to a federal judgeship, his NAACP pay was $18,000.[75]

To successfully lead the Black community today, to radically change and transform the attitudes of the impoverished Black majority and effectively improve their conditions, a Black leader must demonstrate a willingness to sacrifice, or surrender personal success or desires to serve the poor and disadvantaged members of the Black community. Such sacrifice includes demonstrating one's love and commitment to the group through continued contribution to the sustainment and protection of the group and its collective interests. To surrender one's self-interest and personal aggrandizement to improve the condition of the Black masses demonstrates the type of attitude that if all members of the community had, solving the problems in the Black community would be effortless.

Humility

As a leader of the Black community, whose main responsibility is to work with and be one of the people, it is essential to refrain from thinking one is better or more important than poor Blacks who leaders intend to help. Humility (modest opinion or estimate of one's own importance, and rank) is required. Instead, a leader should emphasize the importance of the masses and their importance and contribution to their own struggle and the success in improving their conditions. It is necessary at times to deflect one's role and importance in the struggle to others; accomplishments can be credited to staff, advisors, and other members of the Black community. One way that this can be done is to refrain from talking about oneself. When dealing with issues of importance to the Black community using "we" instead of "I" deflects attention away from individual leaders and gives credit back to the masses that can use the attention and confidence to further proceed in their quest.

A significant portion of Martin Luther King, Jr.'s legacy of leadership is encompassed in his perception as a humble leader. He would participate firsthand in marches and rallies, engage in civil disobedience, get arrested, jailed, and abused alongside his supporters, even when friends and colleagues would offer him a way out. Additionally, King embraced a humble lifestyle. When awarded the Noble Peace Prize in 1964, King turned over the $54,000 prize money to groups involved in the Civil Rights Movement rather than spend it on a better home and car for his family.

As a leader, one can also gain the perception of humility by the people in the fight for liberation by joining in communal activities, festivals, and traditions. By participating in the same routines and activities as other members of the Black community and a leader reinforces commitment to unity and solidarity. Ultimately, the leader must make the same sacrifices and have the same standard and level of accountability as other members of the community; the key is that the leader is not above participating in activities and taking part in similar traditions as the majority of members of the Black community. Finally, a symbol of humility takes place when the leader admits shortcomings, mistakes and pitfalls. Illustrate to the people that you are not infallible in a manner to which members of the Black community can relate.

Although a leader has a position of esteem and may have certain privileges or advantages over the majority of the Black community, it is important to remain humble and exercise a modest opinion of one's importance in the Black struggle for racial equality. The majority of Blacks already sense a pattern of elitism in the current model of Black leader-

ship. To demonstrate this aspect of a leader's character they must participate in the liberation of the poor as any other contributing member of a
team who has a particular role to fill, and yet as vital as any other. A
leader must hold oneself to the same standard (sometimes higher) and
level of accountability to sacrifice and contribute as all other members of
the community. No leader will be perfect and being conscience of one's
shortcomings will make it easy to empathize with the most disadvantaged members of the community. Thus it is imperative that a leader acts
like they are no better than any one member of the Black community
despite their position in society.

Courage

A Black leader will need the courage (the quality of mind or spirit that
enables a person to face difficulty, danger, and pain without fear; brav-
ery) to take an uncompromising stance within the Black community,
while at the same time be willing to point out the contradictions and tools
of manipulation within the American system. To be strong in convictions
and confident in moral character requires courage from the leader. In
both cases, a Black leader will face ridicule and contention from the people. It is difficult to risk being shunned and ostracized by one's own
community. The task of liberation is difficult and any time you seek to
take people out of their comfort zone you risk the chance that they will
rebel against you. But an effective Black leader must demonstrate the will
to overcome those difficult times with confidence.

Despite threats to her personal safety, eviction from her home, ridicule by some factions of the Civil Rights Movement, and a life-debilitat-
ing jail house beating, Fannie Lou Hamer played a significant role in
securing voting rights for Blacks in Mississippi.[76] Hamer braved intense
racial hatred; she was once evicted immediately from her home after she
attempted to register to vote in 1972.[77] She was willing to take great risk
to achieve the greater good and consistently eschewed opportunistic motives for personal gain. Her courage demonstrates uncompromising, persistent determination to serve the lowliest people in the Black community.

Martin Luther King, Jr. needed significant courage to debunk popular
myths of American innocence and goodness and remind the nation that
its wealth rested upon the bones of exploited slaves. He also placed the
heavy burden of self-sacrificing morality on an already oppressed people, which was courageous, and often noble, but cost him the loyalty of
adolescent males.[78] King also advocated radical redistribution of political
and economic power to restructure society towards the end of life.

As a leader of the Black community it is important to not be afraid of
taking risks; attempting to lead the impoverished Black majority in contemporary society is a risky endeavor as it is. One cannot be afraid of

taking a hard stance and say and do things that must be said or done even though they may not be popular. Be willing to face ridicule from Blacks and people of influence outside of the Black community as well. To do so will require thick-skin on your part to survive the personal and potential physical attacks that come with attempting to accomplish the common good in a corrupted society. To take society to unsuspected possibilities and accomplish unachieved common goals and interests will require the Black community to be challenged, but at the same time the leader must challenge mainstream society, its institutions, and the existing conditions. Part of the challenge will be to hold strong conviction and commitment to one's goal and vision for the community while living an alternative lifestyle to the rest of the corrupt community.

One has to be willing to take the risk of telling White Americans that they are not holding up to their end of the deal of democracy and equality, while at the same time confront the Black community with the truth: that they are not holding up their end of the bargain by taking responsibility for their own actions and negative attitudes towards one another and being committed to improve their conditions. A lot of the problems facing the Black community cannot be solved by White America and the Black community must be ready and willing to face these challenges head on, and alone. It takes courage to tell Blacks when they do not measure up to fulfilling their obligations to one another.

Responsibility

In the process of taking on new challenges and exploring new avenues for the Black community to express self-determination and assume control in the Black community, it is imperative that a Black leader assume responsibility (answerable and accountable to one's self and others) for the conditions of the Black masses and also for the successes and failures of their programs and institutions when they arise. This includes also being accountable for their actions and the outcomes of their methods. Having to be responsible and accountable for behavior and outcomes to the Black community will compel a leader to work continually in the best interests of the most disadvantaged; this is the constituency to whom they will be responsible to explain themselves to. Win or lose, a leader must confront the Black community with results. Responsibility of leadership also means taking a hard stance on issues that the majority of Blacks may not like but is in the overall best interest of the community as a whole. Booker T. Washington abhorred ignorance, drunkenness, poverty, and apathy.[79] Since a leader is responsible for the health and advancement of the community, they have to protect the Black community from itself at times.

Together with Du Bois, Washington espoused a strong principle of communal responsibility within the Black community, a significant effort to prevent the development of deep divisions within the Black community based on class, culture, and color.[80] Washington commissioned graduates to go forth and teach and lead their people into a better life. Du Bois argued that our duties as members of the Black community compelled forward-looking, virtuous citizens to act on behalf of the common good of the present society and of their children as well.

Responsibility was particularly significant for Du Bois and he paid special concern to the unique qualities of responsibility pertaining to Blacks. The thinking class of Black Americans, Du Bois argued, would shirk a heavy responsibility; a responsibility to themselves, a responsibility to the struggling masses, a responsibility to the darker races of men whose future depends on so largely on this American experiment, but especially a responsibility to this nation.[81] The concept of the "Talented Tenth" was based entirely on the concept of the wealthy and educated Blacks accepting the responsibility to uplift their struggling brethren. He made clear his position on the intellectual's responsibility to oppressed populations wherever found.

Du Bois spread the share of responsibility among the wealthy class of the Black intelligentsia and the parents of Black children. He stated, "the day will dawn when mothers must explain but clearly why the little girls next door do not want to play with 'niggers'; what the real cause of the teachers' unsympathetic attitude is, and how people may ride on the backs of street cars and the smoker end of trains, and still be people, honest high-minded people."[82] It was Black parents' obligation not to thrust Black children into a racist society prematurely, without the proper foundation of self-respect, and knowledge and pride in their heritage.

Additionally, Du Bois took an active stance in proposing that Whites take a certain level of responsibility for the condition of Blacks in America and the subjugation of Africans worldwide. He declared that certain supplementary truths about the American race problem must never be forgotten, specifically, that slavery and race prejudice from Whites are potent if not sufficient causes of Blacks' position. White Americans as a group are heavily bombarded with racial stereotypes. Du Bois recognized that White America's newspapers, radio networks, and other communication systems perpetuated racial stereotypes. The cultural institutions that produced popular music, theater, films, professional athletics, and public amusements of all types reinforced White superiority and Black inferiority. Rather than by a search for common human characteristics and mutual respect, their relations with Blacks as individuals and as a group have been largely predetermined, and structured on a basis of antagonistic conflicts, competition, and hatred.[83]

In the end, leaders take responsibility for the outcome of the constituents for which they are responsible. As a leader, if you succeed you will get credit for transforming the community, and if you fail, you should receive the blame. Thus, one should hold all parties accountable and responsible for their participation in Blacks' fight for racial equality and justice; Whites and Black, male and female, alike. The historical injustices and remaining remnants of racism and discrimination cannot be erased from White's consciousness and they must take responsibility for healing past wounds and making future concessions. Whites should not be let off the hook in dealing with societal conditions that will eventually impact their lives. At the same time, Blacks can no longer blame Whites and racism for all their problems and must take responsibility for their own communities and the fight for equality. Ultimately, American society will grow numb to Blacks' cry of racism and discrimination if they do not make considerable progress and rely on blaming Whites as the fundamental cause for their conditions and standing in American society.

In order to sufficiently hold the community accountable for its progress and participation in protecting and promoting its collective interests, part of responsibility and strong moral character means that the leader has to be careful not to participate in behavior unflattering to the majority of the Black community's interests or that puts it in an unfavorable light. While looking after the community, in particular the poor and ignorant, leaders must act on high standards and moral character, demonstrating by example the commitment and accountability necessary to radically transform the habits of the majority of members of the Black community. The strongest level of responsibility consists of a strong commitment to take it upon oneself to look after the community and the future of the Black community.

Flexibility

While developing and instituting new methods and practices to solve the issues plaguing the majority of Blacks, a leader must exhibit flexibility (susceptible of modification or adaptation). Leadership requires the ability to modify plans and adapt new strategies based on conditions and circumstances. To be successful, a leader must be capable of fitting in and adapting to a plethora of different groups and situations while never losing sight of the objectives and purpose of their appointment.

Most importantly, leaders must be willing to change course when times change and explore other ideas and methods when they may be effective in achieving the desired outcome. For instance, Du Bois appeared to promote Black integration, nationalism, communism, and capitalism at different times throughout his career. After the assassination of Martin Luther King, Jr., Whitney Young Jr. altered his thinking about civil rights strategies, which resulted in more aggressive program strategies. This new civil rights strategy included working more directly with the Black community by moving away from integration and gradualism, and consequently, Young took a new attitude about Black Power.[84] Although criticism was painful for Young to hear, he demonstrated his willingness to change ineffective management and operating practices.[85] Thus, it is imperative that a leader be willing to change course and explore any and all possibilities to achieve the type of radical change that is needed to transform the attitude and values of the Black community.

A Black leader must approach the solving of the wide array of problems by using a variety of techniques from a diverse range of political perspectives. Many of the problems faced by the Black community, such as poor performance by Black males, relocation/ outsourcing of jobs overseas, and the feminization of poverty, have become social issues within the White community.[86] Consequently, a Black leader needs to have flexibility, imagination, and creativity as they attempt to solve the Black community's pressing issues.

An efficient and effective Black leader should never be afraid to change course in order to accomplish one's vision. The vision may not change, but the path and methods one uses to get there may change for many reasons. Effective leaders adapt to the new circumstances, events, and possibilities that one will assuredly experience while trying to radically transform the habits and conditions of the poor Black majority. Leaders must be flexible enough to modify strategy or platform when necessary and beneficial to the Black majority, but refrain from appearing fickle and disorganized. It is ok to change one's mind and demonstrate one's open-mindedness, but it is wise not to appear inconsistent and indecisive. In the end, one must be willing to adapt one's vision and strategy to uplift the Black masses when new circumstances, conditions, and uncontrollable events present themselves. To appear too rigid and unable to adapt to new conditions can prohibit the leader's ability to accomplish their vision and ultimately improve the conditions of the Black community.

VIRTÙ IN NEW BLACK LEADERSHIP

Virtù requires that a Black leader be willing to exercise any means necessary in order to achieve their vision of the Black community and to make that vision a reality. In addition to intellectual and moral character, an effective leader must exercise political virtù: *the complete set of political skills that enable a leader to achieve great things*. Achieving radical change will take exceptional skill and talent on behalf of a Black leader to confront various obstacles and barriers within and without the Black community. To shake the people out of their comfort zone and confront inevitable backlash will require a set of political skills, not practiced by modern Black leaders.

Washington's authoritarian measures at Tuskegee put his exercise of political virtù on display. Black ministers and educators who favored an aggressive approach to civil rights were dismissed or demoted by Washington's surrogates. Spies were planted in civil rights organizations and Black colleges whose faculty or administrators opposed the Tuskegee philosophy were denied funds from White philanthropies and corporations. Even within his own ranks, Washington cautiously looked for signs of insubordination. One Tuskegee Institute instructor expressed misgivings about Washington's authoritarian behavior to his pastor in Boston. Washington's aides managed to steal these personal letters, and the teacher in question was promptly humiliated for actions that "were disloyal to the institution."[87]

Du Bois' display of virtù is demonstrated in his willingness to employ any means necessary to transform the identity and culture of the Black community. His tactics included the spectrum of political ideologies ranging from Black Nationalism to integration and assimilation. He is considered the founder of The Niagara Movement, which is perceived as a nationalist movement and the NAACP, which is considered to practice an assimilationist approach to American racial problems. Du Bois also endorsed the employment of both socialist and communist economic principles to attain African liberation and transform Black culture. At various times, Du Bois was a reformed Republican, a Democrat, a Socialist, a Communist, and a supporter of the Progressive Party of Henry Wallace.[88]

The reputation of the leader is almost as significant as the actual outcomes they bring and their achievement. A leader's reputation can be greatly beneficial and contribute to the ease in which they are able to earn the respect of followers, and thus, get them to take actions they otherwise would not take. It can also be beneficial in how the leader is accepted by other groups and individuals outside of the community. A Black leader's reputation can be a useful tool to diminish confrontation, making their job easier when a leader's healthy reputation precedes them. Thus, how to use one's reputation effectively is a critical political skill of virtù. One of the greatest tools of Martin Luther King, Jr.'s leadership was the reputation that he had among governors and police chiefs throughout the South and in areas plagued by segregation and discrimination. He had a reputation for being able to mobilize large groups to rallies and marches that would intentionally disrupt the status quo in the cities that they would visit and cause police officers and elected officials to be on notice. At times, MLK was able to succeed in the aspirations of his platform before even showing up; his reputation alone preceded him.

Ultimately, virtù for tomorrow's Black leader demands the willingness to achieve their vision and uplift the status and standing of the Black community by any means necessary, doing whatever it takes; no options should be left off the table. In the end, a leader will be judged by what one accomplishes and the improved conditions of their constituents; the methods will either be legendary or forgotten, but the outcome and new position in society will remain a part of the community. One of the great attributes of Machiavelli's virtù is that subjective personality characteristics are potentially irrelevant in the leader's ultimate ability to accomplish one's vision for the community. This means, as a leader, you should not worry about the perception of being mean, liked, or popular.

The main focus is always the same: the radical transformation of the habits by interaction among members of the Black community. Be mean, angry, and revengeful when necessary. Have mercy and show empathy to others to gain the perception of a compassionate person, yet waste no time in displaying one's contempt and aggression when the opportunity presents itself. Effective leaders must be aggressive, take chances, and monitor enemies and those considered to be perpetual violators of the will and aspirations of members of the Black community. Use violence when necessary, if it works and achieves a public good. In a good, directed way, Malcolm X, Fred Hampton, and the Black Power Movement were all able to make the threat and potential violence in self-defense a popular tool.

Goal oriented violence is more legitimate than random acts targeted at unsuspecting and uninvolved individuals. Thus, violence is a tool of virtù that a leader must consider. Once removed as an option off the table, the leaders' ability to accomplish their task is diminished. Certain acts of violence, different from riots, can be beneficial to the Black community when not targeting Blacks or taking place in Black communities; violence towards oppressors and the systems and institutions that perpetuate miserable Black conditions, not in our own communities. Malcolm X proved that oppressed people are redeemable and that Black rage and defiance can be constructively used.[89] Ultimately a leader will be judged based on whether or not you succeed; the methods can always be forgiven based on circumstances. Make example of traitors and disloyal enemies of the community. Disloyalty of any kind cannot be tolerated and must be discouraged at all costs—scores settled, slights paid for. The Black community will respond to a leader who displays their strength and courage toward a hostile mainstream society.

When it is beneficial to the advancement of the interests of the Black community as a whole, a leader must be prepared to demonstrate a wide range of emotions and characteristics; some widely accepted and popular, others to be displayed sparingly. Traditionally, traits such as honesty, moderate temperament, and forgiveness are deemed "good" and beneficial to the upstanding character and personality of the individual, but for the leader, these traits can be detrimental to the leader's ability to attain their vision. Do not tell people everything or be too honest; keep some things (your dreams and goals) to yourself. Be careful of peoples' intentions; people want and intend to do a lot of things that they will never do. Be careful of trust; understand the limitations and shortcomings of society, in addition to their capabilities. This means sometimes a leader may have to lie and act immoral under certain circumstances, conditions, and crowds. As a leader, your job is to put on whatever "hat" fits the situation. The key is to have enough political skill to pull it off successfully. Ultimately what will determine success is accomplishment and vision.

SUMMARY

This research has addressed the conditions of the Black community by investigating their negative patterns of behavior, or "bad habits," and advancing a model of leadership that will radically transform the standing and conditions of the poor and disadvantaged members of the Black community. This includes the development of new habits that reinforce unity and solidarity by all members. The habits of citizenship are measured by examining four major issues: economic standing, educational attainment, involvement in the criminal justice system, and health and family structure. Poor and declining conditions among the lowliest members of the Black community in these areas lead to the conclusion that Blacks have bad citizenship habits, or patterns of interaction among themselves, and lack leadership to transform those habits into community-building at the national level.

The Black community and its leadership have been corrupted. The community has a corrupted perception of citizenship (i.e., what it means and the purpose of being a member of the Black community), and its relationship to the state. Citizens are members of a national community that are committed to a common cause, actively participating and contributing to the sustainment, protection, and improvement of the state or community, or the common good. Citizenship is the transferring of rights, privileges, and obligations between individuals and other members of the community. The purpose of belonging to a community is the exchange of rights, privileges, and obligations that individuals gain from group membership that cannot be earned alone, such as protection. The self-preservation of individuals, their history, identity, heritage, and culture is found and protected by the community and it is in the community where individual rights are protected and knowledge of the common good is established.

Corruption is the process in which Blacks are unable and unwilling to put the good of the community over the good of individual self-interest. Blacks' perception as second-class citizens based on the institution of slavery, the inability to earn a decent wage, the history of segregation, and the restriction of voting rights, contributes to not only their corrupt perception of citizenship, but the erosion of value in belonging to the Black community and the greater American polity. Erosion of value in belonging to the Black community results in Blacks no longer finding being a part of the Black community and contributing to its improvement as significant or relevant. In the worst case, members of the Black community find belonging to the group detrimental to long-term goals.

Corruption and the erosion of value in Black citizenship are preserved through manipulation, cultural invasion, division or lack of trust, and Blacks' over-reliance on liberalism. Corruption is evident in Black community "bad habits," or negative patterns of behavior, such as (1) Blacks' relationship to the economy—meaning how they earn and spend money; (2) participation in the criminal and judicial systems; (3) educational attainment, and (4) health and family structure. Although Blacks earn more money, graduate from high school, and have greater access to White-collar jobs, collectively Blacks have earned less income and gained at a slower rate than all other races in America, resulting in Blacks earning the lowest income in America today.

Additionally, there are more Blacks involved in the criminal justice system, continually falling below Whites and the national average in employment and educational attainment, and suffering disproportionately from increased health and familial structure problems. Erosion of value in belonging to the community and corruption prevents and diminishes the ability to attain the common good. Since not all people will willingly sacrifice self-interest for the common good, everyone does not deserve to be leaders, nor citizens granted with the rights and privileges of community membership.

Blacks have corrupt and ineffective leadership in the post-Civil Rights era (1968) because the conditions and standing of the Black majority have not improved overall; if anything collective standing and conditions have worsened. Leaders are people who guide the people to new heights or unsuspected possibilities. The most important acts by leaders improve the conditions of the public or provide a public good, thus the key to effective leadership includes the promotion and advancement of the conditions of the many. Great leaders take the people beyond what previous leaders have already attained, and beyond what the people thought they were capable of achieving. Effective leaders are contrarian because they are not followers. They are often despised and rejected initially because they are iconoclasts. Leaders pursue their vision for the community, look beyond extant conditions and tap into ignored possibilities in order to radically transform the conditions and status of the impoverished Black majority.

Effective Black leadership radically changes the habits of the Black community via the advancement of the poor and disadvantaged Black majority. With a new set of virtues, leaders create a new type of follower, in a sense, a new citizen. Leaders arouse new or dormant attitudes among the public and develop stable institutions. To change human attitudes requires great leadership skills. Thus, leadership is the ability to transform attitudes of the public in order to achieve unsuspected or unrealized opportunities and demonstrate the habits of virtue that cause the people to fight for their collective interests. Effective leaders set an example of excellence and service. The theory and praxis of excellence and service create new values and institutions that improve the conditions for the poor Black majority.

In attempting to overcome Blacks' bad habits a leader should advocate revolutionary, innovative, and creative ideas to transform the conditions and consciousness of a corrupted society. Radical change includes transformation of the conditions in which Blacks currently find themselves comfortable. This requires clarity of vision, goals, and expectations on the part of leaders and the Black community. Leaders must devote attention to increasing the devotion, enthusiasm, and allegiance of the Black masses so that they will be open to radical changes in their habits and patterns of behavior. To achieve this end, a leader must fight alongside members of the Black community. This requires a leader to trust and love the people. Thus, a leader must work with the people, live amongst them and experience their quotidian conditions firsthand.

By creating values and institutions that reinforce sacrifice to the community, self-help, and an ethos dedicated to taking care of the poor and disadvantaged, a leader can address the bad habits of the community. Independent banks and economic advising centers, Black-owned businesses in predominately Black communities; Black schools and education centers of the highest quality operated by Black professionals; health, medical, and nutrition centers in predominately Black neighborhoods that are committed to serving the Black poor and operated by Black professionals; and parenting, job placement, and crime prevention centers that target poor Blacks, are examples of institutions that Black leaders must build and sustain.

Blacks have the resources to enhance financial independence if leaders could engage Black professionals and entrepreneurs to recycle revenue into Black community-building. It is imperative for Black leaders to create unity and solidarity among members of the Black community to successfully mobilize enough support to convince prospective leaders and professionals to commit resources to expand Black institutions. One way this can be accomplished is by leaders emphasizing Blacks' linked or common fate and transforming a negative perception of Blacks' fate to a positive one. To do so will require radical changes to shake the people out of their comfort zone and transform the attitudes and behavior of the collective Black community.

NOTES

1. Freire, *Pedagogy of the Oppressed*, 164.
2. Ibid.
3. Woodson, *The Mis-Education of the Negro*, 24.
4. Ibid., 182.

5. Freire, *Pedagogy of the Oppressed*, 128.

6. Ibid., 239.

7. Lea E. Williams, *Servants of the People: The 1960s Legacy of African American Leadership* (New York: St. Martin's Press), 226.

8. Fanon, *Black Skin, White Masks*, 182.

9. Freire, *Pedagogy of the Oppressed*, 163.

10. Peter Goldman, "Malcolm X." In *Dictionary of American Negro Biography*, edited by Michael R. Winston, (New York: W. W. Norton), 305.

11. Robert Michael Franklin, *Liberating Visions* (Minneapolis, MN: Fortress Press), 1990.

12. Ibid., 89.

13. Ibid., 165.

14. Freire, *Pedagogy of the Oppressed*, 91.

15. Williams, *Servants of the People*, 238.

16. Ibid.

17. Ibid., 169.

18. Freire, *Pedagogy of the Oppressed*, 148–49.

19. Ibid., 74.

20. Ibid., 177.

21. Franklin, *Liberating Visions*, 17.

22. Ibid., 96.

23. Hadjor, *Another America: The Politics of Race and Blame*, 196.

24. Freire, *Pedagogy of the Oppressed*, 166.

25. Abigail and Stephan Thernstrom, *America in Black and White: One Nation, Indivisible*. 1st Touchstone Edition (New York: Simon & Schuster, 1999), 534.

26. William J. Wilson, *The Declining Significance of Race: Blacks and Changing American Institutions* (Chicago: University of Chicago Press), 1978.

27. Franklin, *Liberating Visions*, 32.

28. Ibid.

29. Michael Dawson, *Behind the Mule: Race and Class in African-American Politics* (Princeton, NJ: Princeton University Press), 1994.

30. Ibid.

31. Cornel West, *Race Matters*. *Race Matters* (New York: Vintage/Random House, 1994).

32. Michael Dawson, *Black Visions: The Roots of Contemporary African American Political Ideologies* (Chicago: University of Chicago Press, 2001).

33. Williams, *Servants of the People*, 206.

34. Tate, *From Protest to Politics: The New Black Voters in American Elections*.

35. J. H. Clarke, *Malcolm X: The Man and His Times* (New York: Macmillan, 1969).

36. Franklin, *Liberating Visions*, 88.

37. bell hooks, *Ain't I A Woman* (Boston, MA: South End Press, 1981).

38. Michelle Wallace, *Black Macho and the Myth of the Superwoman* (Verso: Verso Classics Edition), 1999.

39. hooks, *Ain't I A Woman*.

40. Elaine Brown, *A Taste of Power: A Black Woman's Story* (New York: First Anchor Books Edition), 1994.

41. Ibid.

42. Ibid.

43. Neha Sahgal and Greg Smith, "A Religious Portrait of African Americans," *Pew Research Center's Forum on Religion & Public Life*, January 30, 2009.

44. Ibid.

45. Jeremiah Carma, *Holy Lockdown* (Lilburn, GA: Twelfth House Publishing, 2004).

46. Michael Battle, *The Black Church in America* (Malden, MA: Blackwell Publishing, 2006).

47. Anthony B. Pinn, *The Black Church in the Post Civil Rights Era* (Maryknoll, NY: Orbis Books, 2002).

48. Ibid., xv.

49. Emmitt Price III, *The Black Church and Hip-Hop Culture* (Lanham, MD: Scarecrow Press, 2011), 10.

50. Tyrone Gordon and F. Stewart Carlyle III, *Growing the African American Church* (Nashville, TN: Abingdon Press, 2006), 7.

51. Franklin, *Liberating Visions*, 114.

52. Ibid., 123.

53. Mabee, "The Crisis in Negro Leadership."

54. Ibid.

55. James Q. Wilson, *Negro Politics: The Search for Leadership* (Glencoe, IL: The Free Press, 1960).

56. Smythe, "Changing Patterns in Negro Leadership."

57. Ibid.

58. Ibid.

59. Tilman C. Cothran and William Phillips, Jr., "Negro Leadership in a Crisis Situation," *Phylon (1960–)* 22 no. 2 (1961): 107–18.

60. Ibid., 118.

61. Ibid.

62. Ibid.

63. Franklin, *Liberating Visions*, 13.

64. Ibid., 21.

65. Ibid.

66. Williams, *Servants of the People: The 1960s Legacy of African American Leadership*, 149.

67. K. Mills, *This Little Light of Mine: The Life of Fannie Lou Hamer* (New York: Dutton, 1993).

68. Williams, *Servants of the People: The 1960s Legacy of African American Leadership*, 239.

69. Ibid., 236.

70. Franklin, *Liberating Visions*.

71. Ibid.

72. W. E. B. Du Bois, *Reconstruction in America* (New York: The Free Press, 1992), 34.

73. Franklin, *Liberating Visions*, 65.

74. Ibid., 234.

75. Williams, *Servants of the People: The 1960s Legacy of African American Leadership*, 227.

76. Ibid.

77. Ibid., 226.

78. Franklin, *Liberating Visions*, 122.

79. Ibid., 32.

80. Ibid., 33.

81. Du Bois, *Reconstruction in America*, 43.

82. Marable, *Black Leadership: Four Great American Leaders and the Struggle for Civil Rights*, 53.

83. Ibid., 45.

84. Williams, *Servants of the People: The 1960s Legacy of African American Leadership*, 112.

85. Ibid., 239.

86. Cunnigen, "Black Leadership in the Twenty-First Century," 27.

87. Ibid., 34–35.

88. Marable, *Black Leadership: Four Great American Leaders and the Struggle for Civil Rights*, 76.

89. Franklin, *Liberating Visions*.

Conclusion

Is the Black community better off today than in 1970? In the forty-five plus years since the Civil Rights Movement it is widely accepted by Blacks and Whites alike that the conditions of Blacks in America have substantially improved. Although Blacks have greater access to U.S. political and economic institutions, higher education, and higher wages, whether Blacks' overall conditions have improved is difficult to determine. Whether the conditions of the Black community are better than during the Civil Rights era is a matter of difference in individual versus collective standing. By looking at the collective standing of the Blacks in America, it is possible to discern that the conditions of the Black community overall have not substantially improved in the last half century.

Black leaders today must have the devotion, commitment, and enthusiasm of poor Blacks to radically transform the standing and conditions of the Black community. Black community well-being would improve because willingness to take risks beyond their comfort zone would unleash untapped possibilities to advance communal interests. Blacks would not be afraid to break away from the status quo and take appropriate measures necessary to improve their conditions. It will take courage to realize radical change, and only revolutionary leadership, with the devotion, commitment, and enthusiasm of poor Blacks will create such conditions. It will take courage to face the adversity, ridicule, and resentment from people inside and outside of the Black community while transformation takes place. Here is where strength and solidarity within the community are important. Blacks can rely on and hold each other accountable to the expectations of membership in the community to successfully overcome their collective adversity. Lastly, there will be less justifiable fear of elite Blacks abandoning the values of poor Blacks if the leadership devotes itself to promoting communal interests.

To radically transform the habits of members of the Black community and significantly improve their lives, Blacks have to create ways to hold leaders and other members of the community accountable to the promotion of the common good. This includes elected officials, and other elite Blacks in positions of authority who rely on votes, money, or protection of the Black community. Blacks must discover ways to punish or reward members and leaders of the community based on their contribution to the advancement of the interests of the Black community.

Blacks must recommit to their most disadvantaged. The Black community can no longer offer its resources and protections to groups who have no interests in the values and goals of poor Blacks. Blacks should restrict access and privileges to those candidates and individuals who demonstrate the willingness to serve all members of the Black community. Blacks' endorsement of certain products, their political endorsements and contributions, where and how they spend their income, and what they watch and listen to can all be reevaluated and transformed to produce more tangible improvements to the conditions of the majority of Blacks in America. The Black community, under the right leadership, can radically transform how it spends income and political capital by restricting who they promote, endorse and grant the protections provided by the Black community.

Leaders must take necessary steps to create unity and solidarity to effectively mobilize the Black community to achieve common goals and interests. Leaders must demonstrate a level of commitment and sacrifice to the Black community by serving others, in particular the poor and disadvantaged, and encouraging others to follow suit. An effective leader successfully transforms the habits of the Black community by demonstrating how sacrifice and commitment to the poor can create better living conditions for all members of the community; that by sacrificing self-interest, the conditions of the Black community overall can be improved. By doing so, Black leaders can set new parameters that redefine and reinterpret the significance and perception of Black citizenship.

Black leaders' theory and praxis must demonstrate the ability to achieve unrealized or unanticipated communal accomplishments. Highlighting achievements of individuals does not necessarily demonstrate one's ability to lead others. Rather, great leadership requires that the conditions of the collective be significantly improved. The Civil Rights Movement would not have been as successful if voting rights and the desegregation of public schools and facilities were only extended to middle-class Blacks who could afford it, while poor Blacks remained in an unchanged, oppressive state.

Part of the problem facing the Black majority is that as the demographics of the country continue to change and the issues become more complex, those issues that are specifically detrimental to the Black community will continue to be dismissed. During the 2012 Presidential election, there was little attention given to the specific demands and issues facing Blacks in America. Although the Obama Administration passed comprehensive health care reform that will inevitable benefit members of the Black community, there was no mention of the continuing crisis of violence in Black neighborhoods, such as Chicago and Oakland, the growing number of Black men who are dropping out of high school, and the disproportionately high unemployment facing members of the Black community.

In December 2012, more than sixty leading Blacks from America's civil rights, social justice, business, and community leaders including Marc Morial, President and CEO of the National Urban League, Rev. Al Sharpton, Ben Jealous, President of the NAACP, Melanie Campbell, President of the National Coalition on Black Civic Participation, gathered in Washington, DC to discuss how to provide solutions to "key" issues facing the Black community. The steps to develop a "Black Agenda" for President Obama to address in his second term included: (1) achieve economic parity for Blacks; (2) promote equity in educational opportunity; (3) protect and defend voting rights; (4) promoting a healthier nation and health care disparities; and (5) achieve comprehensive reform of the criminal justice system. While the wish list is unlikely to result in historic legislation by the Obama administration, participants of the conference were touting the unity displayed by various Black advocacy groups. Said Sharpton, "We embrace our historic role as the conscience of the nation. We are united in our mission to support and protect the well-being of the African American community."[1]

Similarly in November 2012, a separate group of Black leaders convened at Howard University to discuss the "State of the Black World" following President Obama's reelection and what it means for the Black community. The discussion focused on emphasizing implementing policies that "directly" targeted the Black community, acknowledging that the Black community has not received nearly as much direct acknowledgement as other communities comprising the Democratic base, such as Latinos and the LGBT community. In question is Blacks' continued support of Democrats who "take them for granted, knowing they have nowhere else to go."[2]

If Blacks do not have adequate leadership and unified citizens to highlight issues specifically troublesome for the Black community, they will continue to go ignored. This means that the Black community as a group will become increasingly politically irrelevant. They will continue to be pawns to the Democratic Party and disregarded by the Republican Party. Ultimately, the rest of the country will get tired and will no longer want to hear Blacks' cries of racism, oppression, and discrimination. As a result of political irrelevancy, the Black community will no longer be able to protect any of its members and members of the Black community will no longer seek the privileges and protection from the Black community.

Citizenship literature has focused heavily on the rights and privileges associated with citizenship and how to include and expand not only the definition of citizenship but its borders as well. Today the role of the citizen is being further studied based on the relationship between the people and the state, whereas the focus of this research is to invite contemporary research to explore the obligations that individuals not only hold to the state, but to one another as members of a national community. In particular, the focus has been on the personal and collective sacrifices that individuals and groups within a national community make to one another and in allegiance to the common good. Lastly, research acknowledges value as a concept of citizenship that influences the interaction among members of a national community and their willingness to sacrifice and commit resources to the state. Treating value in being a member of a national community or citizen as a good or commodity is significant to group identity and goals. The importance placed on group membership will depend on how much sacrifice and commitment to other members advances the common good, and is perceived as a positive value within the community.

Black leadership literature focused heavily on the different types of leaders throughout Black American history, the models of previous leaders, and the historical trends and transformations of Black leaders from slavery to Civil Rights. In contrast, the purpose behind this research was to investigate a prototype: what do leaders do and what is their role and relationship to their followers or citizens? More importantly, what makes for effective and great leadership? What the Black community needs today is great leadership. Only great leadership can radically transform the collective habits of the impoverished Black majority. The contribution made by this investigation into the research on Black leadership emphasizes the tools and methods used by transcendent leaders and members of the Black community, including the challenges they face, and how to earn the devotion, admiration, and enthusiasm of poor Blacks.

Black leaders face a multitude of complex issues that demand their attention, and it is important to investigate what some of those issues are and how they can effectively be solved. It appears as though progress in the Black community has been validated based on the wealth and success of the few over the uplifting of the conditions of the many. This research presents a new light on how progress in a national community is measured. Additionally, it offers a portrayal of the common good—those things that benefit all Blacks, or that members of the Black community consider necessary for maintaining allegiance to Blacks. With the separate factions and divisions present within the Black community, it is imperative to identify the conditions, experiences, and history that unites all members of the Black community and that can be the source of their strength as a national community in the United States.

There is a variety of conclusions that may be drawn by looking at the experiences of Blacks in the Caribbean and Latin America. Such an investigation may provide further insight into the mechanisms that Blacks have used to gain wider access to political institutions and achieve racial equality. Additionally, the leadership of Blacks in the Caribbean and Latin America is worthy of further exploration. These cases are important to the discussion of the conditions of Blacks because these groups were directly involved in the transportation of Africans during the Atlantic

Slave trade and thus, had a set of experiences and history that all Black descendants from Africa share.

Despite similarities such as the experiences of slavery, this research and findings are particular to the experience of Blacks in the U.S. Citizenship has global relevance as the literature has expanded into a cosmopolitan notion of the global citizen, and the experiences of immigrants and the quest for citizenship in America has evolved. Since America is a "nation of immigrants," the various ethnic and racial groups in America have a story of acquiring the rights and privileges of citizenship. Yet, here the conditions of citizenship and group membership have been arrived at under the framework of the Black experience in America.

Other limitations to this research include the limited number of leaders examined, both before and during the Civil Rights Movement, and among Black contemporary leaders. The purpose was not to exclude certain leaders but rather highlight examples of effective leadership traits. It was beneficial that many of the traits and examples can be found within a small sample of leaders. This gives legitimacy to the suggestion that a potential leader of the Black community does not have to "be all things to all people," but rather one individual is capable of wearing multiple hats and fulfilling multiple roles within the Black community.

Furthermore, concerns of contemporary Black leaders that were left unexamined include issues of interracial marriage and the division of light-skinned versus dark-skinned Blacks regarding who is "more Black." Color divisions within the Black community, with phenotypical Whiteness being the ideal, do more harm than good in establishing unity and solidarity. Since before the Civil War, when light-skin slaves were treated better than darker ones, status among Blacks has been connected to skin tone. Having light-skin garners privileges in terms of educational attainment, income, mental health, and spousal status.[3] In addition to interracial marriage, divisions regarding skin tone can present the dilemma of questioning an individual's commitment to the Black community by their willingness to select mates from outside of the race.

Although the antidotes prescribed in this research are directed towards Black leaders and the Black community, the elements of citizenship and the basic foundations for great leadership can be applicable beyond the experiences of Blacks, in that, the same tools and methods can be universally applied to any individual claiming to be a leader. Additionally, the model of the citizen and how it is measured and evaluated can be used by states in addition to minority ethnic or racial groups. What it means to be a contributing member of a national community and the elements of effective leadership transcends the specifics of the Black community, but how they can be established and applied to the contemporary Black community was the primary concern of the research.

To proceed from the current standing and conditions of the Black community and its leadership, further research into Black community-building is needed. It is imperative to investigate ways Blacks can target resources and contributions in predominately Black communities and develop institutions aimed at alleviating the conditions specific to poor and disadvantaged members of the Black community. Issues of leadership and Black community-building will undoubtedly require further exploration into ways to bring unity and solidarity to different members of the Black community; members of different social and economic classes, religious affiliations, sex, and regions. Most importantly, Blacks must investigate new ways to engage the poor and disadvantaged members of the Black community.

The Black community will need creative and unifying ways to get elite and professional Blacks to recommit themselves to the lowliest members of the group. Additionally, members of the Black community must create incentives and create conditions in which leaders and other members of the Black community will be enticed to commit their time and resources to other members of the community. Successful political, social, and economic institution building must be explored. This would include successful ways that groups can hold leaders and other members of a group accountable. Finally, ways to regenerate pride and value in being a member of a disadvantaged or formerly oppressed group is an important element worthy of further exploration by the Black community. Recommendations for future research into theories of citizenship and the relationship to a community's leaders include further exploration into evaluating and measuring the effectiveness of leaders, in addition to investigating ways groups and minorities have done successful community building, especially in the face of discrimination and oppression, and how groups are able to hold leaders and other members of the group committed and accountable to the interests and values of the community overall.

The presence of two town hall conferences by separate groups of Black leaders highlights the significance of the findings presented in this research. The Black community has more leaders, has held more conferences and meetings by CEOs, business, and community leaders to discuss the problems facing the Black community but has failed to provide any tangible resources or conclusions that make a significant impact to the conditions of poor Blacks. Conferences and town hall meetings take place every year across the country, and yet the conditions of the Black majority have not seen significant improvements. What is the relevance and significance of all these conferences and town hall meetings if they do not lead to tangible results for the disadvantaged members of the community? At the end of Black leadership conferences there is not one public display of a specific demand, specific policy suggestion that can reasonably be achieved that targets Blacks specifically, or a tangible idea that Blacks can take back to their communities to hold elected officials and leaders of their community accountable. The presence of leadership at these conferences highlights the lack of new, younger, innovative leaders present within the Black community. Thus, in the end, such conferences are nothing more than opportunities for further posturing by an outdated and out of touch leadership which the government and the current Black President of the U.S. has no incentive or obligation to acknowledge or address.

Post-Civil Rights leaders have concentrated on protecting Black, middle-class interests and newfound wealth over protecting and serving the interests and values of poor Blacks. As a result, Blacks must reassess Black leadership while determining which members of the Black community ought to receive the benefits and privileges of Black citizenship. Not everyone is worthy of Blacks' vote, protection, or allegiance. Blacks should only protect and swear their allegiance to individuals committed to promoting the interests of the Black majority, in particular the poor and disadvantaged. The problem with contemporary Black leaders is that they are no longer able or willing to sacrifice self-interest and personal aggrandizement to serve the interests of the Black community overall; they have not accepted the responsibility to look after the poor and disadvantaged members of the Black community.

Individual Black elites have been able to attain the highest offices in government and positions of authority in major corporations. The number of Blacks earning, above $250,000 has continued to increase since the end of the Civil Rights era. Yet, the majority of the Black community is having a more difficult time navigating its way through a more "diverse" and "free" America. Just as Black women are afraid of the fight for racial equality being confused with Black men's ability to perpetuate the same patriarchal system of White men, so too, must the Black community refrain from confusing freedom and justice for their ability to perpetuate the status quo of denigrating and looking to escape the history and the experiences of Black poverty. Freedom and equality do not mean the ability to pursue unfettered individualism and self-interest at the expense of disadvantaged members and the community as a whole. Although individual Blacks are able to find great success in America today, collectively, the standing and conditions of the majority of Blacks have not significantly improved.

The majority of Blacks have seen incomes grow less and more slowly than any other group, and experience an education system that continues to fail to produce a tangible means for the majority of Blacks to convert access to education into jobs and capital. Crime and single parent families are more of a reality for the majority of Blacks, and overall health and access to medical care continues to fail to meet the demands of the Black community. Despite greater access to U.S. institutions and wealth, elite Blacks have garnished the most benefits while the lives and conditions for the Black majority have not significantly improved. Although blatant and violent racism may be less of a reality, less visible institutional racism can prove to be just as detrimental and oppressive to Black advancement. Structural racism is still alive and functioning throughout American society, and Blacks experience its negative effects. Those negative effects contribute to the deteriorating collective standing and conditions of many Blacks, despite the success and wealth of some individuals.

The reason why the overall condition and standing of the Black community has not significantly improved is because those who took over the mantle of Black leadership aspired to use the advancement and improvements made during the civil rights movement to further their own individual success and status, thereby avoiding a commitment to serve the lowliest members of the Black community. Whereas Black leaders once fought for the freedoms and protections of the oppressed and discriminated, the Black leaders since the end of the civil rights movement have pursued middle-class, White interests. The majority of members of the Black community see little sacrifice made on behalf of the leadership to further lower class interests. Thus, the problem with contemporary Black leaders is the inability or unwillingness to exercise political virtù; accomplish a vision of poor Black advancement by using any means necessary to shake the corrupted society out of its comfort zone and demonstrating sacrifice and commitment to the most disadvantaged. As a result, Black leaders today have not earned the devotion, commitment, and enthusiasm of poor Blacks.

This research is applied a theory of citizenship and leadership to the contemporary conditions of the Black community in order to evaluate what it means to be a member of the Black community, a citizen in the U.S., and the ways that leaders can help produce the radical change that is necessary to improve the conditions of poor Blacks. Using the framework of contribution, service, and sacrifice with the concepts of the citizen, citizenship, and leadership, I found that since 1970, the collective Black leadership has done little to improve the conditions and standing for the majority of Blacks in America and that to effectively address and improve upon the conditions of poor Blacks, a Black leader must be introduced who will demonstrate and set an example of excellent service, sacrifice, and commitment to the values and interests of poor Blacks. In the end, an effective Black leader in contemporary America will improve upon Blacks' collective economic standing and educational attainment, and reverse the lack of value in and commitment to other members of the community resulting in a disproportionate amount of Black on Black crime, and enhance conditions in the Black family and the physical and mental health of the Black community.

The Black community must reevaluate its leaders and how they perceive themselves as citizens and members of the Black community because the current corrupt state will not produce the conditions in which Blacks will be able to effectively mobile to improve their collective conditions. Blacks must evaluate members of the Black community and their standing as U.S. citizens (both are national communities that Blacks belong to) based upon their commitment and contribution to the common good—the protection, sustainment, and improvement of the community. This should cause Blacks to reassess and reinterpret their history based on the contribution made by Blacks during and after slavery.

Additionally, Blacks in America should evaluate citizens and the significance of citizenship based on the standard of one's contribution to the sustainment, protection, and improvement of the Black community overall, in particular the poor and disadvantaged, because it protects the value of the community as a whole. It will ensure that members of the community have the proper relationship with other members and the state. Perceiving citizenship in this way will set a standard by which new members and leaders can be measured. If Blacks do not readdress how they perceive themselves as members of the Black community and the overall American polity, they will continue to fall to the manipulation and exploitation of opportunists and groups outside of the community with no interest or incentive to listen to or address the issues of the Black community. Citizenship based on one's contribution to the community reinforces the unity and solidarity of the group and creates the conditions in which the Black community can effectively challenge American institutions from a position of strength.

It is important to evaluate Black leaders similarly, according to their contributions and how well they address and improve the conditions of the poor and disadvantaged members of the community. Blacks must evaluate their leaders by how effectively they serve the masses and improve the conditions of the impoverished Black majority; not based on their individual success or social status, or because they are elected officials, popular, or rich and famous. Elected officials and anybody claiming to be a Black leader should be held accountable to the Black poor and disadvantaged. If Blacks do not adequately address corrupt leadership, the demands of the poor and disadvantaged will go unheard and unnoticed by government and decision-makers who have the power and authority to help.

To adequately asses what immediate actions need to be taken, it is imperative to first analyze the current atmosphere surrounding the Black community. Most recently, hundreds of Black men and women have died at the hands of Whites and police officers, beginning with the death of Trayvon Martin, who was shot in 2012 by neighborhood watch volunteer George Zimmerman. In addition to Trayvon Martin, the deaths of Eric Garner (July 2014–New York), Laquan McDonald (October 2014–Chicago), Tamir Rice (November 2014–Cleveland), Sandra Bland (July 2015–Texas), Michael Brown Jr. (August 2014–Ferguson, Missouri), Walter Scott (April 2015–South Carolina), and Freddy Gray (April 2015–Baltimore), have made national news highlight the disparaging recent history of Blacks with law enforcement.

To combat these recent atrocities, the Black Lives Matter Movement has arisen with the goal to not only fight killings of Black people by police, but, queer, trans, and Black lives across the gender spectrum. Additionally, campus protests beginning with the Black members of the University of Missouri football team over racist comments and activities on campus led to their walking out on the football program and promising not to play until the president resigned. This led to a firestorm of protests across college campuses as students at Harvard, Princeton, Lewis and Clark College, Portland State, and the University of Puget Sound led protests demanding that university administrations balance the diversity not only of the student body, but the faculty and staff as well.

One of the biggest developments facing the Black community will ultimately be the end of Barack Obama's Presidency, and the predictable policy backlash resulting from the perception of America's first Black President playing favorites. The first major victory of opponents looking to turn the clock back on Obama's Presidency was the repeal of Obamacare in 2015. Once touted as groundbreaking legislation which provides healthcare to millions of Americans, its subsequent repeal should undoubtedly leave Black America wondering what tangible benefits of the first Black Presidency they can rejoice in. This ultimately leaves Black Americans aimlessly looking for policy recommendations to support the perception of a progressive, egalitarian society; as if American democracy was somehow built for the policy needs of Black America to ever be met.

The time for new, revolutionary leadership is now. The call to action demands the exceptional. The servant. The courageous. No longer ashamed of unique intelligence, charisma, discipline, and will. In a world craving to make everyone equals, it us up to the new leadership to no longer be afraid to grab greatness and claim it for their own. The ability to reshape and redefine the experience and history of Black America is within reach. But in a world, wishing to destroy race, "blackness," and the unique history of Black America, it is the wisdom and courage of the leadership to stand with the masses, affirming the significance and importance of the Black community. No longer ashamed of being too smart. Too Black. Too uncompromising. Too nationalistic. Be strong enough to follow your own convictions. The elimination of these virtues is harmful to the ability of an effective Black leader to flourish. What is good for the rest of society may not fit the plan of the exceptional. Effective leadership requires that ability to demonstrate your own skill and statecraft. Do not be afraid to step out on your own ideas, theories, and methods.

The call to action is for the exceptional. Willing to risk and sacrifice it all for the sake and enhancement of the Black community. By demonstrating such sacrifice and commitment, the exceptional leader affects and influences the lives of others. Sacrifice and service which transforms the path and capabilities of an entire community, through nothing other than the will and virtues of exceptional leadership cannot help but affect and essentially, dominate others. An attitude and way of life, so affirming to the needs of the Black community, they have no other options but to follow. The spirit of the exceptional has the ability to govern the personal, economic, and professional will of the masses. But first, the exceptional leader must demonstrate its use, practicality, and aptitude for success. The exceptional leadership of the Black community affects Black history indefinitely. With nothing but appreciation, the actions taken by the new Black leadership faces the obstacles and barriers of the Black community with appreciation; facing Black life and the adversity that comes with transforming a troubled community in a selfish, disillusioned world with gratitude. Knowing that the basic conditions of Black life will not change unless one faces a life full of suffering and absurdity.

The call to action for effective Black leadership is for the exceptional. No longer afraid to be called an elitist, an intellectual, too driven. In a world that screams for the rights and privileges of individuality, the actions of effective leadership are community confirming. Through the confirmation of community and value in the Black community, the effective Black leader of tomorrow essentially creates *new* values. By creating new values within the Black community, the new leadership appears as the solution to the community's problem. Pervasive self-interest, materialism, and depleting value in "blackness" and the Black community are ultimately transformed through new values of unity, pride in "blackness," and the uniqueness of intellect and community affirming service. The old values of self-depreciation, alienation, disillusionment, and dependence, shall be replaced with the virtues and self-determining character of the new Black leadership.

Why is the call to action for the exceptional? Make no mistake about it. In a world that pushes low expectations, selfishness and materialism, anti-intellectualism, and the promotion of mediocrity, all of the things that reproduce the miserable conditions of the Black community, it will take exceptional effort. It will take someone exceptional to withstand the plagues of society pushing back against the movement of the oppressed. To take miserable souls, undervalued and underappreciated brothers and sisters from all over the country, and commit to sacrifice and make service and unity a new norm will accept nothing less than the blood, sweat, and tears of someone exceptional. Taking the lowered expectations of the status quo and establishing new values; that one individual can make a change. That the Black community can protect, sustain, and improve itself. Despite our differences the Black community can be united.

The future of Black America depends on the ability of each member to adequately assess the quality of its leadership as more than just being capable of earning fame and fortune for themselves while ignoring the most disadvantaged members of Black society. It depends on how Blacks assess their own commitment and affinity for belonging in the Black community. Together radical changes in the attitude and commitment of the members can transform the Black community into one that alters America's ideals into one of true justice and equality. Achieving this goal can best be realized by Black leaders emphasizing greater responsibility among Blacks to lift each other up rather than be satisfied with individual accomplishments. It will truly take a commitment by the best of the Black community to restore and uplift the majority.

NOTES

1. Elizabeth Flock, "African American Leaders Deliver Agenda for Obama's Second Term," *U.S. News & World Report*, December 3, 2012.

2. Keli Goff, "Will Obama Push a 'Black Agenda' Now?" *The Root*, November 26, 2012.

3. Kathy Russell, Midge Wilson and Ronald Hall, *The Color Complex*. (New York: Anchor Books, 1993).

Bibliography

Adler, Stewart J. "Reducing Obesity: Motivating Action While Not Blaming the Victim." *Milbank Q* 87 (2009): 49–70.

Alexander, Michelle. *The New Jim Crow: Mass Incarceration in the Age of Colorblindness.* New York: The New Press, 2012.

————. "Michelle Alexander: More Black Men In Prison Than Were Enslaved In 1850." *ColorLines*, March 30, 2011. www.colorlines.com/articles/michelle-alexander-more-black-men-prison-were-enslaved-1850.

Alfino, Sean. "Poll: Jesse Jackson, Rice Top Blacks." *CBSNews*, February 15, 2006. www.cbsnews.com/stories/2006/02/15/national/main1321719.shtml.

Allen, Danielle S. *Talking With Strangers: Anxieties of Citizenship since Brown v. Board of Education.* Chicago: University of Chicago Press, 2006.

Apuzzo, Matt. "Obama Confronts Racial Division." *Huntington Post*, March 18, 2008. www.huffingtonpost.com/2008/03/18/obama-confronts-racial-di_n_92064.html.

Aristotle. *Politics.* Indianapolis/ Cambridge: Hackett Publishing Company, 1998.

Barnes, Jack. *Malcolm X, Black Liberation & the Road to Workers Power.* New York: Pathfinder Press, 2009.

Barringer, Felicity. "White-Black Disparity in Income Narrowed in 80s." *The New York Times,* July 24, 1992.

Battle, Michael. *The Black Church in America.* Malden, MA: Blackwell Publishing, 2006.

Bell, Derrick. *Faces at the Bottom of the Well: The Permanence of Racism.* New York: Basic Books, 1993.

Belz, Herman. *A New Birth of Freedom: The Republican Party and Freedmen's Rights, 1861–1868.* Westport, CT: Greenwood Press, 1977.

Bendary, Jennifer. "Allen West: I Am the Modern Day Harriet Tubman." *The Huffington Post,* August 18, 2011. www.huffingtonpost.com/2011/08/18/allen-west-harriet-tubman_n_930052.html.

Benhabib, Seyla. *The Claims of Culture: Equality and Diversity in the Global Era.* Princeton, NJ: Princeton University Press, 2002.

Bogardus, Emory S. "Leadership and Attitudes." *Sociology and Social Research* 13 no. 4 (1929): 377–81.

Brown, Elaine. *A Taste of Power: A Black Woman's Story.* New York: First Anchor Books Edition, 1994.

Brown, Michael K., Martin Carnoy, and Elliott Currie. *Whitewashing Race: The Myth of a Color-Blind Society.* Berkeley: University of California Press, 2003.

Browning, Rufus P., Dale Rogers Marshall, and David H. Tabb. *Protest is Not Enough: The Struggle of Blacks and Hispanics in Urban Politics.* Berkeley: University of California Press, 1986.

Bunche, Ralph J. *A Brief and Tentative Analysis of Negro Leadership.* New York: New York University Press, 2005.

Cain, Hermain. *They Think You're Stupid.* Atlanta, GA: Stroud & Hall Publishers, 2005.

Carens, J. H. *Culture, Citizenship, and Community.* Oxford: Oxford University Press, 2000.

Carma, Jeremiah. *Holy Lockdown.* Lilburn, GA: Twelfth House Publishing, 2004.

Carmichael, Stokely and Charles V. Hamilton. *Black Power: The Politics of Liberation in America.* New York: Vintage Books, 1967.

Chancer, Lynn S. *High Profile Crimes: When Legal Issues Become Social Causes.* Chicago: University of Chicago Press, 2005.

Clarke, J. H. *Malcolm X: The Man and His Times*. New York: Macmillan, 1969.

Cohen, Cathy and Michael C. Dawson. "Neighborhood Poverty and African American Politics." *The American Political Science Review* 87 (1993): 286–302.

Cone, James H. *A Black Theology of Liberation*. Maryknoll, NY: Orbis Books, 1986.

———. *Black Theology & Black Power*. Maryknoll, NY: Orbis Books, 1997.

Constant, Benjamin. "The Liberty of the Ancients Compared with that of the Moderns." Accessed from http://oll.libertyfund.org/title/2251 on 01/16/2011.

Contemporary Black Biography, 67. Gale Research, 2008.

Cothran, Tilman C. and William Phillips, Jr. "Negro Leadership in a Crisis Situation." *Phylon (1960–)* 22 no. 2 (1961): 107–18.

Crowley, Martha, et al. "Education and the Inequalities of Place." *Social Forces* 84 no. 4 (2006): 2121–145.

Cruse, Harold. *The Crisis of the Negro Intellectual*. New York: New York Review Classics, 2005.

Cunnigen, Donald. "Black Leadership in the Twenty-First Century." *Society* (July/August) 43 no. 5 (2006): 25–29.

Darity, Jr. and Samuel L. Myers, Jr. "The Relative Decline in Black Family Income During the 1990s." Presentation at the Southern Economic Association Annual meetings, Washington, DC: November 9–12, 2000.

Davis, Allison. "Black Leadership and Anger." *The School Review* 81 no. 3 (1973).

Davis, Theodore J. *Black Politics Today*. New York: Routledge, 2011.

Dawson, Michael C. *Behind the Mule: Race and Class in African-American Politics*. Princeton, NJ: Princeton University Press, 1994.

———. *Black Visions: The Roots of Contemporary African American Political Ideologies*. Chicago: University of Chicago Press, 2001.

DeYoung, Karen. *Soldier: The Life of Colin Powell*. New York: Knopf, 2006.

Dolbeare, Kenneth M. *American Political Thought*. 4th Edition. Chatham House Publishers, 1998.

Du Bois, W. E. B. *Reconstruction in America*. New York: The Free Press, 1992.

———. *The Souls of Black Folk*. New York: W. W. Norton, 1999.

Ennis, Edward J. "The Meaning of American Citizenship." *Journal of Educational Sociology* 17 no. 1 (1943): 3–7.

Fanon, Frantz. *Black Skin, White Masks*. New York: Grove Press, 2008.

Flock, Elizabeth. "African American Leaders Deliver Agenda for Obama's Second Term." *U.S. News & World Report*, December 3, 2012.

Folbre, Nancy. "Hearts and Spades: Paradigms of Household Economics." *World Development* 14 no. 2 (1986): 245–55.

Franklin, John Hope and Alfred A. Moss, Jr. *From Slavery to Freedom: A History of African Americans*. 8th Edition. New York: McGraw-Hill, 2000.

Franklin, Robert Michael. *Liberating Visions*. Minneapolis, MN: Fortress Press, 1990.

Freire, Paulo. *Pedagogy of the Oppressed*. New York: Continuum, 2006.

Gaines, Kevin K. *Uplifting the Race: Black Leadership*. Chapel Hill: University of North Carolina Press, 1996.

Goff, Keli. "Will Obama Push a 'Black Agenda' Now?" *The Root*, November 26, 2012. www.theroot.com/articles/politics/2012/11/will_obama_address_a_black_agenda_in_his_2nd_term.html.

Goldman, Peter. "Malcolm X." In *Dictionary of American Negro Biography*, edited by Michael R. Winston, 422. New York: W. W. Norton, 1983.

Goldman, Robert M. *Reconstruction and Black Suffrage: Losing the Vote in Reese and Cruikshank*. Lawrence: University Press of Kansas, 2001.

Gordon, Tyrone and F. Stewart Carlyle III. *Growing the African American Church*. Nashville, TN: Abingdon Press, 2006.

Gregory, Sean. "Cory Booker (Still) Optimistic He Can Save Newark." *Time*, Monday, July 27, 2009, www.time.com/time/magazine/article/0,9171,1910983,00.html.

Hadjor, Kofi Buenor. *Another America: The Politics of Race and Blame*. Boston, MA: South End Press, 1995.

Harris, Frederick C. "Black Leadership and the Second Redemption." *Society* July/August 43 no. 5 (2006): 22–29.

Hochschild, Jennifer. "Social Class in Public Schools." *Journal of Social Issues* 59 no. 4 (2003): 821–40.

Honig, Bonnie. *Democracy and the Foreigner*. Princeton, NJ: Princeton University Press, 2001.

hooks, bell. *Ain't I A Woman*. Boston, MA: South End Press, 1981.

Hulse, Carl and David M. Herszenhorn. "Rangel Steps Aside From Post During Ethics Inquiry." *The New York Times*, March 3, 2010.

Hurst, Rodney. *It Was Never About A Hot Dog and A Coke!* Livermore, CA: WingSpan Press, 2008.

Itkowitz, Lenna K. *Shirley Chisholm for President*. New York: Random House Publishing, 1974.

James, Frank. "It's All Politics: Black GOP Lawmakers Face Tricky Relations With Democrats." *National Public Radio*, January 4, 2011. www.npr.org/sections/its allpolitics/2011/01/05/132660518/black-gop-lawmakers-to-face-tricky-relations-with-democrats.

Jencks, Christopher and Meredith Phillips. *The Black-White Test Score Gap*. Washington, DC: Brookings Institute Press, 1998.

Joint Center for Political and Economic Studies. "National Roster of Black Elected Officials." November, 2011, www.jointcenter.org/research/national-rosterof-blac kelected-officials.

Jones, Rick L. "Permanent American Hegemony: Liberalism, Domination, and the Continuing Crisis of Black Leadership." *Black Scholar* 31 no. 2 (2001): 38–48.

———. *What's Wrong with Obamamania?: Black America, Black Leadership, and the Death of Political Imagination*. New York: SUNY Press, 2008.

Kozol, Jonathan. *The Shame of the Nation: The Restoration of Apartheid Schooling in America*. New York: Three Rivers Press, 2006.

Kunjufu, Jawanza. *Black Economics: Solutions for Economic and Community Empowerment*. 2nd Edition. Sauk Village, IL: African American Images, 2002.

Leary, Virginia. "Citizenship, Human rights, and Diversity." In *Citizenship, Diversity, and Pluralism: and Comparative Perspectives*, by Alan C. Cairns, John C. Courtney, Peter MacKinnon, Hans J. Michelmann, David E. Smith. New York: McGill-Queen's Press, 2000.

Litzer, Barry. "The Great Black Hope." *Claremont Review of Books* Winter (2009).

Mabee, Carleton. "The Crisis in Negro Leadership." *The Antioch Review* 24 no. 3 (1964): 365–78.

Machiavelli, Niccolo. *Discourses on Livy*. Oxford: Oxford University Press, 1997.

———. *The Prince*. New York: Random House, 1992.

Macnaw, Glen and Tom Pendergast. "Wilder, L. Douglas," *Contemporary Blacks Biography*. (2005) www.encyclopedia.com/doc/1G23431200029.html.

Malveaux, Juliana. "Maxine Waters: Woman of the House." *Essence* no. 1 (1990): 55.

Marable, Manning. *Black Leadership: Four Great American Leaders and the Struggle for Civil Rights*. New York: Penguin Books, 1999.

———. *Malcolm X: A Life of Reinvention*. New York: Viking, 2011.

Marshall, T. H. *Citizenship and Social Class and Other Essays*. New York: Cambridge University Press, 1950.

McCarthy, Thomas. *Race, Empire, and the Idea of Human Development*. New York: Cambridge University Press, 2009.

Miller, David. *Citizenship and National Identity*. Cambridge: Polity Press, 2000.

Miller, Steve and Jerry Seper. "NAACP Tax Status Questioned." *The Washington Times*, February 4, 2001.

Mills, K. *This Little Light of Mine: The Life of Fannie Lou Hamer*. New York: Dutton, 1993.

Moynihan, Daniel P. "The Negro Family: The Case For National Action." Washington, DC: *Office of Policy Planning and Research, U.S. Department of Labor*. www.dol.gov./asp/programs/history/webid-meynihan.

Myrdal, Gunnar. *The American Dilemma: The Negro Problem and Modern Democracy.* New Jersey: Transaction Publishers, 1999.

NAACP. "Our Mission." *National Association for the Advancement of Colored People.* www.naacp.org/history.

Nealy, Michelle. "Black Males Achieving More on College Campuses." *Diverse: Issues In Higher Education* February (2009).

Nelson, H. Vincent. *The Rise and Fall of Modern Black Leadership.* Lanham, MD: University Press of America, 2003.

Nobles, W. "Extended Self: Rethinking the So-called Negro Self Concept." *Journal of Black Psychology* 2 (1976).

Patton, Charlie. "Does the NAACP Still Matter?" *Florida Times Union* (Jacksonville, FL), February 26, 2009.

Perez-Pena, Richard. "Facebook Founder to Donate $100 million to Help Remake Newark Schools." *The New York Times.* Sept. 23, 2010 (2010): 27.

Perry, Bruce. *Malcolm X: The Life of the Man Who Changed Black America.* Station Hill Press, 1992.

Peterson, Jesse. *SCAM: How the Black Leadership Exploits Black America.* Nashville, TN: WND Books, 2003.

Peterson, Paul. *City Limits.* Chicago: University of Chicago Press, 1981.

Pew Research Center. "Optimism About Black Progress Declines: Blacks See Growing Values Gap Between Poor and Middle Class." *Pew Research Center: A Social & Demographic Trends Report,* Tuesday, November 13, 2007.

———. "The Year in the News 2011: Top Newsmakers." *Project for Excellence in Journalism: Pew Research Center,* December 21, 2011.

Pinn, Anthony B. *The Black Church in the Post-Civil Rights Era.* Maryknoll, NY: Orbis Books, 2002.

Price III, Emmitt. *The Black Church and Hip-Hop Culture.* Lanham, MD: Scarecrow Press, 2011.

Pocock, J. "The Ideal of Citizenship in Classical Times." In *Theorizing Citizenship,* edited by Ronald Beiner, New York: SUNY Press, 1995.

Powell, Kevin. "Black Leadership is Dead." *Ebony* 65 no. 12 (2010): 85–87.

Puddington, Arch. "The Question of Black Leadership." *Commentary* 91 no. 1 (1991): 22–29.

Rawls, John. *Justice as Fairness.* Cambridge, MA: Harvard University Press, 2001.

Reed, Evelyn. "The Family As `Natural' Unit Is A Widespread Myth." *The Militant* 62 no. 1 January 12, 1998.

———. "Women's Oppression Rooted in Class-divided Society." *The Militant* 73 no. 22 June 8, 2009.

Reisenberg, Peter. *Citizenship in the Western Tradition.* Chapel Hill: University of North Carolina Press, 1992.

Rollin, Frank A. *Life and Services of Martin R. Delany.* Krause Reprints, 1969.

Rothstein, Richard. "Class and Schools: Using Social, Economic, and Educational Reform to Close the Black White Achievement Gap." *Economic Policy Institute.* Washington, DC: 2004.

Russell, Kathy, Midge Wilson, and Ronald Hall. *The Color Complex.* New York: Anchor Books, 1993.

Rustin, Bayard. "From Protest to Politics: The Future of the Civil Rights Movement." Reprinted from *Commentary.* February, 1965. digital.library.pitt.edu/u/ulsman uscripts/pdf/31735066227830.pdf.

Sahgal, Neha and Greg Smith. "A Religious Portrait of African Americans." *Pew Research Center's Forum on Religion & Public Life.* January 30, 2009.

Selig Center for Economic Growth. *University of Georgia's Terry College of Business,* 2012. www.selig.uga.edu.

Sellers et al. "Multidimensional Inventory of Black Identity: A Preliminary Investigation of Reliability and Construct Validity." *Journal of Personality and Social Psychology* 3 (1997).

Sing, Robert. *The Congressional Black Caucus: Racial Politics in the U.S. Congress*. California: Sage Publications, 1997.

Shklar, Judith. *American Citizenship: The Quest for Inclusion*. Cambridge: Harvard University Press, 2001.

Smith, Robert C. *We Have No Leaders: African Americans in the Post-Civil Rights Era*. New York: SUNY Press, 1996.

Smith, Todd A. "Black Men, You're Headed for Self-Destruction: Report Shows Rise in Black on Black Crime." *Regal Magazine*, January 8, 2009.

Smothers, Ryan. "Booker Has 100 – Day Plan for Newark's Reorganization." *The New York Times*, July 11, 2006.

Smythe, Hugh H. "Changing Patterns in Negro Leadership." *Social Forces* 29 no. 2 (1950): 191–97.

Standing, T. G. "Nationalism in Negro Leadership." *The American Journal of Sociology* 40 no. 2 (1934): 180–92.

Steinhauer, Jennifer. "Black Hopefuls Pick This Year in G.O.P. Races." *The New York Times*, May 4, 2010.

Stuckey, Sterling. *Slave Culture: Nationalist Theory and the Foundations of Black America*. New York: Oxford University Press, 1987.

Talbert, Marcia Wade and Robin White Goode. "Black America's Education Crisis." *Black Enterprise*, September 2011.

Tate, Katherine. *From Protest to Politics: The New Black Voters in American Elections*. New York: Russell Sage Foundation, 1994.

Taylor, Andrew. "Rich Got Richer, Outpace Middle-class." *USA Today*, October 27, 2011.

Thernstrom, Abigail and Stephan. *America in Black and White: One Nation, Indivisible*. 1st Touchstone Edition. New York: Simon & Schuster, 1999.

Tonry, Michael. *Malign Neglect: Race, Crime and Punishment in America*. New York: Oxford University Press, 1995.

Trowe, Maggie. "Debate Grows on Divorce, Changes in Family." *The Militant* 65 no. 6 (February 12, 2001).

Tucker, Robert C. *The Marx–Engels Reader*. 2nd Edition. New York: W. W. Norton, 1978.

U.S. Census Bureau. *US Census Bureau 2015 American Community Survey*. www.census.gov/. Accessed October 17, 2015.

U.S. Department of Justice. www.justice.gov. Accessed October 17, 2015.

U.S. Department of Labor, Bureau of Labor Statistics. data.bls.gov. Accessed October 17, 2015.

Velasquez, Manual, Claire Andre, Thomas Shanks, S. J., and Michael J. Meyer. "The Common Good." *Issues in Ethics* 5, no.1 (Spring 1992).

Wallace, Michele. *Black Macho and the Myth of the Superwoman*. Verso: Verso Classics Edition, 1999.

Walker, David. *David Walker's Appeal*. New York: Hill and Wang, 1995.

Walters, Ronald W. *White Nationalism, Black Interests: Conservative Public Policy and the Black Community*. Detroit, MI: Wayne State University Press, 2003.

———, and Robert C. Smith. *African American Leadership*. Albany, NY: State University Press, 1999.

Walton, Jr., Hanes and Robert C. Smith. *American Politics and the African American Quest for Universal Freedom*. 3rd Edition. New York: Pearson/ Longman, 2006.

Weber, Max. *The City*. Glencoe, IL: The Free Press, 1968.

West, Cornel. *Race Matters*. New York: Vintage/Random House, 1994.

White, John. *Black Leadership in America: From Booker T. Washington to Jesse Jackson*. 2nd Edition. New York: Longman, 1990.

Williams, Lea E. *Servants of the People: The 1960s Legacy of African American Leadership*. New York: St. Martin's Press, 1996.

Wilson, James Q. *Negro Politics: The Search for Leadership*. Glencoe, IL: The Free Press, 1960.

Wilson, William J. *The Declining Significance of Race: Blacks and Changing American Institutions.* Chicago: University of Chicago Press, 1978.

Woodson, Carter G. "Fifty Years of Negro Citizenship as Qualified by the United States Supreme Court." *The Journal of Negro History* 6 no. 1 (1921): 1–53.

———. *The Mis-Education of the Negro.* Kentucky: Tribeca Book, 2011.

Zwaykin, Vitnia. "Maxine Waters." In *Encyclopedia World Biography* 1, 1313. 1998.

Index

accommodation(ist), 134, 140

alienation, 7, 13, 39, 40–42, 46, 48, 121

Allen, Danielle, 37

Black politics, 67, 70, 78, 90, 107, 113

Black Power, 70, 71, 119, 123, 146, 149

Black Racial Identity Development model (BRID), 12

Booker, Corey, 89

BRID. *See* Black Racial Identity Development model

Brown, Elaine, 128

Cain, Herman, 88, 88–89

Canada, Geoffrey, 106

capitalism, 109–110, 125, 126, 146

CBC. *See* Congressional Black Caucus

Chisholm, Shirley, 71, 74, 83

church, the Black, 130–131

citizenship, 1–4, 8–9, 10, 11, 16, 21, 22, 23, 24–25, 27, 30–32, 33, 37, 38–39, 44, 48, 57, 63, 66, 132, 150, 151; American, 6, 11, 64, 70, 74; duties of, 14, 37; erosion of, 14; habits (of), 13, 23, 39, 41, 46–48, 50, 54, 56, 57, 58–59, 100, 102, 103, 114, 120, 122, 123, 150; privileges of, 4, 12, 24, 30, 39, 59, 64, 65; rights (of), 5, 136

Civil Rights Movement, 37, 43, 45, 49, 68, 71, 74, 76, 77, 79, 106, 112, 120, 128, 131, 133, 140, 142, 143

class(es)/classism, 21, 32, 59, 67, 90, 102, 105, 110, 111, 120, 123, 124–127, 144–145

common good, 3, 4, 25–28, 29–30, 31, 33, 38, 39, 41–42, 50, 57, 64, 65, 97, 100, 104, 108, 131, 132, 137–138, 139, 141, 144, 145, 150, 151

community, Black, 5, 7, 9, 10–13, 14–15, 16–17, 18–19, 20–21, 22, 23, 25, 26, 27, 28, 30, 31, 32–33, 37, 39–40, 41, 42–44, 46–48, 49, 50, 51, 56–58, 58, 63, 64, 65, 67, 68, 70, 72, 74, 87, 89, 93, 97, 98, 100, 102, 103–106, 107–108, 110, 113–114, 117–118, 119–120, 122–123, 136, 147, 148–149, 150–152

Congressional Black Caucus (CBC), 73, 87

corruption, 11–12, 13, 15, 17, 18–19, 20–22, 26, 32, 33, 38, 40, 57, 58, 100–103, 105, 107, 114, 126, 136, 141, 150–151

courage, 99, 100, 119, 120, 143, 144, 149

crime, Black, 45, 50, 103, 124; Black on Black crime, 50, 51, 93, 98, 100

cultural invasion, 15, 17, 19, 151

culture of poverty, 44

Delany, Martin, 6, 8, 9, 69

Depression, the, 67–68

distrust, 18, 39, 40, 46, 48

division, 15, 18, 19, 31, 90, 111, 124, 134, 144, 151

Douglass, Frederick, 8, 66, 67, 128

drive, 137

Du Bois, W. E. B., 9, 47, 67, 108, 138–139, 140, 141, 144–145, 146, 148

economic status, Black, 125

economy, Black, 51

education, Black, 54; Black educational attainment, 114

erosion, 4, 11, 14, 20, 22, 26, 151; in the Black community, 13, 15, 17, 18–19, 20, 21, 22, 32, 33, 37, 57, 58, 63, 102, 103, 150–151; of citizenship habits, 13, 14, 31, 38, 39, 40

exclusion, 23–24, 30

About the Author

Stephen C. W. Graves is a political scientist who specializes in Political Theory, Black Politics, and American Government. He is also the CEO and Founder of *Troublesome*, a non-profit organization that focuses on community outreach and providing educational and professional services to minorities and underprivileged groups. Born in Tulsa, Oklahoma, Stephen's family resides in Portland, Oregon and he continues to call the Pacific Northwest home.